ISLAM DENOUNCES TERRORISM

ISLAM DENOUNCES TERRORISM

Amir Ansari

CYBER TECH PUBLICATIONS
4264/3, Ansari Road, Daryaganj, New Delhi-110002 (India)
Ph.: 011-23244078, 011-43559448 Fax: 011-23280028
E-Mail: cyberpublicationsdelhi@yahoo.com
Website: www.cybertechpublications.com

ISLAM DENOUNCES TERRORISM

Amir Ansari

First Edition 2010

Published by :

G.S. Rawat for **Cyber Tech Publications**
4264/3, Ansari Road, Daryaganj, New Delhi-110002 (India)
Ph.: 011-23244078, 011-43559448 Fax: 011-23280028
E-Mail: cyberpublicationsdelhi@yahoo.com
Website: www.cybertechpublications.com

Printed at: Asian Offset Printers, Delhi-53

Preface

Religion commands love, mercy and peace. Terror, on the other hand, is the opposite of religion; it is cruel, merciless and demands bloodshed and misery. This being the case, the origins of a terrorist act should be sought in disbelief rather than in religion. People with a fascist, communist, racist or materialist outlook on life should be suspected as potential perpetrators. The name or the identity of the triggerman is not important. If he can kill innocent people without blinking an eye, then he is a nonbeliever, not a believer. He is a murderer with no fear of God, whose main ambition is to shed blood and to cause harm. For this reason, "Islamic terror" is an erroneous concept which contradicts the message of Islam. The religion of Islam can by no means countenance terrorism. On the contrary, terror (i.e. murder of innocent people) in Islam is a great sin, and Muslims are responsible for preventing these acts and bringing peace and justice to the world.

As is known, for centuries, various acts of terrorism have been carried out in different parts of the world by different groups for a variety of purposes. Sometimes a communist organisation, sometimes a fascist group, and sometimes radical and separatist factions assume responsibility for these acts. While countries like America often became the target of attacks by racist and marginal terrorist groups, the European countries have been centre stage for violent acts carried out by terrorist groups. 17 November in Greece, RAF (Red Army Faction) and Neo-Nazis in Germany, ETA in Spain, Red Brigades in Italy and many other organisations seek to make their voices heard through terror and violence by killing innocent and defenceless people. The nature of terrorism changes with changing world conditions and increases its impact and power with the new means made possible by developing technology. In particular, mass communication tools such as the Internet extend the scope and influence of the terrorist activities considerably.

This book maintains that the source of the terror that we condemn is definitely not from a divine religion, and that there is no room for terrorism in Islam. This is made clear in the Qur'an, the main source of Islam, and in the practices of all true Muslim rulers, the Prophet Muhammad being the foremost of them. This book reveals, in the light of the verses of the Qur'an and with examples from history, that Islam forbids terrorism and aims to bring peace and security to the world.

—Author

CONTENTS

1

Introduction

The reason why a special chapter is assigned to collapse of the theory of evolution is that this theory constitutes the basis of all anti-spiritual philosophies. Since Darwinism rejects the fact of creation, and therefore the existence of Allah, during the last 140 years it has caused many people to abandon their faith or fall into doubt. Therefore, showing that this theory is a deception is a very important duty, which is strongly related to the deen. It is imperative that this important service is rendered to all people. Some of our readers may find the chance to read only one of our books. Therefore, we think it appropriate to spare a chapter for a summary of this subject.

Another point to be stressed is related to the content of the book. In all the books of the author, faith-related issues are told in the light of the Qur'anic verses and people are invited to learn Allah's verses and live by them. All the subjects that concern Allah's verses are explained in such a way as to leave no room for doubt or question marks in the reader's mind.

The sincere, plain and fluent style employed ensures that everyone of every age and from every social group can easily understand the books. This effective and lucid way of recounting makes the books read quickly. Even those people who rigorously reject spirituality are influenced by the facts recounted in these books and cannot refute the truthfulness of their contents.

This book and all the other works of the author can be read by individuals or studied in a group at a time of conversation. The reading of the books by a group of readers willing to profit from them will be useful in the sense that readers can relate their own reflections and experiences to one another.

In addition, it will be a great service to the deen to contribute to the presentation and reading of these books, which are written solely for the good pleasure of Allah. All the books of the author are extremely convincing. For this reason, for those who want to communicate the deen to other people, one of the most effective methods is to encourage them to read these books.

SEPTEMBER 11

Since the horrific and tragic events of September 11th, nothing has been more discussed and scrutinised in the public arena than Islam. The world at large has been subjected to a wealth of analysis by 'experts' which has further fuelled people's curiosity about this religion. Book-sellers in Europe and the Middle East have reported an upsurge in interest in the Qur'an, which confirms what one British newspaper editor had to say: 'Islam [..] has never been of greater interest to the people of Britain than it is today.' In America, where there are some six million Muslims, Islam is said to be the nation's fastest growing religion, despite there being no systematic form of missionary work.

Contrary to official praise of Islam by the President of America and the Prime Minister of England, some of the media have bluntly suggested that the action taken after September's event is a war and Islam is at its heart. Despite there being a conscious effort to truly understand Islam and Muslims, there seem to be those who are determined to paint terrorism and Islam with the same brush. Simplified and undifferentiated descriptions of Islam help create an image by which Islam is seen as hostile to Western culture, and a religion of backwardness and oppression. 'A selective presentation and analysis of Islam and events by both scholars and political commentators too often inform articles and editorials on the Muslim world', says John Esposito, Director of the Center for Muslim-Christian Understanding, at Georgetown University in Washington. 'This selective analysis fails to tell the whole story [...] While it sheds some light, it is a partial light that obscures and distorts the full picture.'

The world community shares this small planet with the Muslim community which comprises some 1.2 billion adherents to the faith, so anyone who understands Islam to be a religion of terror would naturally be concerned. However, these fears are not well-grounded. Writing in *Time* magazine, Karen Armstrong asserts that: 'If the evil carnage we witnessed on September 11 were typical of the faith, and Islam truly inspired and justified such violence, its growth and the increasing presence of Muslims in both Europe and the U.S. would be a terrifying prospect. Fortunately, this is not the case.'

There seems to be a noticeable discrepancy between knowledge of Islam on the one hand and the certainty of judgements on the other. While the terrorist crime of September 11th may have been the work of some misled individuals, it was certainly not the product of Islam. Islam is a religion that preaches peace, compassion, justice, and frowns upon suicide. The kamikaze assault on innocent civilians stood in direct conflict with Islam's most elementary principles, teachings and spirit – one does not need to be an expert to realise this.

ISLAM AND TRADITION

If Islam is a religion of peace, why the misunderstanding? How can a religion of peace gain a reputation for being a religion of war and terror? The answer lies in the way that Islamic scriptures are misinterpreted to suit perverted agendas. Words and phrases that are often repeated in the media have been misconstrued by individuals to give incorrect meanings. The deliberate blur between 'jihad' and acts of terror has been a phenomenon that has resulted from those unqualified in the science of Sacred Law.

Since the end of the Sunni Ottoman Caliphate in 1924, the Muslim world has been fragmented. The loss of unification created many difficulties from which Muslims are still trying to recover. For one thing, it has seen the loss of the promulgation of traditional Islam, which has now given way to individuals claiming the right to reinterpret Islamic texts to grant them legitimacy in their own ideas. This has seen a tendency 'toward ambiguity and the careless use of many important terms.' Traditional Islam in contrast is related to the notion of orthodoxy, clarity and authority; to continuity and consistency in the transmission of the truth. It places its reliance upon classical scholarship as exemplified in the four schools of Islamic jurisprudence. Within this tradition of Islam, a true Islamic landscape emerges, encompassing the richness of scholarly tradition and its illuminating contribution to the advancement of civilisation.

Sunni Islam engenders a faith and practice that makes the taking of innocent lives unimaginable and which is shared by the vast majority of Muslims worldwide, however the radicals appear to have overlooked this pivotal pillar with their new interpretations of Sacred Law. As noted by Tim Winter, a lecturer on Islam at the faculty of Divinity at Cambridge University 'One of the unseen, unsung triumphs of true Islam in the modern world is its complete freedom from any terroristic involvement [...] Everyone, enemies included, knows that the very idea is absurd.'

The dismantling of the traditional places of learning by the colonialists allowed individuals to make literal and extreme interpretations of Sacred Law that are in contradiction to and radically different from the previous centuries of traditional Islamic practice and learning. Muhammad, the Messenger of God, may God bless him and grant him peace, forewarned of such a time when '[..] people [will] take the ignorant as leaders who are asked for and who give Islamic legal opinion without knowledge [they are] misguided and misguiding.'8 The result has been examples of extreme religious practice devoid of any real knowledge and characterised by bigotry, intolerance, harshness and excessiveness – all of which are in opposition to Islam as exemplified by the Messenger of God, may God bless him and grant him peace, who always advocated the middle way.

TERRORISM

Muhammad, may God bless him and grant him peace, warned his companions to avoid extremes - which he explained was the cause of the destruction of earlier communities. Terrorists it appears, feel that this injunction does not apply to them. Terrorism is an act against God. Anyone who tries to justify such atrocities ultimately fails, since both the Sacred Law and theology abhor such acts as moral sins that run contrary to the essence of Islam. The Qur'an instructs Muslims in times of adversity to act with justice, perseverance and patience. Terrorists apparently never think of relating their acts to the elementary principle that Islam places great value on: the sanctity of human life. 'If someone kills another person – unless it is in retaliation for someone else or for causing corruption in the earth – it is as if he had murdered all mankind' is a verse of the Qur'an, which is disregarded by the fanaticism of hate.

Traditional Muslim jurists considered terrorist attacks against unsuspecting and defenseless victims as heinous and immoral crimes and treated the perpetrators as the worst type of criminals. It is a well-established Qur'anic precept that the injustice of others does not excuse one's own injustice.

JIHAD

In the West, the term 'jihad' has come to be known as something wholly negative – it has been somewhat simplistically described as waging a holy war against infidels. However, in Islam, jihad is something that is positive. It consists of two dimensions: the inner jihad that seeks to curb negative and self-destructive forces within; and the external jihad which is a struggle against violence and tyranny by means of words and actions. As for the latter, it has strict rules of engagement which prohibit destroying civilian life, harming animals and even chopping down trees. The former type of jihad, said to be the most important, is that of the inner self. Muhammad, may God bless him and grant him peace, was reported to have said: "The best jihad one performs is that of helping oneself gain more knowledge of Almighty God." On another occasion, the Messenger of God addressed his companions, saying: "We are now returning from the minor jihad to the major jihad (that of the struggle of the inner self.)"

COMPASSION AND MERCY

In the context of the current atmosphere of violence, one might be excused for assuming that jihad is one of Islam's main pillars. However, this is far from the truth. Islam is 'not addicted to war,' nor does jihad form any one of the five pillars of faith. On the contrary, the Qur'an stresses compassion, benevolence, justice and wisdom. That compassion and mercy are central themes in Islam should be self-evident when almost every chapter of the Qur'an begins with: In the Name of God, The Most Compassionate, The Most Merciful.

In a famous saying of Muhammad, may God bless him and grant him peace, he says: 'The merciful are shown mercy by the Merciful one. Show mercy to those on earth and you will be shown mercy by the One in Heaven.' The Qur'an declares that Muhammad was sent as a Mercy to the worlds (21:107), something to which he himself testified when he refused to curse a warring tribe: 'I have not been sent to curse, but as a summoner and as a mercy'.

Indeed, such is the centrality of mercy and compassion in Islam, that the aforementioned tradition is the first tradition of Muhammad, may God bless him and grant him peace that is taught to the student of Sacred Law. Muslim scholars have said that in every matter, Muslims should be just, merciful and wise – anything that is lacking in any one of these principles cannot be said to be derived from Sacred Law. Compassion in Islam is not restricted to Muslims only, but it also requires sensitivity to the suffering of others. In a tradition, the Messenger of God, may God bless him and grant him peace, declared that 'people are God's children and those dearest to God are the ones who treat His children kindly.'12 A Muslim cannot be considered to be compassionate while there is suffering and injustice around them. It is for this reason, that Islam requires the community of believers to be one in which caring for your neighbours is an integral component of belief. The concern for your neighbour (irrespective of whether they are Muslim or not) is so crucial, that the Prophet, may God bless him and grant him peace, used to say that even if one person remains hungry in a particular area, no angel will descend in that area until that hungry person is fed.

TIME TO REFLECT

We cannot blame religion for the errors of those who use its name or symbols to justify their heinous actions. As Harun Yahya illustrates throughout this book, all religions, have had their share of people who claimed to be strict adherents of their tradition, but who actually grossly misinterpreted their sacred texts to suit their own agendas.

All true religious traditions condemn categorically any sort of act of aggression, and certainly any act of terror. Religion cannot be blamed, but the insanity and hate that drives people to commit such atrocities can be. It would not suffice to leave the condemnation there, it is up to us to seek out the root from which this hate pours forth; what are the causes of their grievances, turmoil, anger, bitterness, frustrations, hopelessness and how can we help to eliminate them? We will soon realise that the causes are not the doing of God or religion, but merely results of regimes that oppress and policies that kill and subvert. Now more than ever there is a need to investigate the link between terrorism and the support that continues for dictatorial regimes, particularly in the Muslim World.

It is not the case that the Muslim world hates the 'West' or indeed America. There are many Muslims living in the West and it would be hypocritical to denounce in a rhetoric of hate the very host country that has welcomed them. Most Muslims realise that there are many similarities extant in the West to Islamic precepts, such as freedom, tolerance, the right to education, and civil liberties. Graham E. Fuller, the former vice-chairman of the National Intelligence Council at the CIA, recently wrote in the L.A Times that: 'If you travel around the Muslim world, it quickly becomes evident that there is immense respect for a great variety of American values.' Rather, the frustration is vented on what is seen as double standards in government policies. People can enjoy such values in the West, but it appears that there has been a concerted effort to keep such values restricted 'fit for home consumption, but not for export.'

The Muslims in the West are facing a defining moment. Muslims must recapture the true spirit of Islam, and reclaim it from those who have harmed its integrity and honour. As Tim Winter asserts'[M]ainstream Islam will be able to make the loud declaration in public that it already feels in its heart: that terrorists are not Muslims. Targeting civilians is a negation of every possible school of Sunni Islam.'

Harun Yahya's elucidation is timely and much needed. It will, God willing, provide Muslims and non-Muslims alike with an essential understanding of the very heart of Islam, and what has been understood and practised by the vast majority of Muslims throughout history. This is orthodox, Sunni, mainstream Islam. He illustrates by using the core text of all Muslims – the Holy Qur'an, that true Islam cannot in any way, shape or form be associated with terrorism. It is in complete contradistinction to it, for without a doubt, Islam itself denounces Terrorism.

As Muslims, we strongly condemn the terrorist attacks on two major cities of the United States of America on September 11, 2001, which caused the death and injury of thousands of innocent people, and we offer our condolences to the American nation. These attacks propelled the important issue of the true source of terrorism to the top of the world agenda. Thus, it has been announced to the entire world that Islam is a religion of peace and tolerance that summons individuals to compassion and justice. Many world leaders, leading media organisations, television and radio stations said that true Islam forbids violence, and encourages peace between people and between nations. The Western circles that have come to a full grasp of the religion of Islam and are well-informed about Islam as commanded by God in the Qur'an noted clearly that the words "Islam" and "terror" cannot stand side by side, and that no divine religion permits violence.

This book maintains that the source of the terror that we condemn is definitely not from a divine religion, and that there is no room for terrorism in Islam. This is made clear in the Qur'an, the main source of Islam, and in the practices of all true Muslim rulers, the Prophet Muhammad being the foremost of them.

As is known, for centuries various acts of terrorism were been carried out in different parts of the world by different groups for a variety of purposes. Sometimes a communist organisation, sometimes a fascist group, and sometimes radical and separatist factions assume responsibility for these acts. While countries like America often became the target of attacks by racist and marginal terrorist groups, the European countries have been centre stage for violent acts carried out by terrorist groups. November in Greece, RAF (Red Army Faction) and Neo-Nazis in Germany, ETA in Spain, Red Brigades in Italy and many other organisations seek to make their voices heard through terror and violence by killing innocent and defenceless people. The nature of terrorism changes with changing world conditions and increases its impact and power with the new means made possible by developing technology. In particular, mass communication tools such as the Internet extend the scope and influence of the terrorist activities considerably.

Besides the Western organisations, there are also other terror organisations of Middle East origin. Terrorist attacks are carried out by these groups in all corners of the world. Sadly, the fact that the perpetrators of various terrorist acts carry Christian, Muslim or

Jewish identities cause some people to put forward claims which do not concur with divine religions. The truth is that even if terrorists have Muslim identities, the terror they perpetrate cannot be labelled "Islamic terror", just as it could not be called "Jewish terror" if the perpetrators were Jews or "Christian terror" if they were Christians. That is because, as will be examined in the following pages, murdering innocent people in the name of a divine religion is unacceptable. We need to keep in mind that, among those who were killed in New York and Washington, there were people who loved Jesus (Christians), the Prophet Moses (Jews) and the Prophet Muhammad (Muslims). Unless forgiven by God, murdering innocent people is a great sin that brings torment in Hell.

The aggressors can commit such violence only with the intention of attacking religion itself. It may well be that those who carried out this violence did so to present religion as evil in the eyes of people, to divorce people from religion and to generate hatred towards those who are religiously inclined. Consequently, every attack on American citizens or other innocent people having a religious facade is actually an attack made against religion.

Religion commands love, mercy and peace. Terror, on the other hand, is the opposite of religion; it is cruel, merciless and demands bloodshed and misery. This being the case, the origins of a terrorist act should be sought in disbelief rather than in religion. People with a fascist, communist, racist or materialist outlook on life should be suspected as potential perpetrators. The name or the identity of the triggerman is not important. If he can kill innocent people without blinking an eye, then he is a nonbeliever, not a believer. He is a murderer with no fear of God, whose main ambition is to shed blood and to cause harm. For this reason, "Islamic terror" is an erroneous concept which contradicts Islam's message. The religion of Islam can by no means countenance terror. On the contrary, terror (i.e. murders committed against innocent people) in Islam is a great sin and Muslims are responsible for preventing these acts and bringing peace and justice to the world.

2

Islamic Morality: The Source of Peace and Security

Some of those who say that something is done in the name of religion may, in fact, misunderstand that religion and as a result, practice it wrongly. For that reason, it would be wrong to form ideas about that religion by taking these people as an example. The best way of understanding a religion is to study its divine source.

Islam's divine source is the Qur'an, which is based on concepts of morality, love, compassion, humility, sacrifice, tolerance and peace. A Muslim who lives by those precepts in its true sense will be most polite, careful of thought, modest, just, trustworthy and easy to get on with. He will spread love, respect, harmony and the joy of living all around him.

ISLAM IS THE RELIGION OF PEACE

Terror, in its broadest sense, is violence committed against non-military targets for political purposes. To put it another way, targets of terror are entirely innocent civilians whose only crime, in the eyes of terrorists, is to represent "the other side".

For this reason, terror means subjecting innocent people to violence, which is an act bereft of any moral justification. This, as in the case of murders committed by Hitler or Stalin, is a crime committed against mankind.

The Qur'an is a Book revealed to people as a guide to the true path and in this Book, God commands man to adopt good morals. This morality is based upon concepts such as love, compassion, tolerance and mercy. The word "Islam" is derived from the word meaning "peace" in Arabic. Islam is a religion revealed to mankind with the intention of presenting a peaceable life through which the infinite compassion and mercy of God manifest on earth. God calls all people to Islamic morals through which compassion, mercy, peace and tolerance can be experienced all over the world. In Sura Baqara, verse 208, God addresses believers as follows:

O You who believe! Enter absolutely into peace (Islam). Do not follow in the footsteps of Satan. He is an outright enemy to you.

As the verse makes clear, security can only be ensured by "entering into Islam", that is, living by the values of the Qur'an. The values of the Qur'an hold a Muslim responsible for treating all people, whether Muslim or non-Muslim, kindly and justly, protecting the needy and the innocent and "preventing the dissemination of mischief". Mischief comprises all forms of anarchy and terror that remove security, comfort and peace. As God says in a verse, **"God does not love corruption".** (Qur'an, 2:205)

Murdering a person for no reason is one of the most obvious examples of mischief. God repeats in the Qur'an a command He formerly revealed to Jews in the Old Testament thus:

... if someone kills another person – unless it is in retaliation for someone else or for causing corruption in the earth – it is as if he had murdered all mankind. And if anyone gives life to another person, it is as if he had given life to all mankind... (Qur'an, 5:32)

As the verse suggests, a person who kills even a single man, "unless it is in retaliation for someone else or for causing corruption in the earth", commits a crime as if he had murdered all mankind.

This being the case, it is obvious what great sins are the murders, massacres and attacks, popularly known as "suicide attacks", committed by terrorists. God informs us how this cruel face of terrorism will be punished in the hereafter in the following verse:

> *There are only grounds against those who wrong people and act as tyrants in the earth without any right to do so. Such people will have a painful punishment. (Qur'an, 42:42)*

All these reveal that organising acts of terror against innocent people is utterly against Islam and it is unlikely that any Muslim could ever commit such crimes. On the contrary, Muslims are responsible for stopping these people, removing "mischief on earth" and bringing peace and security to all people all over the world. Islam cannot be reconciled with terror. Just the contrary, it should be the solution to and the path to the prevention of terror.

GOD HAS CONDEMNED WICKEDNESS

God has commanded people to avoid committing evil: oppression, cruelty, murder and bloodshed are all forbidden. He describes those who fail to obey this command as "following in Satan's footsteps" and adopting a posture that is openly revealed to be sinful in the Qur'an. A few of the many verses on this matter in the Qur'an read:

> *But as for those who break God's contract after it has been agreed and sever what God has commanded to be joined, and cause corruption in the earth, the curse will be upon them. They will have the Evil Abode. (Qur'an, 13:25)*

> *Eat and drink of God's provision and do not go about the earth corrupting it. (Qur'an, 2:60)*

> *Do not corrupt the earth after it has been put right. Call on Him fearfully and eagerly. God's mercy is close to the good-doers. (Qur'an, 7:56)*

Those who think that they will be successful by causing wickedness, upheaval and oppression, and by killing innocent people are committing a great error. God has forbidden all acts of wickedness involving terrorism and violence, condemned those who engage in such acts and said ***"God does not uphold the works of those who cause mischief." in one of His verses. (Qur'an, 10:81)***

In the present age, however, acts of terrorism, genocide and massacres occur all over the world. Innocent people are being savagely killed, and countries where communities are being brought to hate each other for artificial reasons are drowning in blood. These horrors in countries with different histories, cultures and social structures may have causes and sources peculiar to each. However, it is evident that the fundamental cause is a moving away from morality based on love, respect and tolerance that religion brings with it. As a result of lack of religion, communities emerge that have no fear of God and believe that they will not be called to account in the hereafter. Since they believe that, "I will not have to account for my actions to anyone," they can easily act with no compassion, morality or conscience.

The existence of hypocritical people who emerge in the name of God and religion, but actually organise themselves to commit wickedness condemned by God, is indicated in the Qur'an. One verse talks about a gang of nine men who planned to murder the Prophet by swearing in the name of God:

> *There was a gang of nine men in the city causing corruption in the land and not putting things right. They said, "Let us make an oath to one another by God that we will fall on him and his family in the night and then say to his protector, We did not witness the destruction of his family and we are telling the truth." They hatched a plot and We hatched a plot while they were not aware. (Qur'an, 27:48-50)*

As this incident described in the Qur'an reveals, the fact that people do things "in the name of God" or even swear in His name, in other words that they use the kind of language designed to show themselves as very religious, does not mean that what they do is in conformity with religion. On the contrary, what they do can be quite against the will of God and the morality of religion. The truth of the matter lies in their actions. If their actions are "causing corruption and not putting things right", as the verse reveals, then you can be sure that these people cannot be truly religious, and that their aim is not to serve religion.

It is quite impossible for someone who fears God and has grasped the true morality of Islam to support violence or wickedness, or to take part in such actions. That is why Islam is the true solution to terrorism. When the sublime morality of the Qur'an is explained, it will be impossible for people to connect true Islam with those who support or join groups that aim at hatred, war and chaos. That is because God has forbidden wickedness:

> *Whenever he holds the upperhand, he goes about the earth corrupting it, destroying (people's) crops and breeding stock. God does not love corruption. When he is told to have fear of God, he is seized by pride which drives him to wrongdoing. Hell will be enough for him! What an evil resting-place. (Qur'an, 2:205-206)*

As can be seen from the above verses, it is out of the question for someone who fears God to turn a blind eye to even the smallest action that might harm mankind. Someone who does not believe in God and the hereafter, however, can easily do all kinds of evil, since he thinks he will not have to account to anyone.

The first thing that needs to be done to rid the world of the present-day scourge of terrorism is to use education to do away with deviant irreligious beliefs that are put forward in the name of religion, and to teach people true Qur'anic morality and to fear God.

THE RESPONSIBILITY OF BELIEVERS

Those who have no concern for events unless they directly affect them are bereft of the insight that espouses unselfishness, brotherhood, friendship, honesty and the service that religion bestows upon people. Throughout their lives, such people try to satisfy their own egos by merely wasting their means, totally unaware of the threats humanity faces. In the Qur'an however, God praises the morals of those who strive to bring good to their surroundings; those who are concerned about the events that take place around them and who call people to the right way. In a verse from the Qur'an, a metaphor is given for those who offer no good to others and those who always act on the path of goodness:

God makes another metaphor: two men, one of them deaf and dumb, unable to do anything, a burden on his master, no matter where he directs him he brings no good, is he the same as someone who commands justice and is on a straight path? (Qur'an, 16:76)

As the verse points out, it is obvious that those who are "on a straight path", are those who are devoted to their religion; fear and heed God, hold spiritual values in high regard, and are filled with eagerness to serve people. In general, such people are there to serve humanity and bring with them great benefits to mankind. For this reason, it is very important for people to learn about the true religion and live by the morals explained by the Qur'an – the final Revelation from God. In the Qur'an, God defines those people who live by such high morals:

> *Those who, if We establish them firmly on the earth, will keep up prayer and pay the welfare due, and command what is right and forbid what is wrong. The end result of all affairs is with God. (Qur'an, 22:41)*

God Commands Us to Do Good Deeds

A Muslim is someone who abides by the commands of God, tries scrupulously to live by Qur'anic morality, peace and harmony, which make the world a more beautiful place and lead it to progress. His aim is to lead people to beauty, goodness and well-being. The Qur'an says:

> *...And do good as God has been good to you. And do not seek to cause corruption in the earth. God does not love corrupters. (Qur'an, 28:77)*

Someone who adopts the Islamic faith wishes to earn God's pleasure and compassion and to enter heaven. He has to make strenuous efforts to do this, and to adopt a morality acceptable to

God while he is in this world. The clearest manifestations of this morality are compassion, pity, justice, honesty, forgiveness, humility, sacrifice and patience. The believer will behave well towards people, try to perform good deeds and spread goodness. In His verses, God commands:

> *We did not create the heavens and earth and everything between them, except with truth. The Hour is certainly coming, so forgive [men's failings] with fair forbearance. (Qur'an, 15:85)*
>
> *... Be good to your parents and relatives and to orphans and the very poor, and to neighbours who are related to you and neighbours who are not related to you, and to companions and travellers and your slaves. God does not love anyone vain or boastful. (Qur'an, 4:36)*
>
> *... Help one another in benevolence and piety. Do not help each other to wrongdoing and enmity. And fear God. God is severe in retribution. (Qur'an, 5:2)*

As the verses have made clear, God wishes those who believe in Him to behave well towards people, to cooperate with each other when it comes to goodness, and to avoid wickedness. In Sura Anam,verse 160, God promises that "anyone who comes with a fine deed will have ten more like it. But those who produce a bad action will only be repaid with its equivalent and they will not be wronged."

In His book, God describes Himself as He who knows "the secrets of men's hearts", and warns people to "avoid all kinds of evil." A Muslim therefore, which means "one who surrenders himself to God" must evidently be someone who does his best to fight terrorism.

A Muslim does not remain indifferent to what goes on around him, and never adopts the mentality that nothing matters as long as it does not harm him. That is because he has surrendered himself to God. He is His representative, and an ambassador of good. He cannot, therefore, remain indifferent in the face of cruelty and terrorism. In fact, the Muslim is the greatest enemy of terrorism, which kills people who have done no wrong. Islam is against all forms of terrorism, and tries to prevent it right from the beginning, in other words on the level of ideas. It demands peace between people and for justice to prevail, and commands people to avoid discord, conflict and wickedness.

God Commands Us to Be Just

The true justice described in the Qur'an commands man to behave justly, making no discrimination between people, to protect peoples' rights, not to permit violence no matter what the circumstances, to side with the oppressed against the oppressor and to help the needy. This justice calls for the rights of both parties to be protected when reaching a decision in a dispute, assessing all aspects of an incident, setting aside all prejudices, being objective, honest, tolerant, merciful and compassionate.

For instance, someone who cannot assess events in a moderate way, and who is swayed by his emotions and feelings, will fail to arrive at sound decisions and will remain under the influence of those feelings. However, someone who rules with justice needs to set all his personal feelings and views aside. He needs to treat all parties with justice when they ask for help, to side with what is right under all circumstances, and not to diverge from the path of honesty and truthfulness. A person should incorporate the values of the Qur'an into his soul in such a way that he may be able to consider other parties' interests before his own and maintain justice, even if this harms his own interests.

God commands the following in Sura Ma'ida, verse 42:
"... if you do judge, judge between them justly."

In Sura Nisa, God commands believers to act justly even it is against themselves:

> *O You who believe! Be upholders of justice, bearing witness for God alone, even against yourselves or your parents and relatives. Whether they are rich or poor, God is well able to look after them. Do not follow your own desires and deviate from the truth. If you twist or turn away, God is aware of what you do. (Qur'an, 4:135)*

In the Qur'an, God gives a detailed description of justice and informs believers of the attitude they have to adopt in the face of incidents they encounter and of the ways to exercise justice. Such guidance is a great comfort to believers and a mercy from God. For this reason, those who believe are responsible for exercising justice in an undivided manner both to earn God's approval and to lead their lives in peace and security.

The justice God commands in the Qur'an is the justice that is exercised equally among all people, with no consideration of language, race, or ethnicity. The justice in the Qur'anic sense does not vary according to place, time and people. In our day, too, there are people being subjected to cruel and unjust treatment because of the colour of their skin or their race in all corners of the world.

However, God informs us in the Qur'an that the purpose in the creation of different tribes and peoples is "that they should come to know each other". Different nations or peoples, all of whom are the servants of God, should get to know one another, that is, learn about their different cultures, languages, traditions and abilities. In brief, the purpose of the creation of different races and nations is not conflict and war but cultural richness. Such variation is a bounty of God's creation.

The fact that someone is taller than someone else or that his skin is yellow or white neither makes him superior to others nor is it something to feel ashamed of. Every trait a person has is a result of God's purposeful creation, but in the sight of God, these variations have no ultimate importance.

A believer knows that someone attains superiority only by having fear of God and in the strength of his faith in God. This fact is related in the following verse:

> *O Mankind! We created you from a male and female, and made you into peoples and tribes so that you might come to know each other. The noblest among you in God's sight is that one of you who best performs his duty. God is All-Knowing, All-Aware. (Qur'an, 49:13)*

As God informs us in the verse, the understanding of justice recommended by Him calls for equal, tolerant and peaceable treatment of everyone, with no discrimination between them.

Hatred Felt Towards a Community Does Not Prevent Believers From Exercising Justice

Hatred and anger are the major sources of evil, and are likely to prevent people from making just decisions, thinking soundly and conducting themselves rationally. People can readily inflict all kinds of injustice on people for whom they feel enmity.

They may accuse these people of acts they have never committed, or bear false witness against them although their innocence is known to them. On account of such enmity, people may be subjected to unbearable oppression.

Some people avoid bearing witness in favour of people they disagree with, although they know they are innocent, and they keep evidence which would reveal their innocence hidden. Furthermore, they take pleasure in the misery these people face, their encounters with injustice or great suffering. Their greatest worry, on the other hand, is that justice should be done and these peoples' innocence proved.

For these reasons, it is very hard for people in corrupt societies to trust one another. People worry that they can fall victim to someone else at any time. Having lost mutual trust, they also lose their human feelings such as tolerance, compassion, brotherhood and co-operation, and start hating one another.

However, the feelings someone holds in his heart towards a person or community should never influence a believer's decisions. No matter how immoral or hostile the person he is considering may be, the believer sets all these feelings aside and acts and makes his decisions justly and recommends that which is just. His feelings towards that person cast no shadow over his wisdom and conscience. His conscience always inspires him to comply with God's commands and advice, and never to abandon good manners, because this is a command God gives in the Qur'an. In Sura Ma'ida, it is related as follows:

> *O You who believe! Show integrity for the sake of God, bearing witness with justice. Do not let hatred for a people incite you into not being just. Be just. That is closer to faith. Heed God (alone). God is aware of what you do. (Qur'an, 5:8)*

As is related in the verse, displaying a just attitude is what most complies with having fear of God. A person of faith knows that he will attain the pleasure of God only when he acts justly. Every person who witnesses his or her good manners will trust this person, feel comfortable in their presence and trust them with any responsibility or task. Such people are treated with respect even by their enemies. Their attitude may even lead some people to have faith in God.

Islam Defends Freedom of Thought

Islam is a religion which provides and guarantees freedom of ideas, thought and life. It has issued commands to prevent and forbid tension, disputes, slander and even negative thinking among people. In the same way that it is determinedly opposed to terrorism and all acts of violence, it has also forbidden even the slightest ideological pressure to be put on them:

> *There is no compulsion in religion. True guidance has become clearly distinct from error. (Qur'an, 2:256)*

> *So remind them! You are only a reminder. You are not in control of them. (Qur'an, 88:21-22)*

Forcing people to believe in a religion or to adopt its forms of belief is completely contrary to the essence and spirit of Islam. According to Islam, true faith is only possible with free will and freedom of conscience. Of course, Muslims can advise and encourage each other about the features of Qur'anic morality. All believers are charged with explaining Qur'anic morality to people in the nicest manner possible. They will explain the beauties of religion in the light of the verse, "Call to the way of your Lord with wisdom and fair admonition..." (Qur'an, 16:125), however, they must also bear in mind the verse, "You are not responsible for their guidance, but God guides whoever He wills." (Qur'an, 2:272)

They will never resort to compulsion, nor any kind of physical or psychological pressure. Neither will they use any worldly privilege to turn someone towards religion. When they receive a negative response to what they say, Muslims will reply along the lines of: "To you your religion, and to me, mine" (Qur'an, 109:6)

The world we live in contains societies with all kinds of beliefs: Christian, Jewish, Buddhist, Hindu, atheist, deist and even pagan. Muslims living in such a world must be tolerant of all beliefs they come up against, no matter what they may be, and behave forgivingly, justly and humanely. This responsibility placed on believers is to invite people to the beauty of the religion of God by means of peace and tolerance. The decision whether or not to implement these truths, whether or not to believe, lies with the other party. Forcing that person to believe, or trying to impose anything on him, is a violation of Qur'anic morality. In fact, God issues a reminder to believers in the Qur'an:

> *If your Lord had willed, all the people on the earth would have believed. Do you think you can force people to be believers? (Qur'an, 10:99)*

> *We know best what they say and you [O Muhammad] are not a compeller over them. But warn by the Qur'an whoever fears My warning. (Qur'an, 50:45)*

A model of society in which people are forced to worship is completely contradictory to Islam. Belief and worship are only of any value when they are directed to God by the free will of the individual. If a system imposes belief and worship on people, then they will become religious out of fear of that system. From the religious point of view, what really counts is that religion should be lived for God's good pleasure in an environment where peoples' consciences are totally free.

The history of Islam is full of the tolerant practices of Muslim rulers who have respected all religions and built religious freedom with their own hands. For example, Thomas Arnold, a British missionary employed in the service of the Indian government, describes that Islam favours freedom in these words:

But of any organised attempt to force the acceptance of Islam on the non-Muslim population, or of any systematic persecution intended to stamp out the Christian religion, we hear nothing. Had the caliphs chosen to adopt either course of action, they might have swept away Christianity as easily as Ferdinand and Isabella drove Islam out of Spain, or Louis XIV made Protestantism penal in France, or the Jews were kept out of England for 350 years. The Eastern Churches in Asia were entirely cut off from communion with the rest of Christendom, throughout which no one would have been found to lift a finger on their behalf, as heretical communions. So that the very survival of these Churches to the present day is a strong proof of the generally tolerant attitude of the Muhammadan governments towards them.1

God Forbids the Murder of Innocent People

Killing a person for no reason is one of the greatest sins related in the Qur'an:

... if someone kills another person – unless it is in retaliation for someone else or for causing corruption in the earth – it is as if he had murdered all mankind. And if anyone gives life to another person, it is as if he had given life to all mankind. Our Messengers came to them with Clear Signs, but even after that many of them committed outrages in the earth. (Qur'an, 5:32)

...those who do not call on any other deity together with God and do not kill anyone God has made inviolate, except with the right to do so, and do not fornicate; anyone who does that will receive an evil punishment. (Qur'an, 25:68)

As the verse suggests, a person who kills innocent people for no reason is threatened with a great torment. God informs us that killing even a single person is as evil as murdering all mankind on earth. A person who observes God's limits can do no harm to a single human, let alone massacre thousands of innocent people. Those who assume that they can avoid justice and thus punishment in this world will never succeed, for they will have to give an account of their deeds in the presence of God. That is why believers, who know that they will give an account of their deeds after death, are very meticulous to observe God's limits.

God Commands the Faithful to be Compassionate and Merciful

Islamic morality is described in one verse as:

Then to be one of those who have faith and urge each other to steadfastness and urge each other to compassion. Those are the Companions of the Right. (Qur'an, 90:17-18)

As we have seen in this verse, one of the most important features of the morality that will lead believers to salvation on the Day of Judgement and to enter into paradise is "being one of those who urges each other to compassion".

The true source of compassion is love of God. A person's love of God gives rise to his feeling love for the things He has created. Someone who loves God feels a direct link and closeness to the things He has created. This strong love and closeness he feels for the Lord, who created him and all mankind, leads him to display a pleasing morality, as commanded in the Qur'an. True compassion emerges as he lives by this morality. This model of morality, full of love, compassion and sacrifice, is described in these verses:

Those of you possessing affluence and ample wealth should not make oaths that they will not give to their relatives and the very poor and those who have made emigration in the way of God. They should rather pardon and overlook. Would you not love God to forgive you? God is Ever-Forgiving, Most Merciful. (Qur'an, 24:22)

Those who were already settled in the abode and in faith before they came, love those who have migrated to them and do not find in their hearts any need for what they have been given and prefer them to themselves even if they themselves are needy. It is the people who are safe-guarded from the avarice of their own selves who are successful. (Qur'an, 59:9)

> *... those who have given refuge and help, they are the true believers. They will have forgiveness and generous provision. (Qur'an, 8:74)*

Be good to your parents and relatives and to orphans and the very poor, and to neighbours who are related to you and neighbours who are not related to you, and to companions and travellers and your slaves. God does not love anyone vain or boastful. (Qur'an, 4:36)

> *Charity (zakat) is for: the poor, the destitute, those who collect it, reconciling people's hearts, freeing slaves, those in debt, spending in the Way of God, and travellers. It is a legal obligation from God. God is All-Knowing, All-Wise. (Qur'an, 9:60)*

This high level of morality that is demanded from believers, described in the Qur'an, stems from their deep love of God. Thanks to their devotion to Him, they scrupulously abide by the morality revealed by Him in the Qur'an.

Believers never try to make people feel indebted because of the compassion they demonstrate and the help they offer people, and do not even expect to be thanked. Their true aim is to try to gain God's good pleasure by means of the morality they exhibit, because they know that they will be called to account for that morality on the Day of Judgement.

In the Qur'an, God has expressly revealed that hell will be the outcome for those who knowingly refuse to live by the morality of the Qur'an:

> *"What has brought you into hell-fire?" They will say, "We were not among those who prayed and we did not feed the poor." (Qur'an, 74:42-44)*

> *Seize him and bind him, and then expose him to hell-fire, then fasten him with a chain seventy cubits long! For he did not believe in God Almighty, nor did he urge the feeding of the poor. (Qur'an, 69:30-34)*
>
> *Have you seen him who denies the religion? He is the one who harshly rebuffs the orphan and does not urge the feeding of the poor. (Qur'an, 107:1-3)*
>
> *...nor do you urge the feeding of the poor (Qur'an, 89:18)*

As we have seen in these verses, the Muslim described in the Qur'an possesses a most loving and compassionate nature. Nobody who possesses this morality can of course consent to terrorism or acts of violence directed at innocent people. Terrorists' characters are the exact opposite of Qur'anic morality. A terrorist is a ruthless person who looks with hatred on the world, and wants to kill, destroy and shed blood.

A Muslim raised in the morality as revealed by the Qur'an, however, approaches everyone with the love expected by Islam, respects ideas of all kinds, always tries to bring harmony where there is discord, lower tensions, embrace all sides and behave with moderation. Societies consisting of people like this will be ruled by a more developed civilisation, and enjoy greater social morality, harmony, justice and plenty than can be seen in even the most modern nations today.

God has Commanded Forgiveness and Tolerance

The concept of forgiveness and tolerance, described in the words, "Make allowances for people" (Qur'an, 7:199) is one of the most fundamental tenets of Islam.

When we look at the history of Islam, the way that Muslims have translated this important feature of Qur'anic morality into the life of society can be seen quite clearly. As we shall be considering in later parts of the book, Muslims have always brought with them an atmosphere of freedom and tolerance wherever they have gone.

They have enabled people whose religions, languages and cultures are completely different from one another to live together in peace and harmony under one roof, and provided peace and harmony for its own members.

One of the most important reasons for the centuries-long existence of the Ottoman Empire, which spread over an enormous region, was the atmosphere of tolerance and understanding that Islam brought with it. Muslims, who have been known for their tolerant and loving natures for centuries, have always been the most compassionate and just of people. Within this multi-national structure, all ethnic groups have been free to live according to their own religions, and their own rules.

True tolerance can only bring peace and well-being to the world when implemented along the lines set out in the Qur'an. Attention is drawn to this fact in a verse which reads: "A good action and a bad action are not the same. Repel the bad with something better and, if there is enmity between you and someone else, he will be like a bosom friend." (Qur'an, 41:34)

In the verses of the Qur'an, God has always described forgiveness as a superior quality, and in one verse, He has given the good news that such behaviour will be rewarded: "The repayment of a bad action is one equivalent to it.

But if someone pardons and puts things right, his reward is with God. Certainly He does not love wrongdoers." (Qur'an, 42:40) In another verse, He has described believers as: "those who give in times of both ease and hardship, those who control their rage and pardon other people – God loves the good-doers" (Qur'an, 3:134) God has revealed in the Qur'an that it is virtuous behaviour to forgive someone even if he has done wrong. One verse on the subject reads:

> *...You will never cease to come upon some act of treachery on their part, except for a few of them. Yet pardon them, and overlook. God loves good-doers. (Qur'an, 5:13)*

All of this shows that the morality that Islam recommends to mankind brings to the world the virtues of peace, harmony and justice. The barbarism known as terrorism, that is so preoccupying the world at present, is the work of ignorant and fanatical people, completely estranged from Qur'anic morality, and who have absolutely nothing to do with religion.

The solution to these people and groups who try to carry out their savagery under the mask of religion is the teaching of true Qur'anic morality. In other words, Islam and Qur'anic morality are solutions to the scourge of terrorism, not supporters of it.

3

War in the Quran

According to the Qur'an, war represents an "unwanted obligation" which has to be carried out with strict observance of particular humane and moral guidelines and which must not be resorted to except when it is absolutely inevitable.

In one Qur'anic verse, it is explained that those who start wars are the disbelievers and that God does not approve of wars:

> *...Each time they kindle the fire of war, God extinguishes it. They rush about the earth corrupting it. God does not love corrupters. (Qur'an, 5:64)*

In the case of a conflict, before engaging in a war, believers must wait until fighting becomes compulsory. Believers are allowed to fight only when the other party attacks and no other alternative except war remains:

> *But if they cease (fighting), God is Ever-Forgiving, Most Merciful. (Qur'an, 2:192)*

A closer examination of the Prophet Muhammad's life reveals that war was a method resorted for defensive purposes only in unavoidable situations.

The revelation of the Qur'an to the Prophet Muhammad continued for a period of 23 years. During the first 13 years of this period, Muslims lived as a minority under a pagan order in Mecca and faced much oppression. Many Muslims were harassed, abused, tortured, and even murdered, their houses and possessions plundered. Despite this, however, Muslims led their lives without resorting to violence and always called the pagans to peace.

When the oppression of the pagans escalated unbearably, the Muslims emigrated to the town of Yathrib, which was later to be renamed Madinah, where they could establish their own order in a freer and more friendly environment. Even establishing their own system did not prompt them to take up weapons against the aggressive pagans of Mecca. Only after the following revelation, the Prophet commanded his people to prepare for war:

> *Permission to fight is given to those who are fought against because they have been wronged – truly God has the power to come to their support – those who were expelled from their homes without any right, merely for saying, "Our Lord is God"... (Qur'an, 22:39-40)*

In brief, Muslims were allowed to wage war only because they were oppressed and subjected to violence. To put it in another way, God granted permission for war only for defensive purposes. In other verses, Muslims are warned against the use of unnecessary provocation or violence:

> *Fight in the Way of God against those who fight you, but do not go beyond the limits. God does not love those who go beyond the limits. (Qur'an, 2:190)*

After the revelation of these verses, several wars occurred between the Muslims and the pagan Arabs. In none of these wars, however, were the Muslims the inciting party. Furthermore, the Prophet Muhammad established a secure and peaceful social environment for Muslims and pagans alike by signing the peace agreement of Hudaybiya which conceded to the pagans most of their requests. The party who violated the terms of the agreement and started hostilities once again were the pagans. With rapid conversions into Islam, the Islamic armies mustered a great force against the pagan Arabs. However, Muhammad conquered Mecca without bloodshed and in a spirit of tolerance. If he wished,

Muhammad could have taken revenge on pagan leaders in the city. Yet, he did not do harm to any one of them, forgave them and treated them with the utmost tolerance. In the words of John Esposito, a Western expert on Islam, "eschewing vengeance and the plunder of conquest, the Prophet instead accepted a settlement, granting amnesty rather than wielding the sword toward his former enemies."

Pagans, who would later convert to Islam of their own free will, could not help admiring such nobility of character in the Prophet.

Not only during Mecca's conquest, but also in the course of all the battles and conquests made in the time of the Prophet Muhammad, the rights of innocent and defenceless people were meticulously protected. The Prophet Muhammad reminded believers numerous times about this subject and by his own practice became a role model for others to follow. Indeed, he addressed believers who were about to go to war in the following terms: "Go to war in adherence to the religion of God. Never touch the elderly, women or children. Always improve their situation and be kind to them. God loves those who are sincere." The Messenger of God also clarified the attitude Muslims must adopt even when they are in the middle of a raging battle:

> *Do not kill children. Avoid touching people who devote themselves to worship in churches! Never murder women and the elderly. Do not set trees on fire or cut them down. Never destroy houses!*

The Islamic principles God proclaims in the Qur'an account for this peaceful and temperate policy of the Prophet Muhammad. In the Qur'an, God commands believers to treat the non-Muslims kindly and justly:

> *God does not forbid you from being good to those who have not fought you over religion or driven you from your homes, or from being just towards them. God loves those who are just. God merely forbids you from taking as friends those who have fought you over religion and driven you from your homes and who supported your expulsion... (Qur'an, 60:8-9)*

The verses above clarify how Muslims should behave towards non-Muslims: A Muslim should treat all non-Muslims kindly and only avoid making friends with those who show enmity towards Islam. In a case where this enmity causes violent attacks against Muslims, that is, where they wage a war against them, then Muslims should respond to them justly by considering the humane dimensions of the situation. All forms of barbarism, unnecessary acts of violence and unjust aggression are forbidden by Islam. In another verse, God warns Muslims against this and explains that rage felt towards enemies should not cause them to fall into injustice:

> *You who believe! Show integrity for the sake of God, bearing witness with justice. Do not let hatred for a people incite you into not being just. Be just. That is closer to heedfulness. Heed God (alone). God is aware of what you do. (Qur'an, 5:8)*

THE MEANING OF THE CONCEPT OF "JIHAD"

Another concept that deserves clarification due in the context of our discussion is that of "jihad".

The exact meaning of "Jihad" is "effort". Thus, in Islam, "to carry out jihad" is "to show effort, to struggle". The Prophet Muhammad explained that "the greatest jihad is the one a person carries out against his lower soul". What is meant by "lower soul" here is selfish desires and ambitions.

Assessed from the Qur'anic point of view, the word "jihad" can also mean a struggle carried out on intellectual grounds against those who oppress people, treat them unjustly, subject them to torture and cruelty and violate legitimate human rights. The purpose of this struggle is to bring about justice, peace and equality.

Apart from these ideological and spiritual meanings, struggle in the physical sense is also considered as "jihad". However, as explained above, this has to be a struggle carried out solely for defensive purposes. The use of the concept of "jihad" for acts of aggression against innocent people, that is for terror, would be unjust and a great distortion of the true meaning of the term.

Killing Oneself, In Other Words Committing Suicide, is Forbidden in the Qur'an

Another important matter that arose in the wake of the latest terrorist assaults against the United States is that of suicide attacks. Some people who are ill-informed on Islam have made utterly erroneous statements to the effect that this religion of peace allows suicide attacks, whereas in Islam killing oneself and killing other people are both prohibited. In the words, "Do not kill yourselves." (Qur'an, 4:29) God has declared suicide to be a sin. In Islam it is forbidden for anyone to kill himself or herself, for no matter what reason.

The Prophet reveals suicide to be a sin in a parable, when he says that those who commit suicide will be punished:

> *Indeed, whoever (intentionally) kills himself, then certainly he will be punished in the Fire of Hell, wherein he shall dwell forever.*

As this makes clear, committing suicide, and thus carrying out suicide attacks, and causing the deaths of thousands of innocent people while doing so, is a total violation of Islamic morality. God says in the Qur'an that it is a sin to put an end to one's own life. For that reason, it is quite impossible for someone who believes in God and says he abides by the Qur'an to do such a thing. The only people who can do such things are those who have a very mistaken perception of religion, have no idea of true Qur'anic morality, fail to use their reason and conscience, are under the influence of atheist ideologies, and who have been brainwashed with feelings of hatred and revenge. Everybody must oppose such actions.

Compassion, Tolerance and Humanity in the History of Islam

To sum up the facts we have seen so far, we can say that the political doctrine of Islam (in other words, Islamic rules and principles regarding political matters) is exceedingly moderate and peace-loving. This truth is accepted by many non-Muslim historians and theologians.

One of these is the British historian Karen Armstrong, a former nun and an expert on Middle East history. In her book Holy War, which examines the history of the three divine religions, she makes the following comments:

> *... The word 'Islam' comes from the same Arabic root as the word 'peace' and the Koran condemns war as an abnormal state of affairs opposed to God's will... Islam does not justify a total aggressive war of extermination... Islam recognises that war is inevitable and sometimes a positive duty in order to end oppression and suffering. The Koran teaches that war must be limited and be conducted in as humane a way as possible. Mohammad had to fight not only the Meccans but also the Jewish tribes in the area and Christian tribes in Syria who planned on offensive against him in alliance with the Jews. Yet this did not make Mohammed denounce the People of the Book. His Muslims were forced to defend themselves but they were not fighting a 'holy war' against the religion of their enemies. When Mohammad sent his freedman Zaid against the Christians at the head of a Muslim army, he told them to fight in the cause of God bravely but humanely. They must not molest priests, monks and nuns nor the weak and helpless people who were unable to fight. There must be no massacre of civilians nor should they cut down a single tree nor pull down any building.*

After the death of the Prophet, the Caliphs who succeeded him were also very sensitive in exercising justice. In conquered countries, both the indigenous people and the newcomers led their lives in peace and security. Abu Bakr, the first Caliph, demanded his people adopt just and tolerant attitudes in these lands. All these attitudes were in compliance with the values of the Qur'an. Abu Bakr gave the following command to his army before the first Syrian expedition:

> *Stop, O people that I may give you ten rules to keep by heart: Do not commit treachery, nor depart from the right path. You must not mutilate, neither kill a child or aged man or woman. Do not destroy a palm tree, nor burn it with fire and do not cut any fruitful tree. You msut not slay any of the flock or herds or the camels, save for*

your subsistence. You are likely to pass by people who have devoted their lives to monastic services; leave them to that to which they have devoted their lives. You are likely, likewise, to find people who will present to you meals of many kinds. You may eat; but do no forget to mention the name of Allah.

Umar ibn al-Khattab, who succeeded Abu Bakr, was famous for the way he exercised justice and made contracts with the indigenous people of the conquered countries. Each one of these contracts proved to be an example of tolerance and justice. For instance, in his declaration granting protection to Christians in Jerusalem and Lod, he ensured that churches would not be demolished and guaranteed that Muslims would not worship in churches in groups. Umar granted the same conditions to the Christians of Bethlehem. During the conquest of Medain, the declaration of protection given to the Nestorian Patriarch Yeshuyab III (650 - 660 AD) again guaranteed that churches would not be demolished and that no building would be converted into a house or a mosque. The letter written by the patriarch to the bishop of Fars (Persia) after the conquest is most striking, in the sense that it depicts the tolerance and compassion shown by Muslim rulers to the Book of People in the words of a Christian:

They [Abbasids] have not attacked the Christian religion, but rather they have commended our faith, honored our priests... and conferred benefits on churches and monasteries.

All these are very important examples revealing the understanding of justice and tolerance of true believers. In a verse God commands the following:

God commands you to return to their owners the things you hold on trust and, when you judge between people, to judge with justice. How excellent is what God exhorts you to do! God is All-Hearing, All-Seeing. (Qur'an, 4:58)

Canon Taylor, one of the mission leaders of the Anglican Church, expresses the beauty revealed by the Islamic morality in one of his speeches as follows:

> *It [Islam] brought out the fundamental dogmas of religion – the unity and greatness of God, that He is merciful and righteous, that He claims obedience to His will, resignation and faith. It proclaimed the responsibility of man, a future life, a Day of Judgment, and stern retribution to fall upon the wicked; and enforced the duties of prayer, almsgiving, fasting and benevolence. It thrust aside the artificial virtues, the religious frauds and follies, the perverted moral sentiments, and the verbal subtleties of theological disputants… It gave hope to the slave, brotherhood to mankind, and recognition to the fundamental facts of human nature.*

The false assertion that people in conquered countries converted to Islam under threat has also been disproved by Western researchers, and the justice and tolerant attitude of Muslims has been confirmed. L.Browne, a Western researcher, expresses this situation in the following words:

> *Incidentally these well-established facts dispose of the idea so widely fostered in Christian writings that the Muslims, wherever they went, forced people to accept Islam at the point of the sword.*

In his book The Prospects of Islam, Browne goes on to say that the real motive behind the Muslims' conquests was the brotherhood of Islam. The vast majority of Muslim administrators who have reigned over the Muslim lands throughout history continued to treat the members of other religions with the utmost tolerance and respect. Within the borders of all Islamic states, both Jews and Christians lived in safety and enjoyed freedom.

Georgetown University's Professor of Religion and International Relations John L. Esposito describes how Jews and Christians who came under the administration of Muslim states met with enormous tolerance:

> *Muslim armies proved to be formidable conquerors and effective rulers, builders rather than destroyers. They replaced the indigenous rulers and armies of the conquered countries, but preserved much of their government, bureaucracy, and culture. For many in the conquered territories, it was no more than an exchange of masters, one that*

brought peace to peoples demoralized and disaffected by the casualties and heavy taxation that resulted from the years of Byzantine-Persian warfare. Local communities were free to continue to follow their own way of life in internal, domestic affairs. In many ways, local populations found Muslim rule more flexible and tolerant than that of Byzantium and Persia. Religious communities were free to practise their faith-to worship and be governed by their religious leaders and laws in such areas marriage, divorce, and inheritance. In exchange, they were required to pay tribute, a poll tax (jizya) that entitled them to from Muslim protection from outside aggression and exempted them from military service. They were therefore called the "protected ones" (dhimmmi). In effect, this often meant lower taxes, grater local autonomy, rule by fellow Semites with closer linguistic and cultural ties than the hellenized, Greco-Roman elites of Byzantium, and greater religious freedom for Jews and indigenous Christians. Most of the Christian churches, such as the Nestorians, Monophysites, Jacobites, and Copts, had been persecuted as heretics and schismatics by Christian orthodoxy. For these reasons, some Jewish and Christian communities aided the invading armies, regarding them as less oppressive than their imperial masters. In many ways, the conquests brought a Pax Islamica to an embattled area.

Another "Pax Islamica" brought by Islam was to women, a segment of society that was tremendously abused in the pre-Islamic times. Professor Bernard Lewis, known to be one of the greatest Western experts on the Middle East, makes the following comment:

In general, the advent of Islam brought an enormous improvement in the position of women in ancient Arabia, endowing them with property and some other rights, and giving them a measure of protection against ill treatment by their husbands or owners. The killing of female infants, sanctioned by custom in Pagan Arabia, was outlawed by Islam. But the position of women remained poor, and worsened when, in this as in so many other respects, the original message of Islam lost its impetus and was modified under the influence of pre-existing attitudes and customs.

The reign of the Seljuk Turks and that of the Ottoman Empire were also marked by the just and tolerant outlook of Islam. In his book, *The Spread of Islam in the World*, Sir Thomas Arnold, the British researcher, explains the Christians' willingness to come under Seljuk rule because of this attitude:

> *This same sense of security of religious life under Muslim rule led many of the Christians of Asia Minor, also, about the same time, to welcome the advent of the Saljuq Turks as their deliverers... In the reign of Michael VIII (1261-1282), the Turks were often invited to take possession of the smaller towns in the interior of Asia Minor by the inhabitants, that they might escape from the tyranny of the empire; and both rich and poor often emigrated into Turkish dominions.*

Malik Shah, the ruler of the Islamic Seljuk Empire during its brightest age, approached the people in the conquered lands with great tolerance and compassion and thus was remembered with respect and love by them. All objective historians refer to the justice and tolerance of Malik Shah in their works. His tolerance also kindled feelings of love towards him in the hearts of the People of the Book. For this reason, unprecedented in history, many cities came under Malik Shah's rule of their own free will. Sir Thomas Arnold also mentions Odo de Diogilo, a monk of St. Denis, who participated in the Second Crusade as the private chaplain of Louis VII, refers in his memoirs to the justice administered by Muslims regardless of the subjects' religious affiliation. Based on the graphic account of Odo de Diogilo, Sir Thomas Arnold writes:

> *The situation of the survivors would have been utterly hopeless, had not the sight of their misery melted the hearts of the Muhammadans to pity. They tended the sick and relieved the poor and starving with open-handed liberality. Some even bought up the French money which the Greeks had got out of the pilgrims by force or cunning, and lavishly distributed it among the needy. So great was the contrast between the kind treatment the pilgrims received from the unbelievers and the cruelty of their fellow-Christians, the Greeks, who imposed forced labour upon them, beat them, and robbed them of what little they*

had left, that many of them voluntarily embraced the faith of their deliverers. As the old chronicler [Odo de Diogilo] says: "Avoiding their co-religionists who had been so cruel to them, they went in safety among the infidels who had compassion upon them, and, as we heard, more than three thousand joined themselves to the Turks when they retired."

These statements by historians reveal that Muslim administrators who truly adopted the morality of the Islam always ruled with tolerance, compassion and justice. Likewise, the history of the Ottoman Empire which ruled lands on three continents for centuries abounds with examples of tolerance.

The way the Jews settled in Ottoman lands during the time of Sultan Beyazid II, after being subjected to massacre and exile in the Catholic kingdoms of Spain and Portugal, is a fine example of the tolerance that Islamic morality brings with it.

The Catholic monarchs who ruled much of Spain at the time brought grave pressure to bear on the Jews who had formerly lived in peace under Muslim rule in Andalusia. While Muslims, Christians and Jews were able to live side by side in peace in Andalusia, the Catholic monarchs tried to force the whole country to become Christian, and declared war on the Muslims while oppressing the Jews. As a result, the last Muslim ruler in the Granada region of southern Spain was overthrown in 1492. Muslims were subjected to terrible slaughter, and those Jews who refused to change their religion were sent into exile.

One group of these Jews without a homeland sought shelter in the Ottoman Empire, and the state allowed them to do so. The Ottoman fleet, under the command of Kemal Reis, brought the exiled Jews, and those Muslims who had survived the slaughter, to the land of the Ottomans.

Sultan Beyazid II has gone down in history as a most pious believer, and in the spring of 1492 he settled these wronged Jews who had been expelled from Spain in certain parts of his empire, around Edirne, and Thessalonica in present-day Greece. Most of the 25,000 Turkish Jews living in Turkey today are the ancestors of those Spanish Jews. They have adapted their religion and customs, which they brought from Spain some 500 years ago, to the conditions in Turkey, and continue to live most comfortably with their own schools, hospitals, old people's homes, cultural associations and newspapers. In the same way that they have traders and businessmen, they also have representatives in numerous professions, from technical subjects to advertising, with increasingly developing intellectual circles. While Jewish communities in many countries in Europe have for centuries been exposed to the fear of anti-Semitic racist attacks, those in Turkey have lived in peace and security. This example alone is enough to demonstrate the tolerance that Islam brings with it and its understanding of justice.

The compassion and tolerance exhibited by Sultan Beyazid II applied to all the Ottoman sultans. When Sultan Mehmet the Conqueror captured Constantinople, he allowed the Christians and the Jews to live freely there. André Miquel, who is known for the valuable works he has written about the just and tolerant practices of Muslims and the world of Islam, says:

> *Christians lived under a very well-administered government which they were unable to find in the time of the Byzantine and Latin states. They at no time saw any systematic oppression. On the contrary, the empire, and Constantinople in particular, became a shelter for those Spanish Jews who had been tortured. There was no forced imposition of Islam anywhere.*

As is clear from these facts, Muslims have at no time in history been oppressive. On the contrary, they have brought peace and security to all nations and beliefs wherever they have gone. They have abided by God's verse which says: "Worship God and do not associate anything with Him. Be good to your parents and relatives and to orphans and the very poor, and to neighbours who are related to you and neighbours who are not related to you, and to companions and travellers and your slaves. God does not love anyone vain or boastful." (Qur'an, 4:36) and have behaved well to all people.

In short, friendship, brotherhood, peace and love are the bases of Qur'anic morality, and it is to these superior virtues that Muslims try to adhere.

THE REAL FACE OF THE TERRORISTS WHO ACT IN THE NAME OF RELIGION

All these examples reveal that organising acts of terror against innocent people is utterly against Islam and it is unlikely that any Muslim could ever commit such crime. On the contrary, Muslims are responsible for stopping these people, removing "mischief on earth" and bringing peace and security to all people all over the world.

It is not possible to talk about "Christian terror", "Jewish terror" or "Islamic terror". Indeed, an examination into the background of the perpetrators of these acts reveal that the terrorism in question is not a religious but a social phenomenon.

CRUSADERS: BARBARIANS WHO TRAMPLED THEIR OWN RELIGION

The true message of a religion or a system of belief can be at times distorted by its own pseudo-adherents. The Crusaders, whose period constitutes a dark episode in Christian history, are an example of this type of distortion.

The Crusaders were European Christians who undertook expeditions from the end of the 11th century onwards to recover the Holy Land (Palestine and the surrounding area) from the Muslims. They set out with a so-called religious goal, yet they laid waste each acre of land they entered spreading fear wherever they went. They subjected civilians along their way to mass executions and plundered many villages and towns.

Their conquest of Jerusalem, where Muslims, Jews and Christians lived under Islamic rule in peace, became the scene of immense bloodshed. They massacred all the Muslims and Jews in the city without mercy.

In the words of one historian, "They killed all the Saracens and the Turks they found... whether male of female."16 One of the Crusaders, Raymond of Aguiles, boasted of this violence:

> *Wonderful sights were to be seen. Some of our men (and this was more merciful) cut off the heads of their enemies; others shot them with arrows, so that they fell from the towers; others tortured them longer by casting them into the flames. Piles of heads, hands and feet were to be seen in the streets of the city. It was necessary to pick one's way over the bodies of men and horses. But these were small matters compared to what happened at the Temple of Solomon, a place where religious services are normally chanted ... in the Temple and porch of Solomon, men rode in blood up to their knees and bridle reins.*

In two days, the Crusader army killed some 40,000 Muslims in the barbaric ways just described.

The Crusaders' barbarism was so excessive that, during the Fourth Crusade, they plundered Constantinople (present-day Istanbul), a Christian city, and stole the golden objects from the churches.

Of course, all this barbarism was utterly against Christian doctrine. Christianity, in the words of the Bible, is a "message of love". In the Gospel according to Matthew, it is said that Jesus said to his followers, "Love your enemies and pray for those who persecute you" (Matthew, 5:44). In the Gospel according to Luke, it is said that Jesus said, "To him who strikes you on the cheek, offer the other also." (Luke, 6:29) In no part of the Gospels is there any reference to the legitimacy of violence; thus murdering innocent people is unimaginable. You can find the concept of "murdering the innocent" in the Bible; but only in the cruel Jewish King Herod's attempt to kill Jesus while he was a baby.

If Christianity is a religion based on love that accommodates no violence, how did Christian Crusaders carry out some of the most violent acts in history? The major reason for this was that the Crusaders were mainly made up of ignorant people who could better be defined as "rabble". These masses, who knew almost nothing about their religion, who had probably never read or even seen the Bible once in their lifetime, and who were for the most part completely unaware of the moral values of the Bible, were led into barbarism under the conditioning of Crusaders' slogans which presented this violence as "God's Will". Employing this fraudulent method, many were encouraged to commit dreadful acts strictly forbidden by the religion.

It is worth mentioning that in that period, Eastern Christians – the people of Byzantium, for instance – who were culturally far ahead of Western Christians, espoused more humane values. Both before and after the Crusaders' conquests, Orthodox Christians managed to live together with Muslims. According to Terry Jones, the BBC commentator, with the withdrawal of the Crusaders from Middle East, "civilized life started again and members of the three monotheistic faiths returned to peaceful coexistence."

The example of the Crusaders is indicative of a general phenomenon. The more the adherents of an ideology are uncivilised, intellectually underdeveloped and ignorant, the more likely they are to resort to violence. This also holds true for ideologies that have nothing to do with religion. All communist movements around the world are prone to violence. Yet the most savage and bloodthirsty of them were the Red Khmers in Cambodia. This was because they were the most ignorant.

THE BEDOUIN CHARACTER IN THE QUR'AN

In the period of the Prophet Muhammad, there existed two basic social structures in Arabia. City-dwellers and Bedouins (desert Arabs). A sophisticated culture prevailed in Arab towns. Commercial relations linked the towns to the outer world, which contributed to the formation of "good manners" among Arabs dwelling in cities. They had refined aesthetic values, enjoyed literature and especially poetry. Desert Arabs, on the other hand, were the nomad tribes living in the desert who had a very crude culture. Utterly unaware of arts and literature, they developed an unrefined character. Islam was born and developed among the inhabitants of Mecca, the most important city of the peninsula. However, as Islam spread to the rest of the peninsula, all the tribes in Arabia embraced it. Among these tribes were also desert Arabs, who were somehow problematic: their poor intellectual and cultural background prevented some of them from grasping the profundity and noble spirit of Islam. Of this God states the following in a verse:

> *The desert Arabs are the worst in disbelief and hypocrisy, and more fitted to be ignorant of the limits which God has sent down to His Messenger. But God is Knowing, Wise. (Qur'an, 9:97)*

The desert Arabs, that is, social groups who were "worst in disbelief and hypocrisy" and prone to disobey God's commands, became a part of the Islamic world in the Prophet's time. However, in later periods, they became a source of trouble for the house of Islam. The sect called "Kharijis" that emerged among the Bedouins was an example. The most distinctive trait of this perverse sect (which was called "Kharijis", the "rebels", because they greatly deviated from Sunni practices), was their wild and fanatical nature. The "Kharijis", who had little understanding of the essence of Islam or of the virtues and the values of the Qur'an, waged war against all other Muslims basing this war on a few Qur'anic verses about which they made distorted interpretations. Furthermore, they carried out "acts of terrorism". Ali, who was one of the closest companions of the Prophet and was described as the "gate of the city of knowledge", was assassinated by a Kharijite.

In later periods, "Hashashis", another brutal organisation, emerged; this was a "terrorist organisation" made up of ignorant and fanatical militants bereft of a profound understanding of the essence of Islam and thus who could be readily influenced by simple slogans and promises.

In other words, just as the Crusaders distorted and misinterpreted Christianity as a teaching of brutality, some perverted groups emerging in the Islamic world misinterpreted Islam and resorted to brutality.

What is common to these sects and the Crusaders was their "Bedouin" nature. That is, they were ignorant, unrefined and uncultivated, lacking a true understanding of their religion. The violence they resorted to resulted from this lack of understanding, rather than from the religion they claimed to espouse.

A TERRORIST IS WTIHOUT PITY WHOSE ONLY PURPOSE IS TO DESTROY

The founder of Russian Anarchy, Michael Bakunin and his disciple Nechayev define an ideal terrorist in this way:

> *The whole work of his [a revolutionist's] existence, not only in words, but also in deeds, is at war with the existing order of society, and with the whole so-called civilized world, with its laws, morals and customs, he is an uncompromising opponent... He knows only one science; the science of destruction.* (The Alarm *Newspaper Article, "Bakunin's Ground-Work for the Social Revolution," 1885 Dec. 26, 8 p.)*

As understood from these words of Bakunin and Nechayev, terrorists are people who sever their relationship with every material and spiritual institution thereby rejecting every moral value, and who view these institutions as impediments to their designs.

Bakunin also said, "Day and night dare he [a revolutionist] have only one thought, one aim: the unmerciful destruction; while he, cold-blooded and without rest, follows that aim, he himself must be ready to die at any time and ready to kill with his own hands any one who seeks to thwart his aims." In his Ground-Work for the Social Revolution, there is this description of what kind of person a terrorist must be:

> *Stringent with himself he must also be to others. All weak sentiment towards relation, friendship, love and thankfulness must be suppressed through the only cold passion of the revolutionary work.*

These words lay bare the dark face of terrorism and show that it is completely opposed to the religion of Islam which is founded on peace, tolerance and love. In this verse, God reveals that peace is the real salvation of humanity and that pursuing the opposite, that is war and conflict, is to walk in the steps of Satan:

> *O You who believe! Enter absolutely into peace (Islam). Do not follow in the footsteps of Satan. He is an outright enemy to you. (Qur'an, 2:208)*

The Mass Psychology of Terrorism

Another important characteristic of terrorists is that they act with a collective spirit. Within this spirit, individual ideas and personal choice are disregarded as everyone is directed toward one single goal. Those who act within this collective spirit may do things they would never do in their right mind and commit acts without using their own will and consciousness. In many countries of the world, terror groups composed of a few unintelligent and uneducated people get caught up in the emotional hysteria of mass meetings, slogans, and without even knowing what they are doing or why, they get involved in committing mass atrocities.

In one moment, such people can turn into killers with blood on their hands, and even terrorists who are able to commit inhuman acts. A person may seem quiet and calm when he is alone, but when he becomes a part of a terrorist group, he may become capable of committing acts of arson and assault for no apparent reason. Such spells are cast over individuals that they are even willing to be killed for their cause.

The majority of those who take part in acts of terror often have weak wills and consciences, and they become like a flock of sheep under the influence of mass psychology. Good sense and judgment are substituted by excessive and extravagant emotionalism and a tendency toward violence and aggression. Such people are easily provoked, intolerant and know no limitation set by any law.

The error of this mass psychology is revealed in the Qur'an where it says that human beings must act according to their own will and intelligence:

Do not pursue what you have no knowledge of. Hearing, sight and hearts will all be questioned. (Qur'an, 17:36)

One of the Sources of Terrorism: Third World Fanaticism

These examples from history may help us gain better understanding of the present phenomenon, the so-called "Islamic terror", which is nowadays at the top of the international agenda. That is because those who emerge and carry out acts of terrorism in the name of Islam and those who back such acts, representing a tiny minority in the world of Islam, stem from this "character peculiar to Bedouins", not from Islam itself. Failing to understand the essence of Islam, which is essentially a religion of peace and justice, they make it a tool of barbarism, which is simply an outcome of their social and cultural structure. The origin of this barbarism, which may well be called "Third World Fanaticism", is the benighted initiatives of people who are devoid of love for their fellow human-beings.

It is a fact that, for the last few centuries, Muslims in all corners of the Islamic world, have been subjected to violence by Western forces and their allies. The colonialist European states, local oppressive regimes or colonialists backed by the West (Israel, for example) have caused great suffering to Muslims at large. However, for Muslims, this is a situation that has to be approached and responded to from a purely Qur'anic stance.

In no part of the Qur'an does God command believers to respond to violence with violence. On the contrary, God commands Muslims to "respond to evil with goodness":

A good deed and a bad deed are not the same. Repel the bad with something better and, if there is enmity between you and someone else, he will be like a bosom friend. (Qur'an, 41:34)

It is no doubt a legitimate right of Muslims to react against this cruelty. However, these reactions should never turn into a blind hatred, an unjust enmity. God warns about this in the following verse:

> *...Let not the hatred of a people [who once] obstructed you from the Sacred Mosque lead you to transgress. Help one another in benevolence and piety, and help not one another in sin and transgression... (Qur'an, 5:2)*

Consequently, carrying out terrorist acts against the innocent people of other nations under the pretence of "representing the innocent nations in the world", is by no means compatible with Islam.

Another point that deserves a special mention here is that all Western nations and communities cannot be held responsible for the aforementioned violence and oppression against Muslims. Actually, the materialist, irreligious philosophies and ideologies that prevailed in the 19th century are in the main responsible for these dismal acts. European colonialism did not originate from Christianity. On the contrary, anti-religious movements opposing the values of Christianity led the way to colonialism.

At the roots of the greatest brutalities of the 19th century lies the Social Darwinist ideology. In the Western world today, there are still cruel, mischievous and opposing factors, as well as a culture dominated by peaceful and just elements that have its roots in Christianity. As a matter of fact, the main disagreement is not between the West and Islam. Contrary to the general opinion, it is between the devout people of the West and of the Muslim world on the one hand, and the people opposing religion (materialists, atheists, Darwinists etc.) on the other.

Another indication that Third World Fanaticism has nothing to do with Islam is that, until recently, this fanaticism had been identified with the communist ideology. As is well-known, similar anti-Western acts of terror were carried out in 1960s and 1970s by Soviet-backed communist organisations. As the impact of the communist ideology faded, some of the social structures which gave birth to communist organisations have turned their attention to Islam. This "brutality presented under the guise of religion", which is formulated by the incorporation of some Islamic concepts and symbols into the former communist literature is entirely against the moral values which constitute the essence of Islam.

A last remark about this issue is that Islam is not peculiar to a particular nation or geographical region. Contrary to the dominant Western perception, Islam is not an "eastern culture". Islam is the last religion revealed to mankind as a guide to the true path that recommends itself to all humanity. Muslims are responsible for communicating the true religion they believe in to all people of all nations and cultures and making them feel closer to Islam.

Consequently, there is a unique solution for people and groups who, in the name of Islam, resort to terror, form oppressive regimes and turn this world into a dreadful place instead of beautifying it: revealing the true nature of Islam and communicating it so that the masses can understand and live by it.

One of The Methods of Terrorism is to Cause Fear and Panicin Society

One of the most important characteristics of terrorism is that it selects its targets indiscriminately. The fact that it determines these targets without discrimination is one of the most important reasons for the spread of fear, because no one can feel secure. If people know that they are possible targets for noreasons, no-one will feel safe from the terrorists. There is nothing a potential target can do to protect themselves, since terrorists act according to their own rules, in a time and place of their own choosing. Thus acts of terror in society are arbitrary and unpredictable.

The Error of Radicalism

There is another idea that we must examine together with that of terror; that is, the phenomenon of radicalism.

Radicalism means supporting sudden revolutionary destructive changes in any sphere and applying a strict uncompromising policy in order to achieve them. Radicals are characterised by their desire for revolutionary change and the stern, sometimes aggressive attitude they adopt.

In this, as in every sphere of life, the guide for the Muslim is the Qur'an. When we look at radicalism in the light of the Qur'an, we see that it has nothing to do with the way in which God commands the believers to behave. When God describes a believer in the Qur'an, He depicts him as a loving, soft-spoken person, shunning conflicts and arguments, approaching even the most hostile people with warmth and friendship.

An example to guide us in this matter is the command given by God to Moses and Aaron to go to Pharaoh and speak gently to him:

> *Go to Pharaoh; he has overstepped the bounds. But speak to him with gentle words so that hopefully he will pay heed or show some fear. (Qur'an, 20:43-44)*

Pharaoh was one of the most cruel and rebellious unbelievers of his time. He was a despot who denied God and worshipped idols; moreover, he subjected believers (the Israelites of the time) to terrible cruelties and murder. But God commanded His prophets to go to such a hostile man and speak to him gently.

You will notice that the way shown by God was the way of friendly dialogue, not the way of conflict with sharp words, angry slogans and agitated protests.

There are a few other examples to show Muslims how to behave in the dialogue between Shu'ayb and the deniers. This dialogue is related in the Qur'an in this way:

> *And to Madyan their brother Shu'ayb. He said, 'My people, worship God! You have no deity apart from Him. Do not give short measure and short weight. I see you prospering and I fear for you the punishment of an all-encompassing Day.*

My people! Give full measure and full weight with justice; do not diminish people's goods; and do not go about the earth, corrupting it.

What endures with God is better for you if you are believers. I am not set over you as your keeper."

They said, "Shu'ayb, do your prayers instruct you that we should abandon what our fathers worshipped or stop doing whatever we want to with our wealth? Yet you are such a lenient, normal person!"

> *He said, 'My people! What do you think? If I do possess a Clear Sign from my Lord and He has given me His good provision, I do not want to oppose you in what way I am forbidding you. I only want to put things right as far as I can. My success is with God alone. I have put my trust in Him and I turn to Him." (Qur'an, 11:84-88)*

When we examine what he says, we see that Shu'ayb invited the people to believe in God and to adopt high moral principals and he did this with friendliness and humility. We can explain some of the reasons behind of the things said in these verses:

* When Shu'ayb says "I am not set over you as your keeper." to the people, he does not want to dominate them; his only intention is to inform them of the truth that God has revealed.
* "You are clearly the forbearing, the rightly-guided": These words of the deniers to Shu'ayb show his warm, gentle and courteous character and that this was particularly appreciated by the deniers.
* "My people! What do you think?" This expression used by Shu'ayb shows that he calls on the deniers to use their intelligence and conscience. In other words, he does not use insistent pressure, but questions their ideas from an opposing stance and invites them to consider and come to a conclusion based on their own free conscience.
* "I do not want to oppose you in what way I am forbidding you". Shu'ayb's prohibition here is not actually a prohibition. He explains that some acts are sinful and invites the people

to abandon them. Moreover, when Shu'ayb says "I do not want to oppose you", it is not his purpose to dispute with the people; he does not want to make them uncomfortable and incite a quarrel; he wants only to invite them to faith and the practice of high moral principles.

If you examine the Qur'an you will see that a warm, gentle and tolerant disposition characterized all the prophets. God describes Abraham as "tender-hearted and forbearing." (Qur'an, 9:114) and in another verse, the Prophet Muhammad's moral principles are described in this way:

It is a mercy from God that you were gentle with them. If you had been rough or hard of heart, they would have scattered from around you. So pardon them and ask forgiveness for them, and consult with them about the matter. Then when you have reached a firm decision, put your trust in God. God loves those who put their trust in Him. (Qur'an, 3:159)

An obvious characteristic of radicalism is its anger. This disposition can be clearly seen in the speeches, writings and demonstrations of radicals. However, anger is not an attribute of Muslims. When God describes believers in the Qur'an, he describes, "those who give in times of both ease and hardship, those who control their rage and pardon other people – God loves the good-doers" (Qur'an, 3:134)

There is no situation in which a Muslim displays anger. The only thing a Muslim wants from other people is that they believe in God and live according to moral principles, but this is possible only by the grace of God. No matter what we do, no matter how much we try to explain the truth to people, human hearts are in God's hands. God reminds Muslims of this very important fact in this verse, "...Do those who believe not know that if God had wanted to He could have guided all mankind? ..." (Qur'an, 13:31)

There is another verse that emphasises this same fact;

If your Lord had willed, all the people on the earth would have believed. Do you think you can force people to be believers? (Qur'an, 10:99)

Therefore, it is the duty of a Muslim only to explain the facts and to invite people to accept them. Whether or not people accept the invitation is completely up to their own conscience. God reveals this truth in the Qur'an when He says that there is no compulsion in religion.

There is no compulsion in religion. True guidance has become clearly distinct from error. Anyone who rejects false deities and has belief in God has grasped the Firmest Handhold, which will never give way. God is All-Hearing, All-Knowing. (Qur'an, 2:256)

Therefore, there is no coercion to make people believe and become Muslims, or to make Muslims perform prayers and beware of sin. There is only advice. God reveals in a few verses addressed to the Messenger of God that Muslims are not oppressors:

We know best what they say. You are not a dictator over them. So remind, with the Qur'an, whoever fears My Threat. (Qur'an, 50:45)

Say: 'Mankind! The truth has come to you from your Lord. Whoever is guided is only guided for his own good. Whoever is misguided is only misguided to his detriment. I have not been set over you as a guardian." (Qur'an, 10:108)

Muslims are responsible only for explaining their religion; they apply no pressure or coercion on anyone and are enjoined to speak gently to even the most tyrannical deniers. Such persons cannot be radicals, because radicalism stands for the opposite of those qualities we have enumerated. Indeed, radicalism is an un-Islamic current of thought and a political stance that came into the Islamic world from outside. When we examine social phenomena described in terms of radicalism, it will be seen that these are basically a collection of methods and pronouncements used by communists in the past, or an expression of the "fanatical rage" that has no place in true Islam. (The Qur'an, 48:26)

All Muslims must totally reject an angry, unbending argumentative attitude which goes against the very nature of the Qur'an and in its place adopt a friendly, gentle, tolerant, calm and compassionate one. Muslims must set an example to the world and be admired for their maturity, tolerance, moderation, modesty and peacefulness. Muslims must live Islam in the best possible way and be its representatives to the world, not only in these things, but also by their achievements in the fields of science, culture, art, aesthetics and social order and others.

Explaining Islam to others and defending Islam against ideas alien to it are included in what we have listed above. In the verse below, God clearly reveals what attitude a Muslim must assume with regard to others:

> *Call to the way of your Lord with wisdom and fair admonition, and argue with them in the kindest way. Your Lord knows best who is misguided from His way. And He knows best who are guided. (Qur'an, 16:125)*

Terrorist Methods and Psychology

The concept of terror has a wider meaning in today's language. Generally it refers to the armed conflict carried on by radical ideological groups. In general, terror means intimidation. But this intimidation encompasses a broad field including the whole lives of people who feel the intense threat of fear and violence. Terror includes intense and systematic intimidation designed to make people adopt a certain way of thinking and behaviour, as well as every kind of violent act carried out to produce this intimidation. But in every situation, the target of terrorism is directly or indirectly the citizens themselves.

Terror organisations use terror to rally support. The intimidation they use is calculated to increase their strength and so to gain the support of some or all the citizens.

The first thing that people think of when we mention the word "terror" is generally the kind known as "leftist terror", but there is also a kind of terror found in Third World countries and practiced by dictatorial regimes. Actually the reality here is nothing other than a massive implementation of leftist terror tactics. A dictator or a group in power is oppressive, using their power only for personal gain and for this reason they experience various kinds of social opposition. In this situation, the dictatorial regime always resorts to the same formula to show that it is stronger than the opposition; they inaugurate the use of terror so that citizens will be afraid and their own power are consolidated.

Terror organisations, on the other hand, in accordance with the ideologies they espouse, claim that their aim is to remove a government and its administrators which they regard as illegitimate and cruel and, in so doing, that they will reach their goal of establishing a happier and more just way of life. However, this is not a realistic claim. In the Qur'an, in the first verses of Sura Baqara, God issues this command to those who think in this way:

> *When they are told, "Do not cause corruption on the earth," they say, "We are only putting things right." No indeed! They are the corrupters, but they are not aware of it. (Qur'an, 2:11-12)*

For terrorists, killing people is a way of life. They may shoot innocent people without pity and throw bombs at children. For them shedding blood is a pleasure. They have ceased to be human beings and turned into raving savage beasts. If there is anyone among them who shows the least feeling of compassion, they brand him as a coward or a traitor and demote him. Often they use their guns against one another and carry out bloody purges against internal factions in their own organisation.

It can be seen that terrorism is nothing other than a totally diabolical source of bloodshed. Whoever supports this cycle of savagery is defending a satanic system. If a terrorist uses religious language and symbols, this must not deceive anyone. Terrorists who hide under the cloak of false religion are doubly guilty, both of the blood they have shed and for the anti-religious propaganda they have spread while committing these crimes in the name of religion.

Terror and religion are completely opposed to each other. Terrorism adopts the way of aggression, murder, conflict, cruelty and misery. But according to the Qur'an, all these things are kinds of oppression. God enjoins peace, harmony, goodwill and compromise. He forbids terror and every kind of act that does not promote peace, and, condemns those who commit such acts:

But as for those who break God's contract after it has been agreed and sever what God has commanded to be joined, and cause corruption in the earth, the curse will be upon them. They will have the Evil Abode. (Qur'an, 13:25)

The basic quality that terror and those who are infected by its cruelty have in common is that the fear and love of God is something completely alien to them. Their hearts have become hardened and they are spiritually ill. In the Qur'an, God speaks about the character of such people:

But do not obey any vile swearer of oaths, any backbiter, slandermonger, impeder of good, evil aggressor, gross, coarse and furthermore, despicable.(Qur'an, 68:10-13)

To rebel for no cause and to commit acts of assault are forbidden by God. In Islam, acts of what we call terror and anarchy today are forbidden. In the Qur'an it is said:

Say: "My Lord has forbidden indecency, both open and hidden, and wrong action, and unrightful tyranny, and associating anything with God for which He has sent down no authority, and saying things about God that you do not know." (Qur'an, 7:33)

Acts of Violance - One of the Most Important Methods of Terrorist Propaganda

Terrorists regard acts of violence as propaganda for their organisations. For them, killing innocent people, robbing banks, assassinating people, kidnapping and planting bombs all act as propaganda for their struggle. To the terrorist who is bent on wreaking chaos, what publicity a single act of violence can generate in one day is much more publicity than what millions of hand-out brochures could do.

This idea is totally foreign to every kind of human feeling of compassion, mercy, concord and tolerance; it is alien to the moral teaching of the Qur'an and can gain a following only in those societies in which anti-religious ideologies hold sway. For this reason, the only possible solution that can save humanity from this benighted way of thinking is the widespread acceptance of the moral teachings found in the Qur'an and taken as a way of life.

THE OUTLOOK OF ISLAM ON THE PEOPLE OF THE BOOK

Another important topic that has been on the agenda with the acts of terrorism against the United States is the relation between the Western and Islamic worlds. As is known, by the 90s, some intellectuals were suggesting that the world was due for a struggle that would take place between the West and Islam. This is the basic theme of Samuel Huntington's well-known thesis "The Clash of Civilisations". However, this thesis—better called as "Clash of Ignorance" by Edward W. Said—rests on an imaginary scenario generated by the exaggeration of the influence of some radical and ignorant factions to be found in these two civilisations. Actually, there can be no clash between the Western civilisation and the Islamic civilisation, because the beliefs of Judaism and Christianity, the tenets upon which Western civilisation is based, are in perfect harmony with Islam.

In the Qur'an, Jews and Christians are called the "People of the Book". This is because the members of these two religions abide by the Divine Books revealed by God. The outlook of Islam on the People of the Book is extremely just and compassionate.

This attitude towards the People of the Book developed during the years of the birth of Islam. At that time, Muslims were a minority, struggling to protect their faith and suffering oppression and torture from the pagans of the city of Mecca. Due to this persecution, some Muslims decided to flee Mecca and shelter in a safe country with a just ruler. The Prophet Muhammad told them to take refuge the Christian king of Ethiopia. The Muslims who went to Ethiopia found a very fair administration that embraced them with love and respect. The King refused the demands of the pagan messengers who had travelled to Ethiopia and asked him to surrender the Muslims to them, and announced that Muslims could live freely in his country.

These Christian attitudes of compassion, mercy, and justice, are referred to in a verse of the Qur'an which states:

> ... *You will find the people most affectionate to those who believe are those who say, "We are Christians." That is because some of them are priests and monks and because they are not arrogant. (Qur'an, 5:82)*

COMMON BELIEFS AND VALUES SHARED BY MUSLIMS AND THE PEOPLE OF THE BOOK

Christian and Muslim beliefs have many aspects in common. Judaism too shares many beliefs with Islam. In the Qur'an, God relates that Muslims share the same faith with the People of the Book and that they say to them "We have faith in what has been sent down to us and what was sent down to you. Our God and your God are one and we submit to Him." (Qur'an, 29:46)

All true adherents of these three great religions:

- believe that God has created the entire universe out of nothing and that He dominates all that exists with His omnipotence.
- believe that God has created man and living things in a miraculous way and that man possesses a soul granted him by God.
- believe in resurrection, Heaven and Hell and angels, and that God has created our lives with a certain destiny.
- believe that besides Jesus, Moses or Muhammad, God sent many prophets such as Noah, Abraham, Isaac and Joseph throughout history, and they love all these prophets.

In one verse, that Muslims make no distinction among prophets is related as follows:

> *The Messenger believes in what has been sent down to him by his Lord, and so do the believers. Each one believes in God and His angels and His Books and His Messengers. We do not differentiate between any of His Messengers. They say, "We hear and we obey. Forgive us, our Lord! You are our journey's end."* (Qur'an, 2:285)

The beliefs of the People of the Book are in harmony with Muslims, not only in terms of faith-related issues, but also of moral values. Today, in a world where such immoralities as adultery, homosexuality, drug addiction and a model of egoism and self-seeking cruelty have grown widespread, the People of the Book and Muslims share the same virtues: Honour, chastity, humility, self-sacrifice, honesty, compassion, mercy and unconditional love.

The Common Forces against Faith

Another important fact that draws Christianity, Judaism and Islam together is the atheist philosophies that are so influential in our time.

Among the best-known and most harmful philosophies of our age can be cited materialism, communism, fascism, anarchism, racism, nihilism and existentialism. Many people who believed in the false diagnoses, deceptive descriptions and explanations of these ideas on the universe, society and man, have lost their faith or doubted it. What is more, these ideologies have dragged people, societies and nations into great crises, conflicts and wars. Their share of the blame for the pain and troubles that humanity suffers from today is immense.

While they deny God and creation, all the above-mentioned ideologies are based on a common framework, a so-called scientific basis; Charles Darwin's theory of evolution. Darwinism constitutes the basis of atheist philosophies. This theory claims that living beings have evolved as a result of coincidences and by means of a struggle for life. Therefore, Darwinism sends this deceptive message to people:

"You are not responsible to anyone, you owe your life to coincidences, you need to struggle, and if necessary to oppress others to succeed. This world is one of conflict and self-interest".

The social messages put across by Darwinist concepts such as "Natural selection", "struggle for life", "survival of the fittest" are a means of indoctrination. This evil morality advises people to be egoistical, self-seeking, cruel and oppressive. It destroys such virtues as mercy, compassion, self-sacrifice and humility, the moral values of the three great monotheistic religions and presents this as a necessity of "the rules of life."

This Darwinist indoctrination is just the opposite of the beliefs of the People of the Book and the message of the Qur'an. Consequently, the Darwinist indoctrination constitutes the foundation of a world which inherently opposes all the three divine religions.

This being the case, it is necessary for the People of the Book and Muslims to co-operate, since they believe in God and accept the morality that He teaches. The followers of these three religions should expose to the world the fallacy of Darwinism, which has no scientific basis, but which people are trying to preserve for the sake of materialist philosophy. They should co-operatively carry out an intellectual struggle against all other deceptive ideas (communism, fascism, racism) that serve atheism. Once this is realized, the world will, in a very short time, embrace peace, tranquility and justice.

Antisemitism is a Racism Totally Contrary to Islam

In our times, antisemitism is an ideology which threatens world peace and targets the well-being and security of innocent people. This is racist hatred felt by some for the Jews.

In the 20th century, antisemitism has signed its name to great disasters, one of the most horrible being the cruelty and murder inflicted on the Jews by the Nazis. In addition to this, in many countries authoritarian regimes have targeted Jews and subjected them to cruel treatment. Fascist organisations have harassed Jews and carried out bloody attacks against them.

So how should a Muslim regard antisemitism?

The answer is obvious. Every Muslim must oppose antisemitism as he would oppose every other racist ideology. Although Muslims justly condemn the cruel and aggressive policies of the State of Israel together with their occupation of adjacent territory, to blanket condemn innocent Jews is not acceptable to Muslims: this would be a symptom of antisemitism. However, criticising official Zionist ideology has nothing to do with antisemitism, since to object to Zionism is to object to an intense form of racism. There are many Jews who also criticise the racist policies of Zionism, and to label them as being antisemetic would be absurd.

Never subjecting a community to a blanket criticism is a command stressed in the Qur'an, there is a need to distinguish between the righteous and the wicked, the cruel ones and the innocent. After referring to some Jews and Christians, who violated God's commands, God also mentions some other Jews and Christians who displayed moral perfection:

> *[However] They are not all alike. Among the People of the Book there is an upright community who recite the revelation of God during the night and fall prostrate before Him. They believe in God and the Last Day, enjoin what is right and forbid what is evil, and vie with one another in good works. They are of the righteous. And whatever good they do, its reward will not be denied them. God knows those who fear [Him]. (Qur'an, 3:113-115)*

Antisemitism is an anti-religion ideology that has its roots in neo-paganism. Therefore, it is unthinkable that a Muslim would espouse antisemitism or feel sympathy for this ideology. Anti-Semites have no respect for Abraham, Moses or David who were blessed prophets chosen by God to be examples for humanity.

Antisemitism and other kinds of racism (eg. prejudice against blacks) have no place in true religion; they are perversions arising from various ideologies and superstitions. Furthermore, when we examine antisemitism and other forms of racism, we see clearly that they promote ideas and a model of society that is totally contrary to the moral teachings of the Qur'an, for example, at the root of antisemitism lie hatred, violence, and lack of compassion. An anti-Semite may be so cruel as to support the murder of Jewish people, men, women, children and the aged, and condone their being subjected to torture.

However, the moral teaching of the Qur'an enjoins love, compassion and mercy for all people. It also commands Muslims to show justice and be forgiving even to their enemies.

On the other hand, anti-Semites and other kinds of racists bulk at living together in peace with people of a different race or creed. (eg. German racists (Nazis) and Jewish racists (Zionists) were opposed to Germans and Jews living together; each side rejected this in the name of their respective race as a degeneration.) However, in the Qur'an, there is not the slightest distinction between races; the Qur'an advises that people of different faiths live together in the same society in peace and happiness.

According to the Qur'an, Muslims, Jews and Christians Must Live in Friendship

In the Qur'an, there is a significant difference between the People of the Book and those who have no belief in God. This is especially emphasised in the area of social life. For example, it is said concerning those who associate others with God: "(they) are unclean, so after this year they should not come near the Masjid al-Haram." (Qur'an, 9:28) Those who associate others with God are people who know no divine law, have no moral precepts and who can commit every kind of degrading and perverse deed without hesitation.

But the People of the Book, while they rely basically on God's revelation, have moral precepts and know what is lawful and what is not. In the same way, permission has been given to a Muslim man to marry a woman from among the People of the Book. On this subject God commands:

> *Today all good things have been made lawful for you. And the food of those given the Book is also lawful for you and your food is lawful for them. So are chaste women from among the believers and chaste women of those given the Book before you, once you have given them their dowries in marriage, not in fornication or taking them as lovers. But as for anyone who disbelieves, his actions will come to nothing and in the hereafter he will be among the losers. (Qur'an, 5:5)*

These commands show that bonds of kinship may be established as a result of the marriage of a Muslim with a woman from the People of the Book and that those on each side of the union can accept an invitation to a meal. These are the fundamentals that will ensure the establishment of equitable human relationships and a happy communal life. Since the Qur'an enjoins this equitable and tolerant attitude, it is unthinkable that a Muslim could take an opposing view.

The just and tolerant practices of the Prophet Muhammad towards the people of the Book set very good examples to Muslims. In the contract made with the Christians of Najran, who lived in the south of Arabia, the Prophet Muhammad demonstrates one of the best examples of tolerance and justice. The contract included the following article:

> *The lives of the people of Najran and its surrounding area, their religion, their land, property, cattle and those of them who are present or absent, their messengers and their places of worship are under the protection of Allah and guardianship of His Prophet.20*

By means of such contracts, the Messenger of God secured a social order for Muslims and the People of the Book alike, which was marked by peace and security. This order was a total manifestation of the following verse:

> *Those who believe, those who are Jews, and the Christians and Sabaeans, all who believe in God and the Last Day and act rightly, will have their reward with their Lord. They will feel no fear and will know no sorrow. (Qur'an, 2:62)*

The Constitution of Madinah is the most important contract that secured justice and tolerance among Christians, Jews and pagan communities.

The Constitution of Madinah was prepared under the leadership of the Prophet Muhammad 1,400 years ago, that is in 622 AD, to meet the needs of people of different beliefs, and was put into practice as a written legal contract. Different communities of different religions and races that had harboured deep-seated enmity towards one another for 120 years became parties to this legal contract. By means of this contract, the Prophet Muhammad showed that conflicts between those societies, who had been enemies and quite unable to reach any form of compromise, could come to an end, and they could actually live side by side.

According to the Constitution of Madinah, everyone was free to adhere to any belief or religion or to make any political or philosophical choice. People sharing the same views could come together and form a community. Everyone was free to exercise his own justice system. However, anyone who committed a crime would be protected by no-one. The parties to the contract would engage in co-operation with one another, provide support for each other, and would remain under the protection of the Prophet Muhammad. Conflicts between the parties would be brought to the Messenger of God.

This contract was in force from 622 to 632 AD. Through this document, the tribal structures which had formerly been based on blood and kinship were abolished, and people of different cultural, ethnical and geographical backgrounds came together and formed a social unity. The Constitution of Madinah secured absolute religious freedom.

MONASTERIES, CHURCHES AND SYNAGOGUES MUST BE RESPECTED

Another important fact we learn from the Qur'an is that Muslims must respect Jewish and Christian places of worship. In the Qur'an, the places of worship of the People of the Book, ie. monasteries, churches and synagogues, are mentioned as places of worship protected by God.

> *...if God had not driven some people back by means of others, monasteries, churches, synagogues and mosques, where God's name is mentioned much, would have been pulled down and destroyed. God will certainly help those who help Him – God is All-Strong, Almighty. (Qur'an, 22:40)*

This verse shows every Muslim the importance of respecting and protecting the holy places of the People of the Book.

Indeed, the Prophet Mohammad also made contracts with pagans as well as the people of the Book. Pagans were always treated with justice, and when they asked to be taken under protection, their requests were readily accepted by Muhammad. This meant that these communities sought the protection of the Messenger of God in the face of an attack or a wrongful accusation. Throughout his life, many non-Muslims and pagans requested protection from the Prophet Muhammad, and he took them under his protection and ensured their security. In Sura Tawba, God advises that requests of pagans seeking protection be accepted by believers. Of this, God says the following:

> *If any of the idolaters ask you for protection, give them protection until they have heard the words of God. Then convey them to a place where they are safe... (Qur'an, 9:6)*

Jews and Christians, due to their shared commonalities with Muslims are much closer to Muslims than those who have no faith in God. Each of these religions has its book, that is, they are subject to a book sent down by God. They know what is right and what is wrong, what is lawful and what is unlawful according to their scriptures, and all revere the Prophets and Messengers that accompanied them. They all believe in a hereafter, and afterlife where they will have to give an account to God for all their actions. So, there is a shared foundation from where we all can unite upon.

Rallying to a Common Formula

Concerning the People of the Book, God gives Muslims a command in the Qur'an; to rally to a common formula:

> *Say, "O People of the Book! Let us rally to a common formula to be binding on both us and you: That we worship none but God; that we associate no partners with Him; that we erect not, from among ourselves, Lords and patrons other than God." (Qur'an, 3:64)*

This is indeed our call to Christians and Jews: As people who believe in God and follow His revelations, let us rally to a common formula – "faith". Let us love God, Who is our Creator and Lord, and follow His commands. And let us pray to God to lead us to an even straighter path.

When Muslims, Christians and Jews rally to a common formula this way; when they understand that they are friends not enemies, when they see that the real enemy is the rejection of God, then the world will become a very different place. The wars in many parts of the world, enmities, fears and terrorist attacks will come to an end, and a new civilisation based on love, respect and peace will be established upon this "common formula".

There are important facts to consider for Muslims. What God teaches us in the Qur'an about different peoples and creeds is clear:

* The morality of the Qur'an excludes every kind of racism.
* It is commanded in the Qur'an that, so long as they show no hostility to Islam or Muslims, a tolerant and friendly attitude must be maintained toward other religions.

It is evident that the Jews have committed many errors which the Qur'an points out, criticizes and about which it gives a warning. The crimes committed by Israel in the present day against humanity are painfully well-known, but all this must not be taken by Muslims as a cause to feel hostility against all Jews. Again a basic vantage point prescribed by the Qur'an is not to make judgements about people just because they belong to a particular race, nation or religion. In every community, there are good people as well as wicked people.

The Qur'an draws attention to this differentiation. For instance, right after mentioning the rebellious nature - against God and His religion - of some People of the Book, there is reference to an exception and, said thus:

> *[However] They are not all alike. Among the People of the Book there is an upright community who recite the revelation of God during the night and fall prostrate before Him. They believe in God and the Last Day, enjoin what is right and forbid what is evil, and vie with one another in good works. They are of the righteous and whatever good they do, its reward will not be denied them. God knows those who fear [Him]. (Qur'an 3:113-115)*

In another verse, God commands:

> *We sent a Messenger among every people saying: "Worship God and keep clear of all false gods." Among them were some whom God guided but others received the misguidance they deserved. Travel about the earth and see the final fate of the deniers. (Qur'an, 16:36)*

God revealed to all messengers that He is the Unique and that there is no-one but Him whom people must worship, serve and obey. The divine message, conveyed to the people by God through His messengers, has been communicated to people since the creation of man. Some societies have accepted the message and followed the right path while others have denied and swerved from it. This also holds true for the present day. Some people will side with the righteous, whereas some others will plunge into mischief. This is the law of God. Those who believe should also adopt such an outlook and never forget that there may be sincere, pious people who have fear of God among the members of all religions as well as those who are far removed from the religious tenets.

Our hope is that a world will be established in which people will be able to live together in peace, no matter what race or religion they belong to, in which every racist perversion will be rejected, everyone's rights will be safeguarded and everyone will be respected. The struggle that will have to take place on intellectual grounds against all anti-religious ideologies will hopefully establish the peace that has been longed for. Of this God relates the following in the Qur'an:

> *Those who disbelieve are the friends and protectors of one another. If you do not act in this way (be friends and protectors of one another) there will be turmoil in the land and great corruption. (Qur'an, 8:73)*
>
> *Would that there had been more people with a vestige of good among the generations of those who came before you, who forbade corruption in the earth, other than the few among them whom We saved. Those who did wrong gladly pursued the life of luxury that they were given and were evildoers. (Qur'an, 11:116)*

4

ISLAM HAS BROUGHT PEACE AND HARMONY TO THE MIDDLE EAST

History always witnessed peace, justice and tolerance in the lands ruled by Muslim administrators when they followed Qur'anic guidance. The practices in the lands conquered during the lifetime of the Prophet Muhammad are very important examples, and just administrators succeeding him, who followed in the footsteps of God's messengers and never swerved from the morality of the Qur'an established peaceable societies. The true justice, righteousness and honesty described in the Qur'an persisted in the time of these administrators, thereby providing a role model for the succeeding generations to follow.

The land of Palestine and its capital Jerusalem, where members of the three divine religions reside together, are important in the sense that they show how Muslims bring peace and stability to the lands they rule. Indeed, for most of the last 1400 years, Muslim rule has brought peace to Jerusalem and Palestine.

THE PEACE AND JUSTICE BROUGHT TO PALESTINE BY THE CALIPH UMAR

Jerusalem was the capital of the Jews until A.D. 71. In that year, the Roman Army made a major assault on the Jews, and exiled them from the area with great savagery. As the time of the Jewish diaspora began, Jerusalem and the surrounding area was becoming an abandoned land. However, Jerusalem once again became a centre of interest with the acceptance of Christianity during the time of the Roman Emperor Constantine. Roman Christians built churches in Jerusalem. The prohibitions on Jews settling in the region were lifted. Palestine remained Roman (Byzantine) territory up until the 7th century. The Persians conquered the region for a short time, but the Byzantines later reconquered it.

An important turning point in the history of Palestine came in the year 637, when it was conquered by the armies of Islam. This meant new peace and harmony in Palestine, which had for centuries been the scene of wars, exile, looting and massacre, and which saw new brutality every time it changed hands, a frequent occurrence. The coming of Islam was the beginning of an age when people of different beliefs could live in peace and harmony.

Palestine was captured by Umar, the second Caliph after the Prophet himself. The entry of the Caliph into Jerusalem, the tolerance, maturity and kindness he showed towards people of different beliefs, introduced the beautiful age that was beginning. The British historian and Middle East expert Karen Armstrong describes the capture of Jerusalem by Umar in these terms in her book Holy War:

> *The Caliph Omar entered Jerusalem mounted on a white camel, escorted by the magistrate of the city, the Greek Patriarch Sophronius. The Caliph asked to be taken immediately to the Temple Mount and there he knelt in prayer on the spot where his friend Mohammed had made his Night Journey. The Patriarch watched in horror: this, he thought, must be the Abomination of Desolation that the Prophet Daniel had foretold would enter the Temple; this must be Antichrist who would herald the Last Days. Next Omar asked to see the Christian shrines and, while he was in the Church of the Holy Sepulchre, the time for Muslim prayer came round. Courteously the Patriarch invited him to pray where he was, but Omar as courteously refused. If he knelt to pray in the church, he explained, the Muslims would want to commemorate the event by erecting a mosque there, and that would mean that they would have to demolish the Holy Sepulchre.*

Instead Omar went to pray at a little distance from the church, and, sure enough, directly opposite the Holy Sepulchre there is still a small mosque dedicated to the Caliph Omar.

The other great mosque of Omar was erected on the Temple Mount to mark the Muslim conquest, together with the mosque al-Aqsa which commemorates Mohammed's Night Journey. For years, the Christians had used to the site of the ruined Jewish Temple as the city rubbish dump. The Caliph helped his Muslims to clear the garbage with his own hands and there Muslims raised their two shrines to establish Islam in the third most holy city in the Islamic world.

With the Muslim conquest of Jerusalem, the city became a safe haven in which all three religions could co-exist in peace. John L. Esposito writes:

When the Arab armies took Jerusalem in 638, they occupied a center whose shrines had made it a major pilgrimage site in Christendom. Churches and the Christian population were left unmolested. Jews, long banned from living there by Christian rulers, were permitted to return, live, and worship in the city of Solomon and David.

When Caliph Umar entered Jerusalem, he signed the below agreement with the Patriarch of Jerusalem:

This is the security which 'Umar, the servant of God, the commander of the faithful, grants to the people of Ælia. He grants to all, whether sick or sound, security for their lives, their possessions, their churches and their crosses, and for all that concerns their religion. Their churches shall not be changed into dwelling places, nor destroyed, neither shall they nor their appurtenances be in any way diminished, nor the crosses of the inhabitants nor aught of their possessions, nor shall any constraint be put upon them in the matter of their faith, nor shall any one of them be harmed.

In short, Muslims brought civilisation to Jerusalem and all of Palestine. Instead of beliefs that showed no respect for other peoples' sacred values, and which killed them simply out of differences of faith, there reigned the just, tolerant and moderate culture of Islam. After its capture by Umar, Muslims, Christians and Jews lived together in peace and harmony in Palestine. Muslims never tried to use force to make people convert, although some non-Muslims who saw that Islam was the true religion did so of their own free will.

The peace and harmony in Palestine lasted as long as Muslim rule in the region. However, at the end of the 11th century, a conquering force entered the region from abroad, and the civilised land of Jerusalem was barbarically and savagely plundered, in a way never before seen. These barbarians were the Crusaders.

THE SAVAGERY OF THE CRUSADERS

While members of all three religions were living peaceably together in Palestine, the Christians in Europe decided to organise a crusade. Following a call by Pope Urban II on 27 November 1095 at the Council of Clermont, more than 100,000 people from all over Europe set out for Palestine to free the Holy land from the Muslims and find the fabled wealth of the East. After a long and wearying journey, and much plundering and slaughter along the way, they reached Jerusalem in 1099. The city fell after a siege of nearly five weeks, and the Crusaders moved in. And they carried out a savagery the like of which the world has seldom seen. All Muslims and Jews in the city were put to the sword.

The peace and harmony in Palestine, which had lasted since Umar, ended in terrible slaughter. The Crusaders violated all the ethical laws of Christianity, a religion of love and compassion, and spread terror in the name of Christianity.

THE JUSTICE OF SALADIN

The barbaric Crusader army made Jerusalem their capital, and established a Latin Kingdom whose borders stretched from Palestine to Antioch. However, the Crusaders who brought savagery to Palestine did not last long. Saladin gathered all the Muslim kingdoms under his banner in a holy war, and defeated the Crusaders at the battle of Hattin in 1187. After the battle, the two leaders of the crusader army, Reynald of Chatillon and King Guy, were brought into Saladin's presence. Saladin executed Reynald of Chatillon, who had become infamous for the terrible savagery he had committed against Muslims, but he let King Guy go, as he had not committed the same crimes. Palestine once again saw the true meaning of justice.

Immediately after Hattin, and on the very same day that the Prophet Muhammad had been taken from Mecca to Jerusalem in one night, the day of the Ascent, Saladin entered Jerusalem and freed it from 88 years of Crusader occupation. When the Crusaders took the city 88 years earlier, they killed all the Muslims inside it, and for that reason they were afraid that Saladin would do the same thing to them. However, he did not touch even one Christian in the city. Furthermore, he merely ordered the Latin (Catholic) Christians to leave it. The Orthodox Christians, who were not Crusaders, were allowed to live in the city and worship as they chose. In the words of John L. Esposito, "The Muslim army was as magnanimous in victory as it had been tenacious in battle. Civilians were spared; churches and shrines were generally left untouched.... Saladin was faithful to his word and compassionate toward noncombatants."

Karen Armstrong describes the second capture of Jerusalem in these words:

> *On 2 October 1187 Saladin and his army entered Jerusalem as conquerors and for the next 800 years Jerusalem would remain a Muslim city. Saladin kept his word, and conquered the city according to the highest Islamic ideals. He did not take revenge for the 1099 massacre, as the Koran advised (16:127), and now that hostilities had ceased he ended the killing (2:193-194). Not a single Christian was killed and there was no plunder. The ransoms were deliberately very low... Saladin was moved to tears by the plight of families who were rent asunder and he released many of them freely, as the Koran urged, though to the despair of his long-suffering treasurers. His brother al-Adil was so distressed by the plight of the prisoners that he asked Saladin for a thousand of them for his own use and then*

> *released them on the spot... All the Muslim leaders were scandalised to see the rich Christians escaping with their wealth, which could have been used to ransom all the prisoners... [The Patriarch] Heraclius paid his ten-dinar ransom like everybody else and was even provided with a special escort to keep his treasure safe during the journey to Tyre.*

In short, Saladin and the Muslims in his command treated the Christians with great mercy and justice, and even showed them more compassion than their own leaders had. Not only the Christians but also Jews attained peace and security with the conquest of Jerusalem by Muslims. The well-known Spanish-Jewish poet Yuda Al-Harizi expressed his feelings thus in one of his works:

> *God decided that the sacred place would not stay in the hands of Esav, and warned the sould of Saladin, the Prince of the Children of Ishmael and a cautious and brave man. He conquered Yerashalayim with his army and announced that he would accept all the Children of Ephraim. Now we live in peace.*

After Jerusalem, the Crusaders continued their barbarity and the Muslims their justice in other cities in Palestine. In 1194, Richard the Lionheart, who is portrayed as a great hero in British history, had 3,000 Muslims, among whom were many women and children, basely executed in Castle Acre. Although the Muslims witnessed this savagery, they never resorted to the same methods. They abided by God's command "Let not the hatred of a people [who once] obstructed you from the Sacred Mosque lead you to transgress..." (Qur'an, 5:2) and never used violence against innocent civilians. They never employed unnecessary violence, not even against the Crusader armies they defeated.

The savagery of the Crusaders and the justice of the Muslims once more revealed a historic truth: An administration built on the principles of Islam allowed people of different faiths to live together. This fact continued to be demonstrated for 700 years after Saladin, particularly during the Ottoman period.

THE OTTOMAN EMPIRE'S JUST AND TOLERANT RULE

In 1514, Sultan Selim captured Jerusalem and the surrounding area, and some 400 years of Ottoman rule in Palestine began. As in other Ottoman states, this period would enable Palestine to enjoy peace, stability, and the living together of different faiths.

The Ottoman Empire was administered under what is known as the "nation (millet) system", the fundamental feature of which was that people of different faiths were allowed to live according to their own beliefs and even legal systems. Christians and Jews, described as the People of the Book in the Qur'an, found tolerance, security and freedom in Ottoman lands.

The most important reason for this was that although the Ottoman Empire was an Islamic state administered by Muslims, it had no desire to force its citizens to adopt Islam. On the contrary, the Ottoman state aimed at providing peace and security for non-Muslims, and governing them in such a way that they would be pleased with Islamic rule and justice.

Other major states at the same time had much cruder, oppressive and intolerant views of government. The Kingdom of Spain could not tolerate the existence of Muslims and Jews on the Spanish peninsula and inflicted great violence on both communities. In many other European countries, Jews were oppressed just for being Jews (for instance they were imprisoned in ghettoes), and were sometimes the victims of mass slaughter (pogroms). Christians could not even get on with one another: the fighting between Protestants and Catholics in the 16th and 17th centuries turned Europe into a bloodbath. The 30-Years War between 1618 and 1648 was one result of this Catholic-Protestant conflict. As a result of that war, central Europe became a battleground, and in Germany alone, one-third of the population of 15 million people was killed.

In such an environment, it is an indisputably important truth that Ottoman rule was exceedingly humane.

Many historians and political scientists have drawn attention to this fact. One of these is Columbia University's world-famous Middle East expert Professor Edward Said. Originally from a Jerusalem Christian family, he continues his research far from his homeland in American universities. In an interview in the Israeli newspaper *Ha'aretz* he recommended the "Ottoman nation system" if a permanent peace is to be built in the Middle East. What he said was:

> *A Jewish minority can survive the way other minorities in the Arab world survived. ...it worked rather well under the Ottoman Empire, with its millet system. What they had then seems a lot more humane than what we have now.*

History reveals that Islam is the only system of belief to offer a just, tolerant and compassionate way of government in the Middle East. The Pax Ottomana, which came to an end with the withdrawal of the Ottoman Empire from the region, has still not been replaced.

For this reason, the way to attain peace in the Middle East is to introduce the Ottoman model characterised by tolerance and compromise, the two fundamental teachings of the Qur'an. Islam, truly followed, is the solution to all sorts of violence of all kinds, conflicts, wars and terror and a guarantor of peace, justice and tolerance.

THE REAL ROOT OF TERRORISM: DARWINISM AND MATERIALISM

Most people think the theory of evolution was first proposed by Charles Darwin, and rests on scientific evidence, observations and experiments. However, the truth is that Darwin was not its originator, neither does the theory rest on scientific proof. The theory consists of an adaptation to nature of the ancient dogma of materialist philosophy. Although it is not backed up by scientific discoveries, the theory is blindly supported in the name of materialist philosophy.

This fanaticism has resulted in all kinds of disasters. Together with the spread of Darwinism and the materialist philosophy it supports, the answer to the question "What is a human being?" has changed. People who used to answer: "Human beings were created by God and have to live according to the beautiful morality He teaches", have now begun to think that "Man came into being by chance, and is an animal who developed by means of the fight for survival." There is a heavy price to pay for this great deception. Violent ideologies such as racism, fascism and communism, and many other barbaric world views based on conflict have all drawn strength from this deception.

This part of the book will examine the disaster Darwinism has visited on the world and reveal its connection with terrorism, one of the most important global problems of our time.

THE DARWINIST LIE: "LIFE IS CONFLICT"

Darwin set out with one basic premise when developing his theory: The development of living things depends on the fight for survival. The strong win the struggle. The weak are condemned to defeat and oblivion.

According to Darwin, there is a ruthless struggle for survival and an eternal conflict in nature. The strong always overcome the weak, and this enables development to take place. The subtitle he gave to his book , "*The Origin of Species* by Means of Natural Selection or the Preservation of Favoured Races in the Struggle for Life", encapsulates that view.

Furthermore, Darwin proposed that the "fight for survival" also applied between human racial groups. According to that mythical claim, favoured races were victorious in the struggle. Favoured races, in Darwin's view, were white Europeans. African or Asian races had lagged behind in the struggle for survival. Darwin went further, and suggested that these races would soon lose the struggle for survival entirely, and thus disappear:

At some future period, not very distant as measured by centuries, the civilised races of man will almost certainly exterminate and replace the savage races throughout the world. At the same time the anthropomorphous apes ... will no doubt be exterminated. The break between man and his nearest allies will then be wider, for it will intervene between man in a more civilised state, as we may hope, even than the Caucasian, and some ape as low as a baboon, instead of as now between the negro or Australian and the gorilla.

The Indian anthropologist Lalita Vidyarthi explains how Darwin's theory of evolution imposed racism on the social sciences:

His (Darwin's) theory of the survival of the fittest was warmly welcomed by the social scientists of the day, and they believed mankind had achieved various levels of evolution culminating in the white man's civilization. By the second half of the nineteenth century racism was accepted as fact by the vast majority of Western scientists.

DARWIN'S SOURCE OF INSPIRATION: MALTHUS'S THEORY OF RUTHLESSNESS

Darwin's source of inspiration on this subject was the British economist Thomas Malthus's book *An Essay on the Principle of Population.* Left to their own devices, Malthus calculated that the human population increased rapidly. In his view, the main influences that kept populations under control were disasters such as war, famine and disease. In short, according to this brutal claim, some people had to die for others to live. Existence came to mean permanent war.

In the 19th century, Malthus's ideas were widely accepted. European upper class intellectuals in particular supported his cruel ideas. In the article "The Scientific Background of the Nazi "Race Purification" Programme," by Jerry Bergman, the importance 19th century Europe attached to Malthus's views on population is described in this way:

In the opening half of the nineteenth century, throughout Europe, members of the ruling classes gathered to discuss the newly discovered 'Population problem" and to devise ways of implementing the Malthusian mandate, to increase the mortality rate of the poor: 'Instead of recommending cleanliness to the poor, we should encourage contrary habits. In our towns we should make the streets narrower, crowd more people into the houses, and court the return of the plague. In the country we should build our villages near stagnant pools, and particularly encourage settlements in all marshy and unwholesome situations," and so forth and so on.

As a result of this cruel policy, the weak, and those who lost the struggle for surival would be eliminated, and as a result the rapid rise in population would be balanced out.

This so-called "oppression of the poor" policy was actually carried out in 19th century Britain. An industrial order was set up in which children of eight and nine were made to work sixteen hours a day in the coal mines and thousands died from the terrible conditions. The struggle for survival demanded by Malthus's theory led to millions of Britons leading lives full of suffering.

Influenced by these ideas, Darwin applied this concept of conflict to all of nature, and proposed that the strong and the fittest emerged victorious from this war of existence. Moreover, he claimed that the so-called struggle for survival was a justified and unchangeable law of nature. On the other hand, he invited people to abandon their religious beliefs by denying the Creation, and thus undermined all ethical values that might prove to be obstacles to the ruthlessness of the struggle for survival.

Humanity has paid a heavy price in the 20th century for the dissemination of these callous views which led people to ruthlessness and cruelty.

THE ROLE OF DARWINISM IN PREPARING THE GROUND FOR WORLD WAR I

As Darwinism dominated European culture, the effects of the struggle for survival began to emerge. Colonialist European nations in particular began to portray the nations they colonized as "evolutionary backward nations" and looked to Darwinism for justification.

The bloodiest political effect of Darwinism was the outbreak of World War I in 1914.

In his book *Europe Since 1870,* the well-known British professor of history James Joll explains that one of the factors that prepared the ground for World War I was the belief in Darwinism of European rulers at the time.

...it is important to realise how literally the doctrine of the struggle for existence and of the survival of the fittest was taken by the majority of the leaders of Europe in the years preceding the First World War. The Austro-Hungarian chief of staff for example, Franz Baron Conrad von Hoetzendorff, wrote in his memoirs after the war:

> *Philanthropic religions, moral teachings and philosophical doctrines may certainly sometimes serve to weaken mankind's struggle for existence in its crudest form, but they will never succeed in removing it as a driving motive of the world... It is in accordance with this great principle that the catastrophe of the world war came about as the result of the motive forces in the lives of states and peoples, like a thunderstorm which must by its nature discharge itself.*

Seen against this sort of ideological background, Conrad's insistence on the need for a preventive war in order to preserve the Austro-Hungarian monarchy becomes comprehensible.

We have seen too how these views were not limited to military figures, and that Max Weber for example was deeply concerned with the international struggle for survival. Again Kurt Riezler, the personal assistant and confidant of the German chancellor Theobald von Bethmann-Hollweg, wrote in 1914:

> *Eternal and absolute enmity is fundamentally inherent in relations between peoples; and the hostility which we observe everywhere... is not the result of a perversion of human nature but is the essence of the world and the source of life itself.*

Friedrich von Bernardi, a World War I general, made a similar connection between war and the laws of war in nature. "War" declared Bernhardi "is a biological necessity"; it "is as necessary as the struggle of the elements of nature"; it "gives a biologically just decision, since its decisions rest on the very nature of things."

As we have seen, World War I broke out because of European thinkers, generals and administrators who saw warfare, bloodshed and suffering as a kind of development, and thought they were an unchanging law of nature. The ideological root that dragged all of that generation to destruction was nothing else than Darwin's concepts of the "struggle for survival" and "favoured races."

World War I left behind it 8 million dead, hundreds of ruined cities, and millions of wounded, crippled, homeless and unemployed.

The basic cause of World War II, which broke out 21 years later and left 55 million dead behind it, was also based on Darwinism.

WHAT "THE LAW OF THE JUNGLE" LED TO: FASCISM

As Darwinism fed racism in the 19th century, it formed the basis of an ideology that would develop and drown the world in blood in the 20th century: Nazism.

A strong Darwinist influence can be seen in Nazi ideologues. When one examines this theory, which was given shape by Adolf Hitler and Alfred Rosenberg, one comes across such concepts as "natural selection," "selective mating," and "the struggle for survival between the races," which are repeated dozens of time in the works of Darwin. When calling his book *Mein Kampf* (My Struggle), Hitler was inspired by the Darwinist struggle for survival and the principle that victory went to the fittest. He particularly talks about the struggle between the races:

> *History would culminate in a new millennial empire of unparalleled splendour, based on a new racial hierarchy ordained by nature herself.*

In the 1933 Nuremberg party rally, Hitler proclaimed that "a higher race subjects to itself a lower race... a right which we see in nature and which can be regarded as the sole conceivable right". That the Nazis were influenced by Darwinism is a fact that almost all historians who are expert in the matter accept. Peter Chrisp, the author of the book, *The Rise of Fascism,* expressed this fact as follows:

> *Charles Darwin's theory that humans had evolved from apes was ridiculed when it was first published, but was later widely accepted. The Nazis distorted Darwin's theories, using them to justify warfare and racism.*

The historian Hickman describes Darwinism's influence on Hitler as follows:

> *(Hitler) was a firm believer and preacher of evolution. Whatever the deeper, profound, complexities of his psychosis, it is certain that [the concept of struggle was important because] ... his book,* Mein Kampf, *clearly set forth a number of evolutionary ideas, particularly those emphasizing struggle, survival of the fittest and the extermination of the weak to produce a better society.*

Hitler, who emerged with these views, dragged the world to violence that had never before been seen. Many ethnic and political groups, and especially the Jews, were exposed to terrible cruelty and slaughter in the Nazi concentration camps. World War II, which began with the Nazi invasion, cost 55 million lives. What lay behind the greatest tragedy in world history was Darwinism's concept of the "struggle for survival."

THE BLOODY ALLIANCE: DARWINISM AND COMMUNISM

While fascists are found on the right wing of Social Darwinism, the left wing is occupied by communists. Communists have always been among the fiercest defenders of Darwin's theory.

This relationship between Darwinism and communism goes right back to the founders of both these "isms." Marx and Engels, the founders of communism, read Darwin's *The Origin of Species* as soon as it came out, and were amazed at its dialectical materialist attitude. The correspondence between Marx and Engels showed that they saw Darwin's theory as "containing the basis in natural history for communism." In his book *The Dialectics of Nature*, which he wrote under the influence of Darwin, Engels was full of praise for Darwin, and tried to make his own contribution to the theory in the chapter "The Part Played by Labour in the Transition from Ape to Man."

Russian communists who followed in the footsteps of Marx and Engels, such as Plekhanov, Lenin, Trotsky and Stalin, all agreed with Darwin's theory of evolution. Plekhanov, who is seen as the founder of Russian communism, regarded Marxism as "Darwinism in its application to social science."

Trotsky said, "Darwin's discovery is the highest triumph of the dialectic in the whole field of organic matter."

Darwinist education had a major role in the formation of communist cadres. For instance, historians note the fact that Stalin was religious in his youth, but became an atheist primarily because of Darwin's books.

Mao, who established communist rule in China and killed millions of people, openly stated that "Chinese socialism is founded upon Darwin and the theory of evolution."

The Harvard University historian James Reeve Pusey goes into great detail regarding Darwinism's effect on Mao and Chinese communism in his research book China and Charles Darwin.

In short, there is an unbreakable link between the theory of evolution and communism. The theory claims that living things are the product of chance, and provides a so-called scientific support for atheism. Communism, an atheist ideology, is for that reason firmly tied to Darwinism. Moreover, the theory of evolution proposes that development in nature is possible thanks to conflict (in other words "the struggle for survival") and supports the concept of "dialectics" which is fundamental to communism.

If we think of the communist concept of "dialectical conflict," which killed some 120 million people during the 20th century, as a "killing machine", then we can better understand the dimensions of the disaster that Darwinism visited on the planet.

Dialectical Conflict Does Not Foster the Developmentof Societies, It Destroys Them

As we learned earlier, Darwinism proposed that the struggle between living things is the cause of their development and gained so-called scientific currency for the philosophy of dialectical materialism.

As can be understood from its name, dialectical materialism rests on the idea of "conflict". Karl Marx, the founder of this philosophy, propagated the idea that "if there were no struggle and opposition, everything would stay as it is." In another place he said, "Force is the midwife of every old society pregnant with a new one."40 By saying this, he called people to violence, war and bloodshed in order that they could develop.

The first to apply Marx's theory in the realm of politics was Lenin. Fostering the idea that "progress comes about as a result of the conflict of opposites", Lenin advocated that people with opposing ideas should be in constant conflict. Lenin also repeatedly stated that this conflict would require bloodshed, that is, terrorism. A piece by Lenin titled "Guerrilla Warfare" which was first published in Proletary in 1906, eleven years before the Bolshevik Revolution, shows the terrorist methods he had adopted:

The phenomenon in which we are interested is the armed struggle. It is conducted by individuals and by small groups. Some belong to revolutionary organisations, while others (the majority in certain parts of Russia) do not belong to any revolutionary organisation. Armed struggle pursues two different aims, which must be strictly distinguished: in the first place, this struggle aims at assassinating individuals, chiefs and subordinates in the Army and police; in the second place, it aims at the confiscation of monetary funds both from the government and from private persons. The confiscated funds go partly into the treasury of the party, partly for the special purpose of arming and preparing for an uprising, and partly for the maintenance of persons engaged in the struggle we are describing.1

In the twentieth century, one of the most well known ideologies to oppose communism was fascism. The interesting thing is that, although fascism declared itself opposed to communism, it believed just as much as communism in the concept of struggle. Communists believed in the necessity of the class struggle; the fascists simply changed the arena of the struggle concentrating on the idea of the struggle between races and nations. For example, the German historian Heinrich Treitschke, one of the most important sources for Nazi ideas and a prominent racist, wrote, "nations could not prosper without intense competition, like the struggle for survival of Darwin." Hitler also said that he had taken inspiration from Darwin's understanding of struggle:

The whole world of Nature is a mighty struggle between strength and weakness–an eternal victory of the strong over the weak. There would be nothing but decay in the whole of nature if this were not so. He who would live must fight. He who does not wish to fight in this world where permanent struggle is the law of life, has not the right to exist.

These two social Darwinist ideologies believed that, for a society to grow strong, struggle and bloodshed are necessary; what they created in the 20th century is well known. Countless numbers of innocent people died; countless others were wounded or maimed; national economies crumbled; money that used to be spent on health, research, technology, education and art was spent on arms, on bandages to bind the wounds caused by those arms and to restore ruined cities. It became evident as time went on that struggle and terror did not to promote human development but rather destruction.

Certainly there are contradictions in the world. Just as in nature there are light and darkness, day and night, hot and cold, so there are also contradictions in putting ideas into practice. But a contradiction in ideas does not necessitate conflict. On the contrary, if contradictions are approached with tolerance, peace, understanding, love, compassion and mercy, good results may be achieved. Everyone who compares his own idea with another's may develop his own or see its deficiencies and remedy them. Those who defend opposing opinions could have an exchange of ideas in conversation or engage in a constructive critique. Only the kind of sincere, forgiving, peaceful and humble person who conforms to the moral teaching of the Qur'an can develop this approach.

To kill a person or do him harm because he has different ideas, believes in a different religion or belongs to a different race is an immense act of cruelty. For this reason only, throughout history and all over the world, sons and daughters of the same fatherland have struggled with one another to the death, murdering one another without pity. Or people of different race or nationality, women and children included, have been indiscriminately slaughtered. The only person who could do such a thing is someone who has no respect for a human being, and who regards the person in front of him just as an intelligent animal; it is someone who does not believe that he will have to give an account to God for what he has done.

The best and truest attitude to have towards opposing ideas is revealed in the Qur'an. Clashes of ideas have arisen throughout history and one of the most well-known examples of this is the opposition between Moses and his contemporary Pharaoh. Despite all Pharaoh's cruelty and aggressiveness, God sent Moses to invite him to God's religion, and He explained the method Moses was to use:

> *Go to Pharaoh; he has overstepped the bounds. But speak to him with gentle words so that hopefully he will pay heed or show some fear. (Qur'an, 20:43-44)*

Moses obeyed God's command and explained true religion to him at great length. In order to stop Pharaoh's denial of God and his cruelty to people, Moses patiently explained every matter. However, Pharaoh showed a hostile attitude toward Moses' noble character and patience, threatening to kill him and those who shared his ideas. But it was not Pharaoh's attitude that prevailed; on the contrary, he and his people were drowned. Moses and his people were victorious.

As this example shows, the victory of an idea or the struggle for development does not come about by hostility or aggression. The meeting between Moses and Pharaoh offers a lesson from history: it is not those on the side of contention and cruelty who are victorious, but those who are on the side of peace and justice. The exercise of fine moral principles receives its reward both in this world and in the hereafter

Darwinism and Terrorism

As we have so far seen, Darwinism is at the root of various ideologies of violence that have spelled disaster to mankind in the 20th century. The fundamental concept behind this understanding and method is "fighting whoever is not one of us." There are different beliefs, worldviews and philosophies in the world. It is very natural that all these diverse ideas have traits opposing one another. However, these different stances can look at each other in one of two ways:

1) They can respect the existence of those who are not like them and try to establish dialogue with them, employing a humane method. Indeed, this method conforms with the morality of the Qur'an.
2) They can choose to fight others, and to try to secure an advantage by damaging them, in other words, to behave like a wild animal. This is a method employed by materialism, that is, irreligion.

The horror we call "terrorism" is nothing other than a statement of the second view.

When we consider the difference between these two approaches, we can see that the idea of "man as a fighting animal" which Darwinism has subconsciously imposed on people is particularly influential. Individuals and groups who choose the way of conflict may never have heard of Darwinism and the principles of that ideology. But at the end of the day they agree with a view whose philosophical basis rests on Darwinism. What leads them to believe in the rightness of this view is such Darwinism-based slogans as "In this world, the strong survive," "Big fish swallow little ones," "War is a virtue," and "Man advances by waging war." Take Darwinism away, and these are nothing but empty slogans.

Actually, when Darwinism is taken away, no philosophy of conflict remains. The three divine religions that most people in the world believe in, Islam, Christianity and Judaism, all oppose violence. All three religions wish to bring peace and harmony to the world, and oppose innocent people being killed and suffering cruelty and torture. Conflict and violence violate the morality that God has set out for man, and are abnormal and unwanted concepts. However, Darwinism sees and portrays conflict and violence as natural, justified and correct concepts that have to exist.

For this reason, if some people commit terrorism using the concepts and symbols of Islam, Christianity or Judaism in the name of those religions, you can be sure that those people are not Muslims, Christians or Jews. They are real Social Darwinists. They hide under a cloak of religion, but they are not genuine believers. Even if they claim to be serving religion, they are actually enemies of religion and of believers. That is because they are ruthlessly committing a crime that religion forbids, and in such a way as to blacken religion in peoples' eyes.

For this reason, the root of the terrorism that plagues our planet is not in any of the divine religions, but in atheism, and the expression of atheism in our times: Darwinism and materialism.

Every Person Who Desires Peace Must Recognise the Danger of Darwinism

The solution in the fight against a particular problem lies in doing away with the ideas this problem fundamentally depends on. For instance, no matter how hard one endeavours to keep the surroundings of a stinking garbage bin clean, the garbage will keep on stinking. All solutions will prove to be short-lived. The real solution lies in a thorough cleaning of the garbage's source, removing the trash altogether. Alternatively, this is like spending years raising poisonous snakes on a farm, then letting them go, wondering why they start to bite people and trying to round them all up again. The important thing is not to breed them in the first place.

Consequently, in the fight against terrorism, searching for terrorists one by one and trying to render them ineffectual does not provide a viable and permanent solution. The only way of totally eradicating the scourge of terrorism from the face of the earth is to identify the basic sources that breed terrorists and remove them. The main source of terrorism, on the other hand, is erroneous ideologies and the education received in the light of these ideologies.

In our day, in almost all countries of the world, Darwinism is incorporated into school curricula and is considered to be scientific fact. Young people are not taught that they are created by God, that they are endowed with a spirit, wisdom and conscience. They are not told that they will have to give account of their deeds on the Day of Judgement and accordingly be punished in hell or rewarded with paradise for all eternity. On the contrary, they are taught that they are creatures whose forefathers were animals that somehow came into existence by some random coincidences. Under such indoctrination, they assume themselves to be stray beings who are not answerable to God and see their future –that is their survival- in being victorious through struggle. After this stage, it becomes rather easy to brainwash these people, who have been already indoctrinated all through their school lives, and to turn them into enemies of humanity cruel enough to murder innocent children. Such young people can be readily attracted by any strayed ideology; they can act under the influence of the terrorists' conditioning and engage in inconceivably cruel and violent acts. The communist, fascist and racist terrorist groups that have been in existence since the 19th century are the products of this kind of education system.

The second great harm this education system does is to entirely distance education from religion, thereby limiting the sphere of religion to the world of uneducated people. Thus, while those who have access to education are totally removed from religion thanks to Darwinist-materialist instillation, religion becomes something peculiar to the uneducated. This causes the development of superstitious and erroneous ideas and allows those who put forward ideas totally contrary to religion in the name of religion to take control easily.

The recent events of September 11 are the most obvious examples of this. No one who fears God, loves Him and expects to give an account of his deeds in the hereafter can commit any act that will leave thousands of innocent people dead or wounded and orphan thousands of children. Such a person knows that he will give an account to God for every person he subjected to cruelty and each one of them will become a source of anguish for him in hell.

To conclude, the way to stop acts of terrorism is to put an end to Darwinist-materialist education, to educate young people in accord with a curricula based on true scientific findings and to instill in them the fear of God and the desire to act wisely and scrupulously. The fruits of such an education will be a community made up of peaceable, trustworthy, forgiving and tolerant people.

HOW CAN THE TERRORISM BE DEFEATED

In 2001, jet planes were crashed into the World Trade Center and the Pentagon, injuring and killing thousands. In the days following these attacks—totally unexpected in their timing and method, aimed at the world's only superpower—the world began debating the concept of terrorism that lay behind them.

An atmosphere of fear and panic grew, especially in the United States. But that didn't last long: Soon the entire world began wondering how best to combat terrorism. No longer could any country stand apart from the fight against terrorism and declare, "Those attacks weren't aimed at us." Citizens of every nation realized that the dark face of terrorism could confront them at any time, whether asleep in their beds, while watching television, taking their children to the park, or at work in the office. The terrorists' aim, they realized, was to paralyze society, making civilians reluctant to venture into the street, much less use public transport or go shopping—in short, to create a permanent climate of fear. As soon as America recovered from the shock of 9/11, it joined with a large number of other countries to launch a worldwide war on terrorism. Right from the start, however, officials of this powerful coalition declared openly that it wouldn't be enough for them to fight on the military field alone.

How should the struggle against terrorism be pursued? To answer that question, we need to identify terrorism's roots. To do so, we must examine the course of the past century, during which terrorism first emerged as a major threat.

The 20th century's two World Wars, along with many regional conflicts and various acts of local violence, made it the most bloody century ever. In addition to that, toward the end of the millennium, constant technological advances only helped terrorists widen their reach. Now, just one touch of a button could kill hundreds of innocents. High-tech terrorism could inflict billions of dollars in damage to any nation's economy and shape world politics without ever emerging into the daylight. Clearly, after the attacks on New York and Washington D. C. in the United States—the world's greatest technological power—no other country can consider itself safe from terrorism or beyond its deadly grasp. Worse still, if the necessary countermeasures aren't taken, the 21st-century terrorism will grow even more powerful, until one single chemical, biological, or even nuclear attack can slaughter tens of thousands.

5

The True Definition of Terrorism

With terrorism dominating the world's agenda, the definitions of terror, terrorist, and terrorism assume a whole new importance. Many countries define terrorism, draw up terrorist profiles, and publish lists of terrorist organizations in the light of their own national interests. "Terrorist organizations" to some countries are freedom fighters to others. What one country sees as "terrorist nations," another welcomes as "loyal allies." Therefore, who defines terrorism? Who decides—and how do they decide—what a terrorist is? To establish a criterion, one can point out two distinct characteristics of terrorism:

(1) Targeting civilians: Any occupied country has the right to resist an army occupying its territory. But if that resistance includes attacks on civilian targets, any justification ceases to apply, and terrorism begins. As we'll see later on in this book, this definition is entirely in accord with Islamic rules on war. The Prophet Muhammad (may God bless him and grant him peace) commanded his followers to do battle against those who declared war on them. But he also ordered them to never regard civilians as targets. On the contrary, every Muslim was ordered — and still obliged — to take great care to ensure the safety of non-combatants.

(2) Destroying Peace: If no state of war exists, then terrorism can also include attacks on military or official targets. Attacks intended to break down peaceful relations between countries or communities are acts of terrorism, even when aimed at military targets.

All attacks that threaten peace, or that are aimed at civilian targets, even in a state of war, are terrorism. There can be no question of defending, approving or justifying such attacks. There can be no question of defending, approving or justifying such attacks. However, such violence is very widespread in the modern world. That's why any war on terrorism needs to be wide-ranging. Its every stage should be carefully planned, with its final aim the total eradication of the entire concept. That, in turn, requires individuals in every nation to totally distance themselves from terrorism. Every form of terrorism must be unequivocally condemned—whatever its causes or aims, no matter what its targets, where it arises, or how it is carried out. Similarly, anyone sincerely opposed to terrorism should show the same empathy for the thousands of innocent victims it has slaughtered—not only at the World Trade Center, but in attacks in Japan and Spain, in East Turkestan and Indonesia, in the massacre of more than half a million Hutus in Rwanda, in the murder of defenseless people in Palestine, Israel, and all across the globe.

Once every form of terrorism is fiercely condemned, then no longer will its perpetrators receive support from any country, or be allowed to seek shelter inside its borders. Quite literally, terrorists will have nowhere to hide.

THE IDEOLOGICAL FOUNDATION OF TERRORISM

Before the war against terrorism can come to any definitive conclusion, its underlying philosophy must first be identified, along with the means to be employed. This book, therefore, deals with terrorism's basic starting point, as well as the disasters to which it leads. Its starting point is the assumption that violence is a virtue in itself and a powerful means to solve social or political problems. While killing the innocents, damaging public order, and disrupting peace, any terrorist acts under the influence of ideas that have been imposed on him, coaxing him to believe that he's engaged in a justified struggle.

Terrorism can be healed only when such people understand the mistaken illogic of any ideology that inspires terrorism and incites to violence—and when they realize that going along with it can never get them anywhere. Until those ideologies' errors and contradictions are revealed, all measures taken against terrorism can be short-term only. Soon terrorism will emerge again, in different places and under different circumstances, behind a different mask.

We can put an end to terrorism only by destroying its ideological infrastructure. In later chapters, you'll see that modern terrorism's ideological foundations in fact go back to Social Darwinism and the materialist tendencies derived from it. People exposed to this indoctrination believe that life is a field of struggle, and that only the strong survive. The weak are condemned to be eliminated. Man and, in fact, the entire universe, are both products of chance. Therefore, no one is responsible for his actions to anyone else. These and similar ideas inevitably coax people into leading an animalistic form of life, where ruthlessness, aggression and violence are regarded as acceptable or even virtuous.

Anyone who resorts to terrorism, maintaining that violence is the only way to achieve his aims, is actually under the influence of Social Darwinism and materialist thought, no matter what his religion or race, or what group he belongs to. Modern terrorist groups that claim to act in the name of religion are also under Darwinism's influence and materialism, even though they claim to carry out their terroristic acts in the name of religion. This is because for anyone who lives by the morality of religion revealed by God, it's impossible to approve of violence of any kind, much less achieve a "higher" aim by murdering others. Those who resort to such methods are therefore pursuing the exact opposite of the moral values upheld by religion, carrying out their actions under the influence of materialist ideologies.

In *Islam Denounces Terrorism*, it was made clear that Islam fiercely rejects all forms of terrorism, no matter whom it may be directed against. In the light of verses from the Qur'an, it was explained how religion's morality calls people to peace, tolerance, and convenience. Also stressed was the dishonesty of condemning only those acts of terrorism directed against one's own side: Such an attitude only weakens the fight against terrorism; and anyone living according to Islamic morality needs to fight terror in all its all forms. The foundation of that intellectual struggle is based on revealing the true morality of religion.

Today's politicians, political commentators and academics agree that by itself, military force isn't enough to root out terrorism. This book concentrates on the only way it can be eradicated: by means of peace, tolerance, and love. All the divinely-inspired religions that God sent down by means of His messengers are helpful guides. This book offers examples from the Qur'an as well as from the Bible (even though the latter has been partially distorted) to show how each of the three divine religions forbids the use of unjust violence. It also gives examples to show that the only way to fight terrorism is to heal the root causes through the love, affection, compassion, humility, forgiveness, tolerance and concepts of justice that religion's morality instils in people—whom, following the verse from the Qur'an (10:25): "God calls to the Abode of Peace... " Such fortunates will do their utmost to build a world full of peace and love.

THE BLOODY TOLL OF TERROR

Terrorism is one of the gravest menaces facing our 21st-century world because it sees acts of violence as the only way to achieve political aims. The particular aim or problem depends on the terrorist's individual worldview. In a terrorist's eyes, political dilemmas and conflicts caused by ethnic and cultural differences can be resolved by violence alone. No group can get what it wants, except by "blood and iron". The terrorist believes that his objectives—enforcing his demands, spreading his organization's propaganda—can be attained only by damaging the fabric of society; when unease, fear, and conflict come to dominate daily life.

Some groups aim to take advantage of the climate of chaos that their actions bring about. They think that it will be easier to achieve their aims where social stability has collapsed, individuals are wracked with fear and uncertainty. From the destruction, they claim, will rise what they call "righteousness and justice." But expecting that acts of terrorism can establish righteousness and justice, or that problems can be resolved by violence, is a terrible mistake. Violence is counter-productive: All they that live by the sword shall perish by the sword.

In the Qur'an (13:25), God describes such people as "those [who] cause corruption in the earth." So far, they have managed only to increase the number of deaths among the innocent—and among their own supporters as well. Every year, terrorist attacks cause thousands to live in fear and anxiety and suffer economic harm, not to mention those who are wounded or killed. Terrorism threatens all of mankind, its toll so very terrible that fighting has become urgently essential.

TERRORISM IS CLOSE TO HOME!

There are an estimated 500 terrorist groups in the world. These include international cartels controlling trade in drugs, arms and prostitution, as well as underground organizations, marginal movements, various radical ideological groups, and deviant cults that stage actions allegedly in the name of religion. Many terrorist organizations do operate within their own countries' borders, but a number target what they have decided as "enemy" countries, through attacks on prominent sites and individuals that, they calculate, will elicit a huge public reaction. From the reaction, they seek to achieve fame, in fact notoriety, which they hope that will add to their power.

Though terrorism has existed since the earliest times, through esoteric organizations like the Sicarii or Assassins, and flourished in the modern times through revolutionary cadres like the sans-cullottes of the French Revolution or the Russian Nihilism of the 19th century, its threat really came to the fore in the 20th century, which saw an explosion in acts of terror and in the number of terrorists who committed them. Weapons of mass destruction and the rapid advance of technology made terrorist attacks much easier and vastly increased their destructiveness.

By the 1960s, people began to wonder seriously what might happen, if a terrorist group managed to acquire some kind of nuclear weapon that could result in the deaths of tens of thousands. A biological or chemical attack could wipe entire populations off the map. No such attack happened, fortunately. But by the 1990s, the chances of such attacks increased. These concerns only heightened with the collapse of the Soviet Union and the weakening of control over its nuclear arsenal. The spread of the Internet and the facilitation of all forms of information increased worries still further.1 Fear of terrorism became the subject of hundreds of films and books. Reports were written about the possible consequences; research was carried out. Now, all too obviously, terrorists could go beyond familiar, limited actions like bombings, armed robberies, skyjackings and kidnappings, to attack entire communities. Such attacks could be carried out by remote control or computer, with no direct human intervention.

A number of recent fears in the US involving biological weapons like of the anthrax bacteria revealed the scale of the threat posed by bio-terrorism and biological weapons. With the help of an experienced chemist in a simple laboratory, terrorists can now threaten the lives of thousands. One of the first examples of this occurred in 1984, when 750 people were poisoned in four restaurants in a small town in Oregon.2 Later, it was revealed that a Hindu-inspired New Age cult under the leadership of Baghwan Shree Rajneesh was responsible. Disciples had grown salmonella bacteria on their farms and placed them in salad bars in area restaurants. In 1995, the Aum Shinrikyo ("Higher Truth") cult released the poison gas sarin in the Tokyo underground subway system, leading to the deaths of 12 people and another 5,500 injured. Subsequent inquiries revealed that the cult had tried to construct biological weapons in its own laboratories—revealing just how large a threat terrorism poses to the public.

In the 21st century, computer technology is expected to play an important role in terrorist attacks. Meanwhile, more "conventional" ways of terrorism, like bombings, arson attacks, skyjackings and kidnappings are still going on all over the world, from Europe to America, from Asia to Africa. Since 1962, for example, members of the ETA (Euskadi Ta Askatasuna) terrorist organization, fighting for the Basque region's independence, has carried out many terrorist attacks in Spain, resulting in the deaths of more than 800.4 For years, the Irish Republican Army has seized world headlines with its bloody attacks to gain independence for Northern Ireland. The central aim of the IRA is to end British control of Northern Ireland and to achieve the reunification of the island of Ireland. Generally it has operated in Northern Ireland and London, but has also been involved in bombings in various European countries such as Germany. Since 1969, the IRA's terrorist attacks , and Britain's methods of "counter-terrorism", have caused the deaths of more than 3,200 on both sides of the conflict.5 Millions of dollars' worth of damage has been caused by IRA bombings of airports and underground stations, again aimed at civilians. During a European Football Championship match on June 15, 1996, an IRA car bombing in a Manchester shopping center resulted in some 200 injuries.

Currently, no country can feel safe from this kind of threat. The few examples just cited show just how deeply terrorism has come to influence peoples' lives. No longer the problem of just a few specific nations, it's a threat that faces all mankind. Because no one can tell when, where or how terrorists will strike, the fight against them can no longer be considered the duty of a handful of countries or organizations. Terrorism, threatening the entire world, can be resolved only if well-intentioned people support each other in search of peace, friendship and brotherhood.

TERRORISM'S DARK FACE

Terrorism is currently inflicting suffering and physical damage all over the world, not only in the United States, but in the African countries of Uganda, Angola and Nigeria; in the European nations of Great Britain, France and Spain; in Asian countries like Japan, and throughout the Middle East and Latin America. At any moment, civilians can find themselves facing a terrorist attack, whether sitting at home or at a movie theater, in a shopping center, riding a bus, or at their workplace. Naturally, terrorism's ability to enter peoples' homes has led to considerable anxiety and alarm. People are hesitant to enter crowded areas or use public transport; their daily lives are becoming intolerable. But that is exactly what terrorism wants to see: whole communities living in fear and alarm.

The evidence of terrible attacks throughout in the world certainly confirms that concern. In 1996, there were 296 incidents with 314 people killed and 2,912 injured. In 1997, terrorism's scope began to expand: Out of 439 attacks, 398 were aimed at workplaces or non-official premises, leading to the loss of 139 civilian lives, 39 of them civil servants or military personnel.

According to the U.S. State Department, the number of terrorist attacks in 2000 saw an eight percent rise over 1999, with 423 deaths and 791 injured. Between 1981 and 2000, the total number of dead resulting from terrorist attacks was 9,184. Nor do these figures include all the people who died in all terrorist attacks across the globe. The report considered only attacks by international terrorist organizations, not those inflicted by local terrorist groups. In Turkey alone there were 21,866 terrorist attacks between August 15, 1984 and October 31, 2001, costing the lives of 5,605 security personnel and 4,646 civilians. A further 16,562 security forces and 5,091 civilians were injured.

Terrorist actions' physical damage and economic harm add yet another sobering dimension to the picture. The chaos and anarchy provoked by such incidents prevent investment in the affected regions. Attacks aimed at the economic infrastructure doesn't just hold back development. Existing resources are also destroyed, creating economic difficulties that impede social life across a wide spectrum of areas, particularly education. Military costs of the struggle against terrorism impose yet another burden. This diversion of resources that should be spent on raising standards of living affects not just the nation in question, but the entire global economy.

This summary reveals the grim picture that terrorism represents—bringing destruction all over the world and causing untold harm to human lives.

ATHEIST IDEOLOGIES AND THE RISE OF TERRORISM

If a sick person is to be treated properly, an accurate diagnosis is essential. Whatever treatment follows that diagnosis must be followed meticulously and decisively, until the sickness is finally expelled from the body. If not, the illness will inevitably recur. The same applies to one of the most serious ills affecting society. One of the chief reasons why we can't find effective solutions to this century's social problems is that their causes aren't properly identified. When dealing with any social problem, the first thing to do is establish what causes give rise to it. Otherwise, whatever measures are taken can only be temporary.

The roots of terrorism are often sought in concrete matters; and thus the fight against it, aimed at these superficial targets, cannot provide lasting results. In order to free the world from terrorism, the principal factors behind it must be identified and eliminated.

THE TANGLED WEB OF TERRORISTS' LOGIC

It's not possible to defeat terrorism by security measures. By itself, military force is only likely to meet with increased violence, producing a vicious circle in which bloodshed continues to be answered with more bloodshed. When embarking on the fight against terrorists, we need to understand—and then combat—their way of thinking, the way they view life and other human beings, and how they justify their use of violence.

A terrorist believes that he can succeed only by using violence. He wants people around to fear him, and cloaks himself in pitilessness, ruthlessness and aggression to bring that fear about. Anyone opposing his ideas is an enemy, whom he regards as an object that needs to be eliminated. In his article, "Terrorists View us as Targets, not as Humans," psychotherapist and *Journal Sentinel* writer Philip Chard examines the terrorist mindset and how they justify violent attacks aimed at defenseless people:

> *"Researchers have glimpsed aspects of [the terrorists'] psyches. Most prominent among these is their capacity to view their victims as things, as objects, as statistics that, they hope, will show up on a casualty list.*

"They don't want to experience their victims as human beings, as they would a friend or loved one. Rather, they strive to view them as pawns on a political chessboard. Consequently, from their own vantage point, terrorists don't perceive themselves as killing 'people.' In order to slaughter with ease and callous indifference, they mentally dehumanize us into 'targets' ... Their 'cause,' whatever it may be, is sufficiently sacred, noble or desperate that it justifies the carnage they instigate ... For most terrorists, their chief interest resides in effects, not persons ... They are after ... the impact of the massacre, not the experience of the massacre itself. Terrorists want to murder hope, or a way of life, or the spirit of a group of people or an entire nation. They destroy human beings because they believe doing so is the fastest and most direct route to that goal."

Philip Chard draws our attention to a most important matter: that terrorists feel not the slightest pang of remorse at the death of others. On the contrary, the more they can kill, the more successful they consider themselves to be, and rejoice in that fact. Such minds can quite happily shoot innocent people and bomb small children.

For them, shedding blood becomes a source of pleasure. They cease to be human and turn into savage monsters. If one of them does evidence the slightest remorse, he is immediately branded a traitor by his more radical comrades. Being more radical and more bloody is considered to be more devout in the cause, so the zeal to kill increases constantly. Since any dispute can easily be defined as treacher, terrorists invariably use guns against each other, and carry out attacks on other splinter groups within their own ranks.

This passionate attachment to violence goes deeper beyond political ideologies and in fact stems from an underlying misconception about human nature. The terrorist mindset finds its inspiration from the materialist philosophy and Darwinist thought. Darwinism regards human beings as animals and maintains that living things evolve through a struggle for survival in nature. Eliminating the weak, so that the strong can emerge victorious, forms the essence of any terrorist's twisted thinking.

THE TERRORIST MINDSET

Was Built By Darwinism

According to Charles Darwin's theory of evolution, there is constant conflict in nature, and a ruthless competition for survival. The strong always defeat the weak, thus enabling progress. Out of that concept came the idea of the "struggle for survival" and such terms as "the favored races" (European whites) and "inferior" ones (Asian or African races). This racist logic laid the groundwork for hatred and conflicts all over the world. In turn, Darwin's idea of "the survival of the fittest" justified a great many movements that led mankind to hatred, enmity, conflict and war.

Darwinism still indoctrinates people with the deception that humans are no more than a highly developed animal species, the result of blind chance and have no Creator. This theory maintains that the world once consisted of nothing but inanimate rock, soil, and gasses. By sheer coincidence, life emerged as a result of the effect of natural forces like wind and rain and lightning on organic molecules. The theory goes on to explain all life on earth, including human beings, as a product of the blind forces of nature and mere chance. Yet this theory of evolution is a huge deception that violates the most basic laws of chemistry and biology and defies all reason and logic. (For more on this subject, see Chapter 7, The Evolution Deception). However, the theory is imposed on modern society with an enormous propaganda and people indoctrinated with this idea believe themselves to be the products of chemical and biological accidents — free of all responsibility to the Creator and His moral code. Moreover, those under the spell of Darwinist logic—seeing life as a battlefield and therefore, justifying all kinds of wickedness in the struggle for survival—are brainwashed with the terrible idea that it's normal to treat other people like animals, even to exterminate them.

People educated with such ideas transformed the 20th century into one of savagery, supported conflict as part of Darwinism, and even regarded war as the most important means of furthering their aims. "Dialectical conflict" became the so-called justification for the massacres carried out by Communist ideologues. Over the course of the century, Communist terror cost the lives of some 120 million people. Darwin's nonsensical "struggle for survival between the races " and "natural selection" became the foundations for Nazism. Adolf Hitler claimed that only the superior races could—or should—survive. The Fascist terror he inspired unleashed a wave of slaughter across the entire world. Some 55 million people died in World War II, which began as a result of the Nazis' policies of war and occupation. Those in the 21st century who still follow those ideas, regard violence as the only way and want this century to go down in history as one of terror.

Darwinism's theory that man is a warring animal, with which so many are subconsciously indoctrinated, has wreaked dreadful harm on mankind. Terrorist attacks are echoes of that. Darwinist slogans that maintain that only the strongest can survive, praise violence, support conflict, and see war as a virtue need to be thrown, once and for all, into the dustbin of history. Darwinism's overthrow can undermine all of those ideologies that support conflict and violence.

On the other hand, the definition of human nature by the monotheist faiths is much different Christianity, Judaism and Islam—the three religions believed in by most people in the world—all oppose the Social Darwinist value called conflict. As we'll see in greater detail in subsequent sections, each of these religions aims at bringing peace and security to the world, while opposing the oppression, torture, and killing of the innocent. Conflict and violence, they agree, are abnormal and unwanted concepts, violating the morality that God has set out for Man. Darwinism, on the other hand, regards violence and conflict as essential, and therefore justified. In short, the source of the world's terrorist nightmare lies in atheism and its contemporary equivalents: Darwinism and materialism.

Since schools in many countries teach Darwinism as clear scientific fact, new generations of terrorists are inevitable. From that point of view, it's urgent to prevent young people from being taught that they're the result of chance, descended from animals, totally unfettered with no duties towards God, and can survive only by emerging victorious in the struggle for survival. Anyone brought up to believe such concepts will inevitably be selfish, aggressive, ruthless, and prone to violence. Such young people are easily susceptible to anarchic and terrorist indoctrination. Following such ideologies, they can become cruel enough to kill children and murder their own brothers and sisters, without batting an eyelid. The communist, racist and fascist terror groups that have plagued the world for the last hundred years are the products of just such an educational system.

That being so, we need to expose the true rottenness of terrorist logic. People need to be awakened to the fact, as effectively as possible, that all those who support and believe in Darwinism are mistaken. Man is not unfettered and irresponsible. We do have a Creator Who watches us at all times, knows even our innermost thoughts and Who, in the hereafter, will call us to account for all our deeds. Our Lord has created Man different from the animals, in that we possess a soul, reason, free will, judgment and powers of discrimination. If a weak-willed person, easily angered, regards himself and others as mere animals, he can act in a totally ruthless manner and easily do them harm. It makes no difference if those others are totally innocent children. But anyone who possesses reason and conscience and knows that he bears a soul, given him by God, holds his anger in check—no matter what the circumstances. His judgment and conscience will always prevail. Never will he do the slightest thing for which God might one day call him to account.

In the Qur'an (91: 7-10), God reveals that Man is inspired by both evil and the will to avoid it. Therefore, it's not some imaginary evolutionary process that underlies moral degeneration and the commission of crimes. Immorality and crime come from the evil side of human nature, which can only be defeated by personal devotion to the moral values that God has taught to humanity through religion. If people have no faith in God and don't believe they must ever account to Him for their actions, they have no reason to avoid committing evil in the forms of personal greed and dishonesty or social evils like wars, racist killings, gang wars or ruthless skinhead assaults. On a less dramatic level, it accounts for why people are left to starve, and for the rampant injustice and ruthlessness in the world today. There is no end to the cruelties of those who regard Man as only an animal species, believing that they, like animals, are engaged in a struggle for survival. Not believing in God and the hereafter, they induce others to forget about them too.

Every human being bears a soul breathed into him by God, and is responsible to the Creator Who created him out of nothing. In the Qur'an (75: 36-40), God reminds those who think of themselves as totally unfettered that they were created, and will be resurrected after death: "Does Man reckon he will be left togo on unchecked? Was he not a drop of ejaculated sperm, then a blood clot which

He created and shaped, making from it both sexes, male and female? Is He Who does this, not able to bring the dead to life?"

So far, we have concentrated on how Social Darwinism, believing that violence is the solution to every problem, encourages violence and is the foundation of terrorism. That is why demolishing the Darwinistic theory—which teaches that man is an animal, that only the physically powerful can survive, and that human life is a battleground—will also demolish one of terrorism's mainstays. The most effective means of protecting people from the nightmare of terrorism is spiritual education. Societies can achieve permanent peace only when their individuals learn to live by proper morality. Beyond that, other measures, rules and precautions to regulate the life of society can go only so far, but can never eradicate the scourge of terrorism.

ONLY LOVE CAN DEFEAT TERRORISM

In the Qur'an (32: 9) , God reveals that He has breathed His own soul into Man, His creation, and that Man is His representative on earth (Qur'an, 6: 165). One of the most important differences between Man and the animals is that Man was created with both earthly desires and with a conscience. Every person possesses desires that incite him to evil, along with a conscience that inspires him to avoid it. Alongside such pleasing attributes inspired by that conscience—love, sacrifice, compassion, humility, affection, honesty, loyalty and kindness—he also possesses destructive and undesirable tendencies, stemming from his earthly desires.

Thanks to his conscience, however, the believer can distinguish between right and wrong and opt for what is morally right. Strong belief in and fear of God, faith in the hereafter, powerful fear of the endless torments of hell and a yearning for Paradise all keep the temptations of his earthly desires at bay. Therefore, he always behaves well towards people, is forgiving, responds to wickedness with good, assists those in need, and shows compassion, love, affection and tolerance.

Terrorists, on the other hand, listen to their earthly desire for violence instead of their consciences, and can easily turn to all forms of wickedness. They become loveless, aggressive people who easily hurt others without the slightest pang of conscience. Having no fear of God, they do not know the morality of religion, nor do they practice it. Nothing can stop them from committing crimes.

In restraining its citizens, society's prevailing rules can go only so far. Thanks to its law enforcement units, the state may be able to partially protect streets and public spaces, and—thanks to a powerful system of justice—may be able to take necessary means to ensure public order and ensure that the crime rate drops. But since it's impossible to keep watch on every individual, 24 hours a day, it's essential that peoples' consciences enter the equation at some stage. Someone who doesn't heed the voice of his conscience can easily turn to crime when on his own, or surrounded by people of like mind. The result is a society of individuals who gladly lie when they feel it necessary, have no compunction against enjoying unfair profits, and feel no qualms about oppressing and exploiting the weak. In a society that has lost all spiritual values and has no fear of God, purely physical measures are clearly not going to solve every problem. The morality of religion, on the other hand, commands a person to avoid evil deeds, even when on his own and when he knows that nobody in his community will ever punish him for his misdeeds. The person who knows that God will call him to account for his every deed, his every decision and his every word—and will reward him for them accordingly in the hereafter—will always avoid evil.

Terrorist organizations can't possibly have any place in a society whose people avoid evil of their own free will. Where religion's morality prevails, problems that give rise to organizations supporting the use of violence will disappear naturally. If the whole society possesses superior virtues like honesty, sacrifice, love and justice, there can be no place for such things as poverty, unequal distribution of income, injustice, the oppression of the weak, or limitations on freedoms. On the contrary, a social order will emerge that meets the wants of the needy; where the wealthy protect the poor and the strong, the weak; where everyone can enjoy the very best health care, education, and transport systems. There, tolerance and understanding will dominate the relationships between different ethnic groups, religions and cultures.

For these reasons, proper morality is the key to solving so many social problems. The source of that key, in turn, is the Qur'an, which God has revealed as a guide for mankind.

MODERATE ISLAM-IN OTHER WORDS, TRUE ISLAM

For half a century after the first verse was revealed to the Prophet Muhammad (may God bless him and grant him peace), Islam underwent such an expansion as has seldom been seen. It spread from the Arabian Peninsula to the whole of the Middle East, North Africa and even Spain, drawing the attention of many in the West. In the words of the famous Islamic expert John L. Esposito, "What is most striking about the early expansion of Islam is its rapidity and success.

Western scholars have marveled at it."12 Over the next centuries, Islam reached all corners of the world, from Indonesia to Latin America. Today, Islam is accepted as the fastest growing religion, and its roughly one billion followers represent about one-fifth of the world's population. Interest in Islam particularly increased after the terrorist attacks of September 11, 2001. (For more details, see *The Rise of Islam* by Harun Yahya).

Looking at today's Islamic world today, we see a wide range of religious practices, depending on societies' different customs and traditions, their cultural heritage, and world views. This has led some individuals researching or trying to understand Islam to form mistaken impressions. Those differences may symbolize only the traditional values of the society under examination, but Islam itself. The only way of arriving at an accurate opinion of Islam is to put aside these differences and turn to the Qur'an, where the essence of Islamic morality is set out, and to the actions of our Prophet (may God bless him and grant him peace).

Even if Muslims comprise the majority in a community, that does not mean that community's behavior, views and judgments will necessarily be Islamic, nor that they need be defended in the name of Islam. When evaluating an individual's—or community's—view of Islam, that must always be borne in mind. Differences may stem from prevailing conditions. The only way to ascertain whether those views are correct is by turning to the Qur'an, the most accurate source of truth about Islam, and to the actions of our Prophet (may God bless him and grant him peace). It is most unfair to pass judgment on Islam and Muslims without studying the Qur'an to learn whether a particular practice appears in it. Examining the lifestyle of a single community only can seriously mislead anyone who tries to understand Islam and form opinions about it. First, what needs to be done is to learn about Islam from its true source. Then, once the various models in different parts of the world are considered in the light of those criteria, many who only imagined they knew about Islam will actually come to do so for the first time; and can free themselves from the errors they have been laboring under so far.

Islam Forbids the Killing of Innocents

According to the Qur'an (5:32), it is a great sin to kill an innocent person, and anyone who does so will suffer great torment in the hereafter:

> ... *If someone kills another person—unless it is in retaliation for someone else or for causing corruption in the earth—it is as if he had murdered all mankind. And if anyone gives life to another person, it is as if he had given life to all mankind. Our Messengers came to them with Clear Signs, but even after that, many of them committed outrages in the earth."*

This verse equals the killing of one innocent to slaughtering all of humanity! Another verse (25:68) expresses the importance that the faithful attach to life:

Those who do not appeal to any other deity besides God [alone]; nor kill any soul whom God has forbidden [them to] except with the right to do so; nor fornicate. Anyone who does so will incur a penalty.

In yet another verse (6:151), God issues the following commandment:

Say: "Come, and I will recite to you what your Lord has forbidden for you": that you do not associate anything with Him; that you are good to your parents; that you do not kill your children because of poverty—We will provide for you and them; that you do not approach indecency – outward or inward; that you do not kill any person God has made inviolate – except with the right to do so. That is what He instructs you to do, so that hopefully, you will use your intellect.

Any Muslim who believes in God with a sincere heart, who scrupulously abides by His holy verses and fears suffering in the hereafter, will avoid harming even one other person. He knows that the Lord of Infinite Justice will suitably reward him for all his deeds. In one of the hadiths, our Prophet (may God bless him and grant him peace) listed the kinds of people who are not pleasing to God:

"Those who act cruelly and justly in the sacred lands, those who yearn for the ways of the ignorant, and those who wrongly shed human blood."

Islam Commands People to Behave Justly

Islamic morality commands believers to behave justly and morally in making a decision, speaking, or working—in short, in every area of their lives. God's commandments in the Qur'an and the sunnah of our Prophet (may God bless him and grant him peace) describe that understanding of justice in great detail. With their warnings, all the Messengers revealed to us in the Qur'an brought peace and justice to all the communities where they were sent. The prophets helped lift cruelty and despotism from the shoulders of the community of the faithful. As God has revealed in one verse (10:47):

> *Every nation has a Messenger, and when their Messenger comes, everything is decided between them justly. They are not wronged.*

A most important feature of Islamic understanding of justice is that it commands justice at all times, even if one is dealing with a person who is near and dear. As God commands in another verse (4:135):

> *You who believe! Be upholders of justice, bearing witness for God alone, even against yourselves or your parents and relatives. Whether they are rich or poor, God is well able to look after them. Do not follow your own desires and deviate from the truth. If you twist or turn away, God is aware of what you do.*

That verse clearly states that to a believer, the wealth or social status of whomever one deals with is of no importance. What is important is fairness—no one should be treated unjustly—and to scrupulously implement the holy verses of God. In another verse (5:8), it is commanded:

You who believe! Show integrity for the sake of God, bearing witness with justice. Do not let hatred for a people incite you into not being just. Be just. That is closer to heedfulness. Heed God. God is aware of what you do.

In that verse, God orders the faithful to act justly always, even with their own enemies. No Muslim can make a spontaneous decision, based on the fact that the person he's dealing with has once harmed him or left him in a difficult situation. Even when he is a personal enemy, if the other side is genuinely in the wrong, any Muslim has the duty to respond with good will and to display the morality God has commanded.

To believers, God has issued the following commandment (60:8): "God does not forbid you from being good to those who have not fought you in the religion or driven you from your homes, or from being just towards them. God loves those who are just." Here, He informs Muslims how their relationships with other people should be. These verses are the very foundation of a believer's attitude towards others, formed not by the nature of the people he is dealing with, but by God's revelations in the Qur'an. That is why Muslims with pure hearts always support what is right. Their determination on this matter is revealed in these terms (Qur'an, 7:181): "Among those We have created, there is a community who guide by the Truth and act justly according to it."

Other verses in the Qur'an on the subject of justice read:

> *God commands you to return to their owners the things you hold on trust and, when you judge between people, to judge with justice. How excellent is what God exhorts you to do! God is All-Hearing, All-Seeing. (4:58)*
>
> *Say: "My Lord has commanded justice. Stand and face Him in every mosque and call on Him, making your religion sincerely His. As He originated you, so you will return." (7:29)*
>
> *God commands justice and doing good and giving to relatives. And He forbids indecency and doing wrong and tyranny. He warns you so that hopefully, you will pay heed. (16:90)*

All over the world, people are subjected to cruel treatment because of their race, language or skin color. Yet according to the view of justice as set out in the Qur'an, a person's ethnicity, race or gender are of no importance, because Islam maintains that all people are equal. Our Prophet's (may God bless him and grant him peace) words, *"All of you belong to one ancestry of Adam, and Adam was created out of clay,"*14 stress that there is no difference between people. Skin color, social status and wealth confer no superiority on anyone.

According to the Qur'an, one reason why different tribes, peoples, and nations were created is so that they "might come to know one another." All are servants of God and must come to learn one another's different cultures, languages, customs and abilities. One intent behind the existence of different nations and races is cultural wealth, not war and conflict. All true believers know that only godliness —in other words, the fear of God and faith in Him— can impart superiority. As God has revealed in the Qur'an (49:13):

Mankind! We created you from a male and female, and made you into peoples and tribes so that you might come to know each other. The noblest among you in God's sight is that one of you who best performs his duty. God is All-Knowing, All-Aware.

Elsewhere (30:22), He has revealed that:

Among His Signs is the creation of the heavens and earth and the variety of your languages and colors. There are certainly Signs in that for every being.

History offers many examples of the faithful behaving with complete justice towards other peoples, helping Islam grow with unbelievable speed over a wide area, taking in North Africa, the whole Middle East and even the Iberian Peninsula. By means of these conquests, the civility and tolerance of Islamic morality was spread to many races, nations, communities and individuals, bringing together millions in a bond of mutual tolerance, the likes of which had never been seen before. The renowned researcher Joel Augustus Rogers has examined the various races and the relationship between the black race and other countries. In his book *Sex and Race,* he describes Islam's influence on the world in these terms:

One reason why Islam was able to survive so brightly for centuries is the almost complete absence in this religion of value-judgements based on race and class, the disregarding of the colour of an individual's skin or his social class and the fact that promotion to the highest levels of a community is based on ability alone... Islam established the greatest and at the same time the freest racial melting-pot in history, and the mixing of these races took place within the body of the most extensive empire the world has ever seen. At the height of its power the Islamic Empire stretched from Spain and central France in the West to India, China and the Pacific Ocean in the East, including Central Asia. The rulers of these extensive territories were of various colours. The colour of peoples' skins was even less important for Muslims than the colours of the flowers in a garden is to the flowers themselves.

Professor Hamilton Alexander Rossken Gibb is one of the world's foremost experts on Islam. In his book *Whither Islam?*, he describes the Islamic view of other races:

No other society has such a record of success uniting in an equality of status, of opportunity, and of endeavors so many and so various races of mankind... Islam has still the power to reconcile apparently irreconcilable elements of race and tradition. If ever the opposition of the great societies of East and West is to be replaced by cooperation, the mediation of Islam is an indispensable condition.

Islamic morality aims at a society built on brotherhood and peace, freedom and security. That is why all communities that come into contact with Islam have given up their oppressive, cruel and aggressive ways and have, instead, built peaceful and civilized societies. (For further details, see *Justice and Tolerance in the Qur'an* by Harun Yahya.) In their works, many Western historians have documented Islam's deep and positive affects on communities that came into contact with it. In *The Making of Humanity*, Professor Robert Briffault discusses the relationship between Western society and Islam:

> *The ideas that inspired the French Revolution and the Declaration of Rights, that guided the framing of the American Constitution and inflamed that struggle for independence in the Latin American countries [and elsewhere] were not inventions of the West. They find their ultimate inspiration and source in the Holy Quran.*

These extracts indicate how, down through the centuries, Islamic morality has taught people about peace, tolerance and justice. Nowadays, nearly everyone is seeking just such a model, and there is no reason why such a culture should not come about once again. All that is needed is people's desire to live by the morality of the Qur'an, starting with themselves and later, making efforts to convey it to others. When everyone, from the highest ranks to the very lowest, begins to implement the morality commanded in the Qur'an, they will become just, compassionate, tolerant, full of love, respectful and forgiving. That, in turn, will bring peace to all of society.

The Muslim Should Use Soft Words to Call People to the Morality of Islam

Every Muslim has the duty to call others to the morality of Islam, to inform them of the existence of God and the proofs of His creation. God Himself has revealed that responsibility in Verse 3: 104: "Let there be a community among you who call to the good, and enjoin the right, and forbid the wrong.

They are the ones who have success." He also reveals how that invitation is to be made:

> *Call [them] to the way of your Lord with wisdom and fair admonition, and argue with them in the kindest way. Your Lord knows best who is misguided from His way, and He knows best who are guided. (16:125)*

> *Correct and courteous words accompanied by forgiveness are better than charity followed by insulting words. God is Rich Beyond Need, All-Forbearing. (2:263)*

True believers know the importance of this responsibility, described in Verse 3:114: "They believe in God and the Last Day, and enjoin the right and forbid the wrong, and compete in doing good. They are among the righteous." Therefore, they call on all those around them—friends, relatives, everyone they can reach—to believe in God, fear Him, and display a proper morality. This pleasing characteristic of Muslims is described in Verse 9:71:

> *The men and women of the believers are friends of one another. They command what is right and forbid what is wrong, and perform prayer and pay charity tax, and obey God and His Messenger. They are the people on whom God will have mercy. God is Almighty, All-Wise.*

From this verse, it's clear that all believers, throughout the course of their lives, are charged with explaining that proper morality, living by it themselves, recommending good deeds to others and advising them to avoid evil. God commands believers to use soft words, "Say to My servants that they should only say the best…" (17:53)

God describes good words and bad in this analogy in the Qur'an (14:24-27):

> *Do you do not see how God makes a metaphor of a good word: a good tree whose roots are firm and whose branches are in heaven? It bears fruit regularly by its Lord's permission. God makes metaphors for people so that hopefully they will be reminded. The metaphor of a corrupt word is that of a rotten tree, uprooted on the surface of the earth. It has no staying-power. God makes those who believe firm with the Firm Word in the life of this world and the hereafter. But God misguides the wrongdoers. God does whatever He wills.*

Anyone who wishes to lead a virtuous life should encourage others toward virtue. Anyone who wants to see good should make an effort to help spread it. Anyone who wants to see others behave according to their conscience should encourage them to do so, and anyone who opposes cruelty should warn those who engage in it. In short, anyone who wants right to prevail should call on all others to abide by it.

When issuing that call, however, it's most important to keep in mind that only God can inspire people to become Muslims, and cause words pleasing to them to have any effect. God has revealed that our Prophet (may God bless him and grant him peace), as a result of his noble character and superior morality, always treated people well—and has recommended him as a role model for all mankind.

Islam Commands Solidarity and Cooperation Among People

In the Qur'an (5:2), God has issued this command:

> *... help each other to goodness and godliness. Do not help each other to wrongdoing and enmity. Have fear of God. God is severe in retribution.*

As that verse makes clear, the faithful struggle only for what is good. They consider the words of God in Verse 4:127 of the

Qur'an: "Whatever good you do, God knows it." They never forget that they will be recompensed for all they do in the sight of our Lord, but God reveals that pleasing mutual aid needs to be in a framework of "good and godliness." The meaning of goodness is also explained in Verse 2:177:

> *It is not devoutness to turn your faces to the East or to the West. Rather, those with true devoutness are those who believe in God and the Last Day, the Angels, the Book and the Prophets, and who, despite their love for it, give away their wealth to their relatives and to orphans and the very poor, and to travelers and beggars, and to set slaves free, and who perform prayer and pay charity tax; those who honor their contracts when they make them, and are steadfast in poverty and illness and in battle. Those are the people who act loyal. They are the people who guard against evil.*

True goodness, therefore, is rather different from the way society in general perceives it. Those who do not live by the morality of the Qur'an view good deeds as favors they confer, whenever they happen to feel like it. Usually they restrict such good deeds to giving money to a beggar, or giving up their seat on the bus to an elderly person.

Yet as we have seen from the above verse, the Qur'an describes goodness as a concept encompassing the whole of a believer's life, as an obligation that must be fulfilled throughout the course of his life, not only when he feels like it or happens to remember it. As a servant, any Muslim possesses true sincerity and helps the poor and needy, even if he himself is in need, even giving up the things he loves (Qur'an, 76:8).

In Verse 51:19, which reads, "And beggars and the destitute received a due share of their wealth," God has revealed that rendering assistance, helping others, and doing good are all incumbent upon Muslims. They give help unconditionally; and believers are ready to make any sacrifice to encourage others towards what is good. They expect nothing in return, apart from winning the pleasure of God. In Verse 76:9-10, God describes such behavior by believers:

We feed you only out of desire for the Face of God. We do not want any repayment from you nor any thanks. Truly We fear from our Lord a glowering, calamitous Day.

Muslims know that God is the Lord of infinite justice, and never forget that their good behavior will be suitably rewarded in the hereafter. Nor do they forget that life in this world is only temporary, and that their true home lies in the sight of God. In the Qur'an, He warns people of their inevitable end, and calls on them all to behave in a manner pleasing to Him:

> *We did not create the heavens and earth and everything between them, except with truth. The Hour is certainly coming, so turn away graciously. (15:85)*

> *Worship God and do not associate anything with Him. Be good to your parents and relatives and to orphans and the very poor, and to neighbors who are related to you and neighbors who are not related to you, and to companions and travelers and your slaves. God does not love anyone vain or boastful. (4:36)*

The recompense for those who exhibit pleasing behavior is of great good news for all of mankind, and is revealed in these verses, in these terms:

> *But as for those who believe and do right actions, We will not let the wage of good-doers go to waste. (50:30)*

When those who have done their duty are asked, "What has your Lord sent down?" their reply is, "Good!" There is good in this world for those who do good, and the abode of the hereafter is even better. How wonderful is the abode of those who guard against evil: Gardens of Eden which they enter, with rivers flowing under them, where they have whatever they desire. That is how God repays those who guard against evil. (16:30-31)

Islam Commands Us to Do Good and Avoid Evil

Believers learn the true meaning of good and evil from the Qur'an, a book revealed by God as the Standard by which to discern the true from the false." Concepts such as good and bad, right and wrong, are elucidated in the Qur'an with examples that everyone can understand. The faithful's fear of God gives them light and understanding to help them distinguish between good and bad. (8:29)

Muslims spend their whole lives implementing their awareness of the good and evil, as described in the Qur'an. Yet they take another important responsibility onto their shoulders: inviting others to see the truth, to avoid evil, and live by the morality of the Qur'an. Believers spend their lives telling people about the difference between good and evil, because to the faithful, God has given the following command (3:104):

Let there be a community among you who call to the good, and enjoin the right, and forbid the wrong. They are the ones who have success.

In Verse 3:110, God stresses how those who abide by this commandment are much more auspicious than others:

> *You are the best nation ever to be produced before mankind. You enjoin the right, forbid the wrong and believe in God. If the People of the Book were to believe, it would be better for them. Some of them are believers, but most of them are deviators.*

The faithful perform that Qur'anic duty not only in respect for those ignorant of the difference between right and wrong and with no knowledge of religion, but also in respect for the faithful themselves. People fall into error not only out of ignorance, but sometimes out of forgetfulness, by mistake, or when driven by earthly desires. That being so, the faithful encourage good and prevent evil by reminding one another of the Qur'an's commandments. They warn each other that in this world, those who fail to avoid evil will suffer the torments of hell; that only those who do good and devoutly carry out their religious obligations will be rewarded with Paradise. That delightful responsibility means that they never need feel wearied or discouraged while continuing to warn others compassionately and affectionately, no matter what mistakes they might have made. In many verses, God reveals that He loves those who have patience, and calls on the faithful to be patient when practicing the morality of the Qur'an:

> *You who believe! Seek help in steadfastness and prayer. God is with the steadfast. (2:153)*

> *... Those who are steadfast and do right actions. They will receive forgiveness and a large reward. (11:11)*

Islam Commands us to Repay Evil with Good

A good action and a bad action are not the same. Repel the bad with something better and, if there is enmity between you and someone else, he will be like a bosom friend. (41:34)

Ward off evil with what is better. We know very well what they express. (23:96)

In these verses, God promises the faithful that they can secure positive results, so long as they adopt a pleasant attitude in the face of wrongdoing. The Qur'an emphasizes that even when a believer is dealing with an enemy, still he can establish a warm friendship. Responding to evil with good is also an essential part of compassion. When any believer sees others adopting an attitude that will not be pleasing to God, he considers first of all how that will affect them in the hereafter. Then he approaches them with toleration and humility, refusing to let himself become puffed up with pride.

Over the course of their lives, believers may come across people of very different characters. Yet they will not change their view of morality according to the people they meet. Others may speak mockingly, use ugly words, become angry, or even behave in a hostile manner. Yet the true believer never ceases to be polite, modest, and compassionate. He will not respond to ugly words with more of the same. He will not laugh at those who mock him, nor answer anger with anger, but remains patient and tolerant. In the face of insulting behavior, he will respond with proper morality, and with such compassion that the other will feel ashamed. That is the morality our Prophet (may God bless him and grant him peace) recommends to us. In one of the hadiths, he says, "*You do not return evil for evil, but excuse and forgive.*"— 18 In another hadith, he calls on the faithful in these terms: '*None of you must be the kind of weak person who says, 'He who has no compassion will receive none.*"

In the Qur'an (5:13), our Prophet (may God bless him and grant him peace) was told to be forgiving when betrayed by some of the children of Israel:

> ... *They have forgotten a good portion of what they were reminded of. You will never cease to come upon some act of treachery on their part, except for a few of them. Yet pardon them, and overlook. God loves good-doers.*

As this verse shows, poor morality displayed by someone else is no justification for displaying the same thing. Each individual is solely responsible to God for his actions. According to the Qur'an, acting with compassion, affection and proper morality in the face of someone else's bad behavior is a sign of superior morality that reveals the extent of a believer's devotion to God. One verse (10:26) reveals the reward that such a pleasing attitude will bring:

> *Those who do good will have the best, and more! Neither dust nor debasement will darken their faces. They are the Companions of the Garden, remaining in it timelessly, forever.*

Islam Commands The Faithful to be Forgiving, Always

One important sign of compassion is a person's ability to forgive. In Verse 7:199, God calls upon His servants to "make allowances for people, command what is right, and turn away from the ignorant."

Some may find this attitude difficult, but in the sight of God, it will be well rewarded. Those caught up in anger may well refuse to forgive mistakes. But to the faithful, God has revealed that it is better to forgive and, in Verse 26:40, has recommended this morality:

The repayment of a bad action is one equivalent to it. But if someone pardons and puts things right, his reward is with God...

In another verse (26:43), God reveals, "But if someone is steadfast and forgives, that is the most resolute course to follow." Verse 24:22 emphasizes that this is a very superior form of morality:

Those of you possessing affluence and ample wealth should not make oaths that they will not give to their relatives and the very poor and those who have emigrated in the way of God. They should rather pardon and overlook. Would you not love God to forgive you? God is Ever-Forgiving, Most Merciful."

In these words, He encourages the faithful to consider their own positions when it comes to forgiveness. Because everyone wants God to forgive him, to protect and show him mercy, so do we hope that all others will excuse and forgive our mistakes. Therefore, God has commanded the faithful to treat others in the same way they would like to be treated themselves. That important responsibility encourages the faithful to be forgiving towards one another. Our Prophet (may God bless him and grant him peace) encouraged them in these words: *"That person is nearest to God, who pardons, when he has someone in his power, one who would have injured him."*20

Believers, knowing that at any moment they may make a mistake, behave tolerantly towards others. Those verses in the Qur'an dealing with repentance make it clear that never making mistakes isn't as important as the determination never to repeat them. One of these verses (4:17) reads:

God accepts only the repentance of those who do evil in ignorance and then quickly repent after doing it. God turns towards such people. God is All-Knowing, All-Wise.

Under conditions that reveal an individual's sincerity, the faithful behave forgivingly and compassionately towards one another. If he who has committed error sincerely repents having done so, they cannot judge him for his past deeds. Even when the faithful are totally in the right and the other completely in the wrong, still they have no compunction about forgiveness, because God recommends such behavior as an example of proper morality (3:134):

> *Those who give in times of both ease and hardship, those who control their rage and pardon other people—God loves the good-doers.*

When it comes to forgiving, the faithful don't distinguish between great and small errors, nor do they tailor their view of forgiveness accordingly. Someone may have committed an error inflicting severe harm on others, great financial loss, even loss of life. Yet the faithful know everything happens by the permission of God, as part of His destiny. When it comes to such things, they therefore place themselves in the hands of God and feel no personal anger.

Alternatively, if someone transgresses this Qur'anic rule and exceeds the bounds set by God, only God can judge that person's behavior. It is never up to the faithful to judge—or refuse to forgive—anyone on any matter. The truly sorry and repentant person will have his reward only in the sight of God. In many verses, God has revealed that apart from "associating partners to Him," He will forgive the errors of the faithful who repent sincerely. Since one man cannot know another's repentance, the faithful simply forgive in the manner God revealed to them. If the Qur'an has anything to say on a particular subject, they treat the person who has committed error in that light.

Islam Commands People To Behave Gently

God has infinite compassion, and is forgiving, protective and gentle toward believers. The Compassionate and Merciful has placed all the blessings in the universe at Man's disposal, supporting him with messengers to reveal the true path. He directs all men to be His sincere servants by means of His revelations, each of which is a guidepost to that path. Our Lord is the *Halim* (the Clement), *Adl* (Lord of Infinite Justice), *'Afuw* (the Pardoner), *Asim* (the Protector), *Barr* (the Source of All Goodness), *Ghafir* (the Forgiver), *Hafiz* (the Protector), *Karim* (the Generous One), *Latif* (the Subtle One), ***Muhsin*** (Lord of Infinite Kindness), *Ra'uf* (the Compassionate), ***Salam*** (the

Author of Safety), *Tawwab* (the Accepter of Repentance) and *Wahhab* (the Bestower).

Believers know that they are under our Lord's protection and are aware of His infinite goodness and kindness. For that reason, they are eager to become the kind of servants that are pleasing to Him, who merit His mercy, and Paradise. As we have seen, one characteristic distinguishing believers is they are full of love and compassion. A Muslim behaves very gently, always treating others kindly. God has offered our Prophet's (may God bless him and grant him peace) gentle nature as an example to all believers (3:159):

It is a mercy from God that you were gentle with them. If you had been rough or hard of heart, they would have scattered from around you. So pardon them and ask forgiveness for them, and consult with them about the matter. Then when you have reached a firm decision, put your trust in God. God loves those who put their trust in Him.

That verse describes how our Prophet's (may God bless him and grant him peace) gentle, moral nature exerted a positive influence on people, whereby they grew even more devoted to him. The Qur'an gives the gentle natures of other loving prophets as role models. One verse (11:87) recounts how, when the Prophet Shuayb (peace be upon him) was sent to the people of Midian, they told him, "... You are clearly the forbearing, the rightly-guided!" The superior morality of the Prophet Abraham (peace be upon him) is another example for everyone. The Qur'an tells us that he was sensitive, gentle and full of love. The verses in question read:

Abraham would not have asked forgiveness for his father, but for a promise he made to him, and when it became clear to him that he was an enemy of God, he renounced him. Abraham was tenderhearted and forbearing. (9:114)

Abraham was forbearing, compassionate, penitent. (11:75)

God has commanded his believers always to behave in a pleasant manner, to speak kindly, and to treat others well. His prophets behaved accordingly. For example, when the Prophet Musa (Moses) (peace be upon him) was about to go to Pharaoh, one of the most repressive and cruel rulers of all times, God called on Moses in these terms (20:42-44):

Go, you and your brother, with My Signs, and do not slacken in remembering Me. Go to Pharaoh; he has overstepped the bounds. But speak to him with gentle words so that hopefully, he will be reminded or show some fear.

These verses are an important reminder that everyone has a duty to live by the morality that the Qur'an reveals, and to adopt the morality of the prophets. The Qur'an proposes the following ideals for mankind: Love to all creatures God created; being kind and gentle in the best possible ways; always favoring compromise and tolerance; never speaking harshly, even under the most trying circumstances; making sacrifices happily and willingly; always desiring and seeking the best for others; pushing one's own personal desires to the background; wishing for others exactly what one wishes for oneself; being always quick to offer assistance in cases of need; and rejecting all forms of cruelty. That, no doubt, is exactly the ethical model that mankind is searching for.

Islam Supports Freedom of Belief

In matters of belief, Islam offers people complete freedom, and in the very clearest language. That has been so ever since Islam was first revealed, and forms the basis of today's Islamic morality. The verses on the subject (2:256) are perfectly clear:

There is no compulsion where religion is concerned. Right guidance has become clearly distinct from error. Anyone who rejects false gods and believes in God has grasped the Firmest Handhold, which will never give way. God is All-Hearing, All-Knowing.

According to Islam, people are free to choose whatever beliefs they wish, and nobody can oblige anyone else. Yes, a Muslim has a duty to communicate Islam and explain the existence of God, to state that the Qur'an is the book of His revelation, that the Prophet Muhammad (may God bless him and grant him peace) was His messenger, to speak of the hereafter and the Day of Judgment and of the beauty of Islamic morality. Yet that duty is restricted to explaining the religion only. In one verse (16:125), God informs our Prophet (may God bless him and grant him peace) that he is only a messenger:

> *Call to the way of your Lord with wisdom and fair admonition, and argue with them in the kindest way. Your Lord knows best who is misguided from His way. And He knows best who are guided.*

Another verse (18:29) states, "... It is the truth from your Lord; so let whoever wishes believe and whoever wishes disbelieve..." In Verse 26:3, our Lord warns the Prophet (may God bless him and grant him peace), "Perhaps you will destroy yourself with grief because they will not become believers." He also issues His Prophet (may God bless him and grant him peace) this reminder (50:45):

> *We know best what they say. You are not a dictator over them. So remind, with the Qur'an, whoever fears My Threat.*

People are free to choose correctly or wrongly. When Islam—the true path that God has revealed—is explained, they come to believe of their own free will, reaching this decision with no pressure being put on them. If they make wrong choices, they will face its consequences in the hereafter. On this subject, Verse 10: 99 of the Qur'an contains the clearest command and reminder: "If your Lord had willed, all the people on the earth would have believed. Do you think you can force people to be believers?"

When one of the faithful explains matters, one person might come to believe straightaway, whereas another might adopt a mocking and aggressive attitude. One who follows his conscience might decide to devote his life to pleasing God, even while another, doing as the deniers did, might respond to those same kind words with wickedness. Yet his denial won't lead whoever issued the invitation to suffer or despair. In Verses 12: 103-104, God has stated, "But most people, for all your eagerness, are not believers. You do not ask them for any wage for it. It is only a reminder to all beings."

What's important is that no matter what reaction he meets with, the person who abides by the Qur'an keeps on displaying the kind of morality that is pleasing to God, refuses to make any concessions on it, and leaves matters in God's hands. God has told us that His religion is to be explained in the most pleasing manner. In the words of the Qur'an (29:46):

> *Argue with the People of the Book only in the kindest way—except in the case of those of them who do wrong–saying, "We believe in what has been sent down to us and what was sent down to you. Our God and your God are one and we submit to Him."*

We must not forget that every event, large or small, takes place according to a destiny created by God. He reveals the true path to anyone invited to believe in Him. For that reason, the faithful feel no distress at the behavior of those who reject Him. The Qur'an gives several examples. In Verse 18:6, God tells our Prophet (may God bless him and grant him peace) not to be distressed when those whom he calls on to believe refuse to do so: "Perhaps you may destroy yourself with grief, chasing after them, if they do not believe in these words." Another verse (28:56) reads, "You cannot guide those you would like to, but God guides those He wills. He has best knowledge of the guided."

That means that whatever invitations an individual issues, all his pleasant words, and every detail he goes into can make an effect only by the will of God.

A believer's only responsibility is to call people to the Qur'an. He cannot be blamed for atheists' refusal to amend their ways, nor with how they will earn the torments of hell for themselves. In Verse 2:119, our Lord told our Prophet (may God bless him and grant him peace), "We have sent you with the Truth, bringing good news and giving warning. Do not ask about the inhabitants of the Blazing Fire."

God has given mankind both reason and a conscience. His messengers and the divine books revealed to them have shown the true path, and people are responsible for their own choices. Islamic morality can be lived only by a sincere decision to do so—by surrendering oneself to God and listening to one's conscience, which always commands one to do what is right. It is a total violation of Islamic morality to force anyone to believe, because what matters is an individual's surrendering himself to God with all his heart and believing sincerely. If any system obliges people to have faith, then those "converts" will become religious only out of fear. The only acceptable way to live a religion is within an environment that leaves one's conscience completely free. This is what God revealed to our Prophet (may God bless him and grant him peace) (88:21-26):

So remind them! You are only a reminder. You are not in control of them. But as for anyone who turns away and disbelieves, God will punish him with the Greatest Punishment. Certainly it is to Us they will return Then their Reckoning is Our concern.

It's worth emphasizing that Islam leaves people free to make their own choices regarding religion and commands them to respect other religions. Even if someone believes in what the Qur'an describes as superstition, still he can live in peace and security in Muslim lands and freely perform his own religious obligations. In Verses 109:2-6, God commanded our Prophet (may God bless him and grant him peace) to tell those who denied Him:

"I do not worship what you worship, and you do not worship what I worship. Nor will I worship what you worship, nor will you worship what I worship. You have your religion, and I have my religion."

Under the morality of Islam, everyone is free to carry out the obligations in accord with his own particular belief. Nobody can prevent any others from performing their particular religious duties, nor can he oblige them to worship in the manner he desires. That violates the morality of Islam, and is unacceptable to God. In the

Islamic model of society emerges in which everyone is free to worship and perform the obligations attendant upon his particular chosen beliefs. The Qur'an (22:40) describes monasteries, churches, synagogues, and the places of worship of the Peoples of the Book as all under God's protection:

> ... *If God had not driven some people back by means of others, [then] monasteries, churches, synagogues and mosques, where God's name is mentioned much, would have been pulled down and destroyed. God will certainly help those who help Him—God is All-Strong, Almighty.*

Our Prophet's (may God bless him and grant him peace) life is full of such examples. When Christians came to see him pray in his own mosque, he left it for them to use. 21That kind of tolerance was maintained during the times of the caliphs who succeeded the Prophet (may God bless him and grant him peace). After Damascus was captured, a church that had been turned into a mosque was divided into two, so that Christians might worship in one half and Muslims in the other.22

Islam Commands That Oppression Be Abolished

Muslims should never remain silent in the face of oppression that they witness, or even hear about secondhand. Their compassion, stemming from the morality of the Qur'an, directs them to oppose all tyranny, wickedness and oppression, to defend the oppressed, to wage a war of ideas on their behalf. Whether dealing with their closest friends or with strangers with whom they share no interests in common, they behave in a manner determined to prevent any such oppression. Rather, they seize on this opportunity to win the good pleasure of God and implement the morality of the Qur'an. Because a believer's conscience is so very sensitive, his compassion never lets him turn a blind eye to the slightest injustice or cruelty. He will take his place in the vanguard of that morality by avoiding any actions that might be unfair to or oppress anyone else. Whenever he sees anyone else behaving that way, his conscience gives him no peace until he's done everything possible to right matters. True compassion has no room for forgetting about oppression, ignoring it or underestimating it.

The ignorant seldom act until oppression stands at their very own doorstep. This stems from their forgetting or denying that in the hereafter, they will be brought face to face with all the good and bad deeds that they encountered in this world. But the faithful, well aware of this, will treat even total strangers he has never met with great compassion and seeks to rescue them from oppression. Even if no one else supports him, he will muster all his strength to forestall wickedness. Even though the majority may behave differently, their lack of conscience never rubs off on the true believer. In the hereafter, Muslims know, they will be called to account for what they did to prevent evil. They won't be able to get away with excuses like, "I didn't see it," or, "I didn't hear it," or "I never knew what was going on."

As is revealed in the Qur'an (19:80), "... he [man] will come to Us all alone," every human being will return to his Creator on his own. People will be brought into the presence of God, put to the trial, and called to account for their deeds in this world. Only those who followed the dictates of their conscience will come out of that questioning at all well. Those who have behaved well, opposed all forms of cruelty, fought evil, and remained on the path of God can expect a suitable reward. God mentions this matter in another verse (2:112):

All who submit themselves completely to God and are good-doers will find their reward with their Lord. They will feel no fear and will know no sorrow.

6

TOLERANCE AND MORALITY IN THE TESTAMENTS

The preceding section considered the Qur'an's calls for people to live in love and security, emphasizing that Islam is a religion of peace. Like other divine religions, Islam proposes a model society of compassionate, mature, moderate, mild, gentle, kind, sympathetic, loyal, understanding, forgiving and tolerant people who avoid fighting and conflict. It also commands believers to strive to bring such a society about.

Divine books revealed before the Qur'an may have undergone a number of distortions, but they still contain sections that agree with it. These books are the Torah and the Gospels. Today, although mixed with human words and thus distorted, they make up the core of what is called the Bible. The Bible's two basic parts, the Old and the New Testaments, are based on the Torah and the Gospels relatively, including many other books and letters. Both the Old and New Testaments favor love, peace and tolerance, also prohibiting terror and oppression. In this section, we'll consider how Jews and Christians from all over the world must take action in light of these commands to oppose terrorism.

The Old Testament consists of five books comprising the Torah given to the Prophet Moses (peace be upon him), the Book of Psalms, and other writings by Jewish prophets and accounts of their lives. Jews believe in the Old Testament. Christians also believe in the New Testament, an addition to the Old, which consists of the four gospels, the Acts of the Apostles following Jesus's death, and a number of letters. According to the Qur'an, however, the divine books of the Bible were distorted after being revealed to mankind. That means that both the Old and New Testaments are no longer the uncorrupted word of God. We should regard them as containing divine elements that agree with the Qur'an, but also various human errors. When making use of the Old and New Testaments, therefore, we need to consider whether their contents are in harmony with the Qur'an.

STATESMENTS FROM THE OLD TESTAMENT COMDEMNING TERROR AND ENCOURAGING LOVE AND PEACE

Seek good and not evil, that you may live; so the Lord God of hosts will be with you, as you have spoken. Hate evil, love good… (Amos 5, 14-15)

As emphasized earlier, the divine books sent down by God to guide His servants describe an ideal society full of love, peace, tolerance and justice. In the Qur'an, for example, God describes the Torah revealed to the Jews as a guide:

> *We sent down the Torah containing guidance and light, and the prophets who had submitted themselves gave judgment by it for the Jews—as did their scholars and their rabbis--by what they had been allowed to preserve of God's Book to which they were witnesses... (5:44)*

Today, we can find part of the Torah's divine commandments in the Old Testament, directing people to avoid evil, tyranny, theft, corruption, falsehood and cruelty; and to display proper morality. In fact, God states in the Qur'an that:

> *He [God] said, "Moses, I have chosen you over all mankind for My Message and My Word. Take what I have given you and be among the thankful." We wrote about everything for him on the Tablets as*

> *an admonition and making all things clear. "Seize hold of it vigorously and command your people to adopt the best in it. I will show you the home of the deviators!" (7:144-145)*

ALL FORMS OF VIOLENCE AND OPPRESSION ARE FORBIDDEN

The Old Testament describes in considerable detail the fate awaiting those who commit evil and want to spread it, and warns people against going down that road. Flying into a rage and harming others, trying to turn them away from the true path, shedding blood and quarrelling are all described as forms of behavior displeasing to God, which He has forbidden. He condemns all those who go down the path of evil and oppression, revealing that such people will never be saved. Some Old Testament accounts emphasize this:

> *Simeon and Levi are brothers; instruments of cruelty are in their dwelling place. Let not my soul enter their council; let not my honor be united to their assembly; for in their anger they slew a man, and in their self-will they hamstrung an ox. Cursed be their anger, for it is fierce; and their wrath, for it is cruel! (Genesis 49, 5-7)*

> *But the wicked are like the troubled sea, when it cannot rest, whose waters cast up mire and dirt. "There is no peace," says my God, "for the wicked." (Isaiah 57, 20-21)*

> *You children of Israel... "There is no truth or mercy or knowledge of God in the land. By swearing and lying, killing and stealing and committing adultery, they break all restraint, with bloodshed upon bloodshed. Therefore the land will mourn; and everyone who dwells there will waste away with the beasts of the field and the birds of the air; even the fish of the sea will be taken away. " Now let no man contend, or rebuke another; for your people are like those who contend with the priest. (Hosea 4, 1-4)*

> *Gilead is a city of evildoers and defiled with blood. As bands of robbers lie in wait for a man, so the company of priests murder on the way to Shechem; surely they commit lewdness. (Hosea 6, 8-9)*

> *The merciful man does good for his own soul, but he who is cruel troubles his own flesh... But he who sows righteousness will have a sure reward. As righteousness leads to life, so he who pursues evil pursues it to his own death... The wicked will not go unpunished; but the posterity of the righteous will be delivered. (Proverbs 11, 17-21)*

> *An ungodly man digs up evil, and it is on his lips like a burning fire. A perverse man sows strife, and a whisperer separates the best of friends. A violent man entices his neighbor, and leads him in a way that is not good... He who is slow to anger is better than the mighty. . . (Proverbs 16, 27-32)*

> *The Lord is far from the wicked... (Proverbs 15, 29)*

The Old Testament describes in considerable detail the deeds of people who did evil and acted tyrannically, making it clear that the wicked will receive their just deserts. But it also states that those who repent will be accepted as good, if they abide by God's religion:

> *Yet the house of Israel says, "The way of the Lord is not fair." O house of Israel, is it not My ways which are fair, and your ways which are not fair? When a righteous man turns away from his righteousness, commits iniquity, and dies in it, it is because of the iniquity which he has done that he dies. Again, when a wicked man turns away from the wickedness which he committed, and does what is lawful and right, he preserves himself alive. Because he considers and turns away from all the transgressions which he committed, he shall surely live; he shall not die. Yet the house of Israel says, "The way of the Lord is not fair." O house of Israel, is it not My ways which are fair, and your ways which are not fair? Therefore I will judge you, O house of Israel, every one according to his ways," says the Lord God. "Repent, and turn from all your transgressions, so that iniquity will not be your ruin. Cast away from you all the transgressions which you have committed, and get yourselves a new heart and a new spirit. For why should you die, O house of Israel? For I have no pleasure in the death of one who dies," says the Lord God. "Therefore turn and live!" (Ezekiel 18, 21-32)*

... Thus says the Lord: "... I am fashioning a disaster and devising a plan against you. Return now every one from his evil way, and make your ways and your doings good." And they said, "That is hopeless! So we will walk according to our own plans, and we will every one obey the dictates of his evil heart." (Jeremiah 18, 11-12)

Do not be like your fathers, to whom the former prophets preached, saying, "Thus says the Lord of hosts: 'Turn now from your evil ways and your evil deeds.'" But they did not hear nor heed Me," says the Lord. (Zechariah 1, 4)

IT IS FORBIDDEN TO HARM OTHERS

Many Old Testament commandments prohibit doing harm to others, killing, ruling without justice, or behaving unfairly.

You shall not murder. You shall not commit adultery. You shall not steal. You shall not bear false witness against your neighbor. You shall not covet your neighbour's house... (Exodus 20, 13-17)

You shall do no injustice in judgment ... nor honor the person of the mighty. In righteousness you shall judge your neighbor. You shall not go about as a talebearer among your people; nor shall you take a stand against the life of your neighbor: I am the Lord... You shall not take vengeance, nor bear any grudge against the children of your people, but you shall love your neighbor as yourself: I am the Lord. (Leviticus 19, 15-18)

Lest innocent blood be shed in the midst of your land which the Lord your God is giving you as an inheritance, and thus guilt of bloodshed be upon you. (Deuteronomy 19, 10)

Deliver those who are drawn toward death, and hold back those stumbling to the slaughter. If you say, "Surely we did not know this," Does not He who weighs the hearts consider it? He who keeps your soul, does He not know it?.. (Proverbs 24, 11-12)

BE GOOD TO OTHERS

The Old Testament contains a number of statements commanding brotherhood and love, sacrifice and humility. Just like

Muslims, the Jews and Christians have been ordered to treat others well, to do good deeds, never to deviate from the path of righteousness, and to be mild-mannered, tolerant and forgiving. Some examples include:

> *Sow for yourselves righteousness; reap in mercy... You have plowed wickedness; you have reaped iniquity. You have eaten the fruit of lies, because you trusted in your own way, in the multitude of your mighty men... (Hosea 10, 12-13)*

> *They hate the one who rebukes in the gate, and they abhor the one who speaks uprightly. Therefore, because you tread down the poor and take grain taxes from him, though you have built houses of hewn stone, yet you shall not dwell in them; you have planted pleasant vineyards, but you shall not drink wine from them. For I know your manifold transgressions and your mighty sins: Afflicting the just and taking bribes; diverting the poor from justice at the gate. Therefore the prudent keep silent at that time, for it is an evil time. Seek good and not evil, that you may live; so the Lord God of hosts will be with you, as you have spoken. Hate evil, love good; establish justice in the gate... (Amos 5, 10-15)*

PEOPLE ARE INVITED TO CONDUCT THEMSELVES WELL

He has shown you, O man, what is good; and what does the Lord require of you but to do justly, to love mercy, and to walk humbly with your God? (Micah 6, 8)

How long will you judge unjustly, and show partiality to the wicked?.. Defend the poor and fatherless; do justice to the afflicted and needy. Deliver the poor and needy; free them from the hand of the wicked. (Psalms 82, 2-4)

The integrity of the upright will guide them, but the perversity of the unfaithful will destroy them. Riches do not profit in the day of wrath, but righteousness delivers from death. The righteousness of the blameless [man] will direct his way aright, but the wicked will fall by his own wickedness. The righteousness of the upright will deliver them, but the unfaithful will be caught by their lust. (Proverbs 11, 3-6)

The desire of the righteous is only good, but the expectation of the wicked is wrath. (Proverbs 11, 23)

He who earnestly seeks good finds favor, but trouble will come to him who seeks evil. (Proverbs 11, 27)

The way of the wicked is an abomination to the Lord, but He loves him who follows righteousness. (Proverbs 15, 9)

In mercy and truth atonement is provided for iniquity; and by the fear of the Lord one departs from evil. When a man's ways please the Lord, he makes even his enemies to be at peace with him. Better is a little with righteousness, than vast revenues without justice. (Proverbs 16, 6-8)

The highway of the upright is to depart from evil... (Proverbs 16, 17)

Do not be envious of evil men, nor desire to be with them; for their heart devises violence, and their lips talk of troublemaking. (Proverbs 24, 1-2)

Do not lie in wait, O wicked man, against the dwelling of the righteous; do not plunder his resting place; for a righteous man may fall seven times and rise again, but the wicked shall fall by calamity. Do not rejoice when your enemy falls, and do not let your heart be glad when he stumbles; lest the Lord see it... Do not fret because of evildoers, nor be envious of the wicked; for there will be no prospect for the evil man… (Proverbs 24, 15-20)

MAN IS COMMANDED TO BE ON THE SIDE OF PEACE

Just like Muslims, Jews and Christians are commanded to avoid war and in particular, to establish peace. The book *Hristiyan Ahlaki* (Christian Morality) describes the kind of behavior a Christian should display, according to the Old and New Testaments, and sums this situation up in these terms: "The conflicts mentioned in the

Holy Book are for the purposes of self-defense."23 It is forbidden to harm non-combatants, like children in the event of war.

Now it happened, as soon as the kingdom was established in his hand, that he executed his servants who had murdered his father the king. But the children of the murderers he did not execute, according to what is written in the Book of the Law of Moses, in which the Lord commanded, saying, "Fathers shall not be put to death for their children, nor shall children be put to death for their fathers..." ... (2 Kings 14, 5-6)

WHEN THE MORALITY OF RELIGION PREVAILS, ACCORDING TO THE OLD TESTAMENT

In the same way as Islam, Judaism and Christianity propose an exemplary model for society. With their strong faith, proper morality and the scrupulous adherence to His verses, the messengers whom God sent as guides to Man are the very finest examples. For this reason, it's most important for believers to try to adopt the prophets' morality of as their own, and to live similarly. If features of religion's proper morality can spread throughout all mankind, the resulting atmosphere will closely resemble heaven. In such a society, the nightmares of anarchy and terror will disappear. Scrupulous adhering to God's commands, those who fear and believe in Him will eagerly avoid all forms of wickedness and mischief. The world will come to be filled with peace and tolerance, moderate and understanding people. The Old Testament describes with a number of examples the life style, once the morality of religion prevails:

Then justice will dwell in the wilderness, and righteousness remain in the fruitful field. The work of righteousness will be peace, and the effect of righteousness, quietness and assurance forever. My people will dwell in a peaceful habitation, in secure dwellings, and in quiet resting places. (Isaiah 32, 16-18)

The wilderness and the wasteland shall be glad for them, and the desert shall rejoice and blossom as the rose; it shall blossom abundantly and rejoice, even with joy and singing... They shall see the glory of the

Lord, the excellency of our God. Strengthen the weak hands, and make firm the feeble knees. Say to those who are fearful-hearted, "Be strong, do not fear!.. " Then the eyes of the blind shall be opened, and the ears of the deaf shall be unstopped. Then the lame shall leap like a deer, and the tongues of the dumb sing. For waters shall burst forth in the wilderness, and streams in the desert. (Isaiah 35, 1-6)

He who walks righteously and speaks uprightly, he who despises the gain of oppressions, who gestures with his hands, refusing bribes, who stops his ears from hearing of bloodshed, and shuts his eyes from seeing evil: He will dwell on high; his place of defense will be the fortress of rocks; bread will be given him, his water will be sure. (Isaiah 33, 15-16)

... To loose the bonds of wickedness, to undo the heavy burdens, to let the oppressed go free, and that you break every yoke? Is it not to share your bread with the hungry, and that you bring to your house the poor who are cast out; when you see the naked, that you cover him, and not hide yourself from your own flesh? Then your light shall break forth like the morning, your healing shall spring forth speedily, and your righteousness shall go before you; the glory of the Lord shall be your rear guard. Then you shall call, and the Lord will answer; you shall cry, and He will say, "Here I am." If you take away the yoke from your midst, the pointing of the finger, and speaking wickedness, if you extend your soul to the hungry and satisfy the afflicted soul, then your light shall dawn in the darkness, and your darkness shall be as the noonday. (Isaiah 58, 6-10)

THE NEW TESTAMEN'S RECOMMENDATIONS FOR A WORLD OF LOVE AND

"... You shall love the LORD your God with all your heart, with all your soul, and with all your mind." This is the first and great commandment. And the second is like it: "You shall love your neighbor as yourself." (Matthew 22, 37-39)

The Christian New Testament also contains many sections forbidding evil and oppression. People are called on to be forgiving, peaceful, tolerant and compromising at all times. For these reasons, Christianity expects people to be understanding and joyful, and to refrain from conflict. Christians who abide by the injunctions revealed by the Prophet Jesus (peace be upon him) and who take his morality as their own are described in these terms in the Qur'an (57: 27):

Then We sent Our Messengers following in their footsteps and sent 'Isa (Jesus) son of Maryam (Mary) after them, giving him the Gospel. We put compassion and mercy in the hearts of those who followed him . . .

In another verse (5:82), God states, "... You will find the people most affectionate to those who believe are those who say, 'We are Christians.' That is because some of them are priests and monks and because they are not arrogant," and praises Christians who turn to God with a sincere heart.

This positive morality of Christians is based on the commandments in the Bible. They are commanded to return good for evil, to love their fellow human beings unconditionally and to help the needy in the same manner. In fact, the New Testament uses a special word for the "unconditional love" that believers have for Our Lord and the faithful. One work dealing with Christianity describes the situation in these terms:

The word agape is used 116 times in 105 verses of the New Testament. It is a very high form of love. Agape Enterprises simply means "Love Enterprises." Our ministry reaches out to those who need, and have nothing to repay. A number of extracts from the New Testament command people to avoid evil and bloodshed and encourage them to display proper morality.

UNCONDITIONAL LOVE AND COMPASSION

"A new commandment I give to you, that you love one another; as I have loved you, that you also love one another." (John 13, 34)

Let love be without hypocrisy. Abhor what is evil. Cling to what is good. Be kindly affectionate to one another with brotherly love, in honor giving preference to one another; not lagging in diligence, fervent in spirit, serving the Lord; rejoicing in hope, patient in tribulation, continuing steadfastly in prayer; distributing to the needs of the saints, given to hospitality. Bless those who persecute you; bless and do not curse. (Romans 12, 9-14)

Owe no one anything except to love one another, for he who loves another has fulfilled the law. For the commandments, "You shall not commit adultery," "You shall not murder," "You shall not steal," "You shall not bear false witness," "You shall not covet," and if there is any other commandment, are all summed up in this saying, namely, "You shall love your neighbor as yourself." Love does no harm to a neighbor; therefore love is the fulfillment of the law. (Romans 13, 8-10)

And may the Lord make you increase and abound in love to one another and to all, just as we do to you. (1 Thessalonians 3, 12)

Then one of the scribes came... and asked him, "Which is the first commandment of all?" Jesus answered him, "The first of all the commandments is: 'Hear, O Israel, the Lord our God, the Lord is one. And you shall love the Lord your God with all your heart, with all your soul, with all your mind, and with all your strength.' ... And the second, like it, is this: 'You shall love your neighbor as yourself.' There is no other commandment greater than these."

So the scribe said to him, "Well said, Teacher. You have spoken the truth, for there is one God, and there is no other but He. And to love Him with all the heart, with all the understanding, with all the soul, and with all the strength, and to love one's neighbor as oneself, is more than all the whole burnt offerings and sacrifices." (Mark 12, 28-33)

Since you have purified your souls in obeying the truth through the Spirit in sincere love of the brethren, love one another fervently with a pure heart... (1 Peter 1, 22)

Finally, all of you be of one mind, having compassion for one another; love as brothers, be tender hearted, be courteous; not returning evil for evil or reviling for reviling, but on the contrary blessing, knowing that you were called to this, that you may inherit a blessing… (1 Peter 3, 8-10)

And above all things, have fervent love for one another, for "love will cover a multitude of sins." Be hospitable to one another without grumbling. As each one has received a gift, minister it to one another, as good stewards of the manifold grace of God. (1 Peter 4, 8-10)

LOVING YOUR ENEMY

"You have heard that it was said, 'You shall love your neighbor and hate your enemy.' But I say to you, love your enemies, bless those who curse you, do good to those who hate you, and pray for those who spitefully use you and persecute you. (Matthew 5, 43-44)

"But I say to you who hear: Love your enemies, do good to those who hate you, bless those who curse you, and pray for those who spitefully use you. To him who strikes you on the one cheek, offer the other also. And from him who takes away your cloak, do not withhold your tunic either. Give to everyone who asks of you. And from him who takes away your goods, do not ask for them back. And just as you want men to do to you, you also do to them likewise. But if you love those who love you, what credit is that to you? For even sinners love those who love them. And if you do good to those who do good to you, what credit is that to you? For even sinners do the same. And if you lend to those from whom you hope to receive back, what credit is that to you? For even sinners lend to sinners to receive as much back. But love your enemies, do good, and lend, hoping for nothing in return; and your reward will be great..." (Luke 6, 27-35)

A PROPER MORALITY

"Blessed are the merciful, for they shall obtain mercy. Blessed are the pure in heart, for they shall see God. Blessed are the peacemakers..." (Matthew 5, 7-9)

"Judge not, and you shall not be judged. Condemn not, and you shall not be condemned. Forgive, and you will be forgiven. Give, and it will be given to you: good measure, pressed down, shaken together, and running over will be put into your bosom. For with the same measure that you use, it will be measured back to you." (Luke 6, 37-38)

And why do you look at the speck [of sawdust] in your brother's eye, but do not perceive the plank in your own eye? Or how can you say to your brother, "'Brother, let me remove the speck that is in your eye,'" when you yourself do not see the plank that is in your own eye? Hypocrite! First remove the plank from your own eye, and then you will see clearly to remove the speck that is in your brother's eye. (Luke 6, 41-42)

Therefore, as the elect of God, holy and beloved, put on tender mercies, kindness, humility, meekness, longsuffering; bearing with one another, and forgiving one another, if anyone has a complaint against another... But above all these things put on love, which is the bond of perfection. (Colossians 3, 12-14)

Finally, brethren, whatever things are true, whatever things are noble, whatever things are just, whatever things are pure, whatever things are lovely, whatever things are of good report, if there is any virtue and if there is anything praiseworthy—meditate on these things. (Philippians 4, 8)

"... God resists the proud, but gives grace to the humble." Therefore submit to God. Resist the devil, and he will flee from you. Draw near to God, and He will draw near to you. Cleanse your hands, you sinners; and purify your hearts, you double-minded. Lament and mourn and weep! Let your laughter be turned to mourning and your joy to gloom. Humble yourselves in the sight of the Lord, and He will lift you up. Do not speak evil of one another, brethren. He who speaks evil of a brother and judges his brother, speaks evil of the law and judges the law. But if you judge the law, you are not a doer of the law but a judge. There is one Lawgiver, who is able to save and to destroy. Who are you to judge another? (James 4, 6-12)

HELPING THE NEEDY AND DOING GOOD DEEDS

"For a good tree does not bear bad fruit, nor does a bad tree bear good fruit. For every tree is known by its own fruit. For men do not gather figs from thorns, nor do they gather grapes from a bramble bush. A good man out of the good treasure of his heart brings forth good; and an evil man out of the evil treasure of his heart brings forth evil. For out of the abundance of the heart his mouth speaks." (Luke 6, 43-45)

But as for you, brethren, do not grow weary in doing good. And if anyone does not obey our word in this epistle, note that person and do not keep company with him, that he may be ashamed. Yet do not count him as an enemy, but admonish him as a brother. (2 Thessalonians 3, 13-15)

So the people asked him, saying, "What shall we do then?" He answered and said to them, "He who has two tunics, let him give to him who has none; and he who has food, let him do likewise." Then tax collectors also came to be baptized, and said to him, "Teacher, what shall we do?" And he said to them, "Collect no more than what is appointed for you." Likewise the soldiers asked him, saying, "And what shall we do?" So he said to them, "Do not intimidate anyone or accuse falsely, and be content with your wages." (Luke 3, 10-14)

I have shown you in every way, by laboring like this, that you must support the weak. And remember the words of the Lord, that He said, "It is more blessed to give than to receive." (Acts 20, 35)

Or ministry, let us use it in our ministering; he who teaches, in teaching; he who exhorts, in exhortation; he who gives, with liberality; he who leads, with diligence; he who shows mercy, with cheerfulness. (Romans 12, 7-8)

For this is the will of God, that by doing good you may put to silence the ignorance of foolish men - as free, yet not using liberty as a cloak for vice, but as bondservants of God. Honor all people. Love the brotherhood. Fear God… (1 Peter 2, 15-17)

For "He who would love life and see good days, let him refrain his tongue from evil, and his lips from speaking deceit. Let him turn away from evil and do good; let him seek peace and pursue it. For the eyes of the Lord are on the righteous, and His ears are open to their prayers; but the face of the Lord is against those who do evil." (1 Peter 3, 10-12)

AVOIDING EVIL AND ADVOCATING PEACE

Where do wars and fights come from among you? Do they not come from your desires for pleasure that war in your members? You lust and do not have. You murder and covet and cannot obtain. You fight and war. Yet you do not have because you do not ask. You ask and do not receive, because you ask amiss, that you may spend it on your pleasures. Adulterers and adulteresses! Do you not know that friendship with the world is enmity with God? Whoever therefore wants to be a friend of the world makes himself an enemy of God. (James 4, 1-4)

Let all bitterness, wrath, anger, clamor, and evil speaking be put away from you, with all malice. And be kind to one another, tender hearted, forgiving one another, just as God forgave you. (Ephesians 4, 31-32)

"Blessed are the peacemakers..." (Matthew 5, 9)

If it is possible, as much as depends on you, live peaceably with all men. Beloved, do not avenge yourselves... for it is written, "Vengeance is Mine, I will repay," says the Lord. Therefore "If your enemy is hungry, feed him; if he is thirsty, give him a drink; for in so doing you will heap coals of fire on his head." (Romans 12, 18-20)

Take heed to yourselves. If your brother sins against you, rebuke him; and if he repents, forgive him. (Luke 17, 3)

THE PROPHET'S NOBLE MORALITY

Our earlier chapters concentrated on the physical and spiritual damage that terrorism inflicts, and cited how conveying the morality of religion on the level of ideas is the most important step in the cultural struggle against terrorism.

Explaining the features of proper morality described in the Old and New Testaments and the Qur'an—love, compassion, tolerance and moderation—is the only way to do away with terrorism's endless bloodshed. In particular, the solution to terrorism in the name of religion in particular lies in religion being correctly explained—in other words in understanding the model of morality we discussed earlier. Whatever model people take for themselves must be a source they can regard as a guide. That source is the Qur'an; the model is the life of our Prophet (may God bless him and grant him peace). This chapter examines his life in the light of the Qur'an's verses and the *hadiths*—his teachings and sayings.

At every moment, our Prophet (may God bless him and grant him peace) displayed a morality that was pleasing to God and lived in the most perfect manner. Any society that model itself on the exemplary messengers of God will provide a most significant obstacle to social evils such as terrorism, which will be unable to survive in such an environment. Terrorists lack any concept of human love. Aggressive, uncompromising, intolerant, incapable of entering a dialogue with those who think differently, seeing no value in others' ideas, they try to resolve every argument through violence. In any social morality built on love and tolerance, they can never achieve their aims.

OUR PROPHET (MAY GOD BLESS HIM AND GRANT HIM PEACE) WAS A MAN OF TOLERANCE AND LOVE

In the time of the Prophet Mohammed (may God bless him and grant him peace), Arabia was home to communities of different religions, cultures and ideas. Jews, Christians, Sabians, Zoroastrians and idol worshippers all lived side by side, together with many different tribes hostile to each other. Yet no matter what their tribe or beliefs, our Prophet (may God bless him and grant him peace) called people to religion with affection, patience, tolerance and love.

The Qur'an (3:19) describes his pleasing attitude to those around him:

> *It is a mercy from God that you were gentle with them. If you had been rough or hard of heart, they would have scattered from around you. So pardon them and ask forgiveness for them...*

As pointed out earlier, the Qur'an reveals that no one should be pressured to embrace Islam. Muslims are charged only with explaining the religion of God. No one can force anyone else to believe or worship. Only by the will of God can another find the true path and come to believe. Our Prophet (may God bless him and grant him peace) always scrupulously abided by that prohibition and stated frequently that a man could live by religion only when, in his heart, he really wanted to. God told our Prophet (may God bless him and grant him peace) in one holy verse (50:45) how he should behave towards those around him:

> *We know best what they say. You are not a dictator over them. So remind, with the Qur'an, whoever fears My Threat.*

Our Prophet (may God bless him and grant him peace) once told the faithful, "I have been sent to show mercy."25 The key to his noble morality is also described in these terms:

> *Those who have mercy will receive the mercy of the Most Merciful.*

A great many hadiths concern our Prophet's (may God bless him and grant him peace) compassion, affection and tolerance. For example, he once said, *"Those who show no mercy will be shown no mercy.*"27 Other words of his include:

My Cherisher has ordered me nine things: To reverence Him, externally and internally; to speak true, and with propriety, in prosperity and adversity…

*I swear by whom my soul is in his hand, you will not enter paradise until you believe, and you will not believe until you love each other. Do you want me to guide you to something which if you practice, you will love each other? Spread greeting with peace among of you.*29

In his collection of information from the world of the hadiths, the great Islamic scholar Imam Ghazali sums up our Prophet's (may

God bless him and grant him peace) attitude to those around him in these terms:

... *Everyone thought that the Prophet (may God bless him and grant him peace) honored him more. Whoever came to him could see his face.*

... He used to call his companions by their surnames with honor and he used to give one surname who had no surname.

... He was very affectionate and kind in dealing with the people.

... *Nobody could speak loudly in his assembly.*

Our Prophet's (may God bless him and grant him peace) love of his fellow man, his consideration and affection, tied those around him and encouraged them to believe. His superior example of morality is one that all Muslims should dwell on. One verse (9: 128) describes the features of our Prophet (may God bless him and grant him peace) that set an example to all mankind:

A Messenger has come to you from among yourselves. Your suffering is distressing to him; he is deeply concerned for you; he is gentle and merciful to the believers.

Love and affection, tolerance and compassion are common traits of the messengers whom God has sent as leaders to the true path. The Qur'an states that the other prophets have been honored with "loving sensitivity" and gives the Prophet John (peace be upon him), to whom He gave wisdom, as an example in this regard to all mankind. Verse 19:13 describes that holy personage in these terms:

... and tenderness and purity from Us – he was conscientious.

OUR PROPHET'S (MAY GOD BLESS HIM AND GRANT HIM PEACE) GENTLE CONSIDERATION

Our Prophet (may God bless him and grant him peace) was in constant contact with all sections of society and spoke to everyone, from those at the very pinnacle of power to prisoners of war, children and orphans. With people of all different social standings, lifestyles, natures and customs, he established positive dialogues, winning their affection and treating them all with kind patience and pleasant understanding.

As reported by those companions who were close to him, our Prophet (may God bless him and grant him peace) was "most kind, morally above reproach, graceful, amiable and considerate." His words, *"I have been sent to perfect good qualities of character"* are an expression of his high nature. Aisha, who knew him very well, described his pleasant morality in the following words: "The Prophet's (may God bless him and grant him peace) nature was the Qur'an."

Anas, who was brought up in the Prophet's (may God bless him and grant him peace) house and served him for years, describes his courtesy in these terms:

God's Messenger (may God bless him and grant him peace), *when he shook hands with anyone, he did not withdraw his hands till the other man withdrew his. Similarly, he did not turn away his face from anyone till that man turned his face to the other side. And he was never seen to put forward his knees in front of one with whom he was sitting.*

Whenever one spoke to him the other would keep quiet and listen till he would finish.

Anas bin Malik ("may Allah be pleased with him") says, 'I remained in the service of the Rasulullah (saas) for ten years. He never once spoke me a word of contempt. When I did something, he never asked me. "Why did you do so?" When I did not do a certain task, he never asked me why I did not do it.

Throughout his life, our Prophet (may God bless him and grant him peace) educated thousands. Through his influence, people who knew nothing about religion came to be considerate, willing to make sacrifices, have a pleasing attitude and possess a superior morality. Even now, centuries after his death, Our Prophet (may God bless him and grant him peace) remains the very best guide and teacher, whose words and morality continue to inspire billions.

OUR PROPHET (MAY GOD BLESS HIM AND GRANT HIM PEACE) ADVISED THE FAITHFUL TO BE FULL OF LOVE

Our Prophet (may God bless him and grant him peace) declared it was particularly important for the faithful to love one another with sincere affection, taking no account of personal interests, and never to harbor negative emotions like hatred, anger or jealousy.

In the Qur'an (42:23), God commands His Prophet (may God bless him and grant him peace) to say the following:

> *That is the good news which God gives to His servants who believe and do right actions. Say: "I do not ask you for any wage for this– except for you to love your near of kin. If anyone does a good action, We will increase the good of it for him. God is Ever-Forgiving, Ever-Thankful."*

Some hadiths regarding the Prophet's (may God bless him and grant him peace) affection, friendship and brotherhood read:

A believer loves for others what he loves for himself.

God's Apostle (saas) used to accept gifts and used to give something in return.

He who is presented with a flower of sweet basil should not reject it, because it is light in weight and pleasant in odor.

Don't hate one another, don't envy one another don't sell over the sale to another, don't dispute with one another and don't back-bite one another. The servants of God are brethren to one another.

The habits of earlier generations have attacked you--envy and hatred. Hatred is shaving. You will not enter Paradise till you believe. You will not believe till you love one another. Shall I not inform you what thing will establish you on it? Spread peace among you.

The strong man is not the one who is strong in wrestling, but the one who controls himself in anger.

Beware of envy, for envy devours good [deeds] as fire devours firewood.

Muslims are brothers to one another. They should neither cheat, lie, nor humiliate each other.

OUR PROPHET (MAY GOD BLESS HIM AND GRANT HIM PEACE) COMMANDED JUSTICE

With the rules he gave to the Muslims; with his just and tolerant attitude towards other religions, languages, races and tribes; and in his equal treatment of everybody, rich and poor, our Prophet Mohammed (may God bless him and grant him peace) is a great example to all of mankind. In one verse (5:42), God tells him "But if you do judge, judge between them justly. God loves the just." The Prophet (may God bless him and grant him peace) never made the slightest concession on that justice, not even under the most difficult conditions.

Many incidents from his life bear witness to the Prophet's (may God bless him and grant him peace) exemplary attitude. In the land where he lived, a variety of religions, races and tribes all lived together. These communities found it very difficult to live together in peace and security, much less restrain those who wanted to sow dissent. However, our Prophet's (may God bless him and grant him peace) justice was a source of peace and security, as much for these non-believers as it was for Muslims. During his lifetime, everyone on the Arabian Peninsula— Christian, Jew, or pagan—was treated justly, with no discrimination.

Our Prophet's (may God bless him and grant him peace) pleasing attitude, in conformity with the Qur'an, sets an example for those of different religions and shows how they should behave to one another. His justice brought about compromise between people of different races. In many of his addresses, even in his Farewell Sermon, he made it known that no one's race or class endowed him with any superiority. This lay only in godliness, as God has revealed in the Qur'an (49:13). Other hadiths on this subject say:

You are sons of Adam, and Adam came from dust. Let the people cease to boast about their ancestors.

These genealogies of yours are not a reason to revile anyone. You are all children of Adam. No one has any superiority over another, except in religion and taqwa [godliness].

OUR PROPHET (MAY GOD BLESS HIM AND GRANT HIM PEACE) ALWAYS FAVORED PEACE

Our Prophet (may God bless him and grant him peace) never desired war but over the years, made great efforts to spread Islam by peaceful means. He was patient in the face of heavy assaults and pressure, except when dealing with such pressure became imperative, he did give permission for war, in the light of a revelation from God. He never declared war so long as there was still the slightest possibility of peace, and as long as an enemy's attacks and pressure represented no mortal danger.

During our Prophet's (may God bless him and grant him peace) lifetime, the Mu'tah Expedition was the bloodiest and most difficult waged by the Muslims. He appointed Zayd ibn Harithah to command the army, and admonished the troops:

*Wage war in the name of God, on the path of God, against those who deny God. Engage in no treachery. Do not cut off ears and noses and other parts of the body. Do not kill women and children, the elderly, and men of religion in their places of worship. Do not cut down date and other trees, and do not tear down buildings.*46

Based on the prophetic orders on war, the following principles, which may be called "The Islamic Principles of Combat", are outlined by Muslim scholars:

1. War is to be waged only with those who encourage and engage in it.
2. Priests in churches, children, women, and the elderly must never be harmed.
3. Sown fields must not be damaged.
4. Treaties and agreements must not be broken.
5. Animals must not be harmed.

6. There must be no cruelty and torture.

7. Towns must not be destroyed.

The Treaty of Medina, signed by our Prophet (may God bless him and grant him peace) and the Jewish and polytheist communities in the city, was also an important example of justice and mutual respect between different communities. The treaty, drawn up to establish a kind of constitution between communities of different beliefs and allowing each one to observe its own principles, brought peace to those who for years had been hostile to one another. One of its most striking features was how it enshrined freedom of belief. The article on that subject reads:

*The Jews of Banu 'Awf are one nation with the Muslims; the Jews have their religion, and the Muslims have theirs...*48

Article 16 of the Treaty of Medina reads, *"The Jew who follows us is surely entitled to our support and the same equal rights as any one of us. He shall not be wronged nor his enemy be assisted."*49 The Prophet's (may God bless him and grant him peace) successors stayed loyal to that rule he agreed to, extending it even to Berbers, Buddhists, Hindu Brahmans and those of other beliefs.

One reason why the time of the Prophet (may God bless him and grant him peace) was blessed with peace and security was his position of justice, so in line with the morality of the Qur'an. Foreign writers, too, have been impressed by his superior character and praise our Prophet's (may God bless him and grant him peace) morality in their works. In *The Genuine Islam*, George Bernard Shaw described these superior traits:

I have always held the religion of Mohammed in high estimation because of its wonderful vitality. It is the only religion which appears to me to possess that assimilating capacity to the changing phase of existence which can make itself appeal to every age. I have studied him ... he must be called the Savior of Humanity. I believe that if a man like him were to assume the dictatorship of the modern world, he would succeed in solving its problems in a way that would bring it the much needed peace and happiness... In our own time as well, abiding by the Qur'an's morality is the only answer to all the conflicts, fighting, and instability of the world. Like our Prophet (may God bless him and grant him peace), never we should depart from the path of justice, and should always respect the rights of different communities and indiviudals, whatever their beliefs and identities may be.

SOLUTIONS TO TERROR AND ANARCHY, FROM BEDUIZZAMAN SAID NURSI

Throughout history, there have been periods when the scourges of terror and anarchy have intensified, posing a threat to entire populations. Numerous solutions have been proposed. One of those who stressed the importance of an all-out struggle against terror and anarchy was the great Turkish Islamic scholar, Bediuzzaman Said Nursi (1877-1960). He said that the first thing people must do is spread the morality of the Qur'an; to that end, he made a number of recommendations.

At the time Bediuzzaman lived, the world was going through radical changes. The First World War had a particularly impact on his life. During the War, he had led the Ottoman militia forces on the Caucasian Front against the invading Russians for which he was later awarded a War Medal. He was taken prisoner in March 1916 and was held in Russia for two years. In early 1918, he escaped from prison and made his way back to Istanbul via Warsaw, Berlin and Vienna.

Thus he had a front-row seat to witness the collapse of the Ottoman Empire and the establishment of the Turkish Republic. He also saw the Russian Revolution bring Communism to power, the conflict between the great European powers, and the difficulties that both World Wars inflicted on the Turkish Republic. As can be seen in his writings, he made a detailed analysis of all these events, evaluating all political developments in the light of the verses of the Qur'an. Always he emphasized how any society that turns its back on religion will suffer great damage; and that only if Muslims joined forces, could they enjoy great success against atheist ideologies.

Bediuzzaman knew that terror and anarchy would emerge in his own time, and afterwards. He therefore tried to alert people to a number of possible solutions for these terrible problems. In his words, "... Religion fiercely condemns strife and anarchy. Anarchy recognizes no rights. It turns human morality and the works of civilization into the morality of animals,"51 This was the best possible expression of Islam's views on terror and violence, which Bediuzzaman spent his life expounding. As he once said, "Patience and endurance to put a stop to anarchy and maintain public order are necessary, with all sincerity in the service of the faith. I am therefore perfectly content to sacrifice my repute to that end."52 He stated that in the fight against anarchy and terror—a fight that required patience and endurance—believers bore a great responsibility.

His experience and guiding words are of great value today. We should carefully consider every statement made by this worthy individual, who spent his life trying to build a world of love and wisdom, based on the morality of the Qur'an.

ONLY BY LOVE, BEDIUZZAMAN ALWAYS SAID, COULD TERRORISM BE OVERCOME

The most noteworthy aspect of his statements is the importance he attaches to human love and life, inspired by the morality of the Qur'an. As he once said,

The true lesson from the Qur'an is this: If there are ten monsters and one innocent person in a house... is it permissible to burn that house... even though the morality of the Qur'an forbids such a thing... [to] ruin ten innocent people for the sake of one monster? Would not burning that house down be the greatest possible cruelty and betrayal? ... the morality of the Qur'an forbids the endangering of the lives or the harming of the 90 percent of innocent people for the sake of the ten percent of monsters who threaten security. We must be aware that we are bound by religion to preserve security and abide by that lesson from the Qur'an... In these words, Bediuzzaman revealed the great importance of human life, that every possible sacrifice should be made to save the life of just one individual, that doing the opposite means committing great cruelty. Muslims should work to establish peace and security. Because that responsibility is a command from God, believers use all means at their disposal to help spread the morality of religion. Where terror and anarchy become terrible scourges, an environment in which Islamic morality is lived resembles heaven. Bediuzzaman said as much in a number of statements:

> *If a Muslim departs from the Muslim community, he turns from the religion and becomes an anarchist and has a poisonous effect on society. Because anarchy recognizes no rights, and turns the proper nature of mankind into the morality of savage animals.*

A true Muslim, a sincere believer, never supports anarchy and wickedness... the religion fiercely condemns strife and anarchy. Because anarchy recognizes no rights, and turns the proper nature of mankind and the works of civilization into the morality of savage animals.55

He made it clear that conveying the morality of religion would open up a great dialogue, even in the hearts of the intolerant, the uncompromising and aggressive. The love of God would keep people from all forms of tyranny. He stressed that every Muslim's duty is to relate the beauties of religion and the truths of the Qur'an, so as to bring that love into peoples' hearts. Bediuzzaman once stressed that his *Risale-i Nur* ("Letters of Light", a collection of all his writings) fulfilled that function:

> *Yes, the* Risale-i Nur *and faith based on truth and proof and the truths of the Qur'an, explains and elucidates matters in a manner appropriate to the times and in such a way that the community can accept them, has led to millions of people examining faith and belief, awoken Islamic love and dialogue in their souls, and built a spiritual wall against atheism and immorality, the signs of anarchy. Yes, the union of the sacred ideal and purpose form an invincible force, an impassable wall, a spiritual power in peoples' souls, hearts and minds.56*

THE IMPORTANCE OF QUR'ANIC MORALITY IN THE CASE AGAINST TERROR

At every opportunity, Bediuzzaman reminded people that in the fight against terror and anarchy, the most important weapon was the spread of religious morality. As he commented,

Towns are also households for their inhabitants. If belief in the hereafter does not govern the members of that large family, vices like malice, self-interest, false pretences, selfishness, artificiality, hypocrisy, bribery, and deception will dominate—displacing sincerity, cordiality, virtue, zeal, self-sacrifice, seeking God's pleasure and the reward of the hereafter, which are the bases of good conduct and morality. Anarchy and savagery will govern under the superficial order and humanity, poisoning the life of the town. Children will become troublemakers, the youth will take to drink, the strong will embark on oppression, and the elderly start to weep.57

In societies that turn their back on religion, deceit, oppression, anarchy, violence and terror emerge. Virtues like cooperation, sacrifice and honesty go by the board. People think only of their own self-interests, desiring only their own comforts and working only for themselves. Yet when a society lives by religion, then cooperation, friendship and brotherhood prevail. Later in this same statement, Bediuzzaman gives examples of the advantages that religious morality can bring to family and social life:

By analogy, the country is also a household, and the fatherland, the home of the national family. If belief in the hereafter rules, then true respect, earnest compassion, disinterested love, mutual assistance, honest service and social relations, unhypocritical charity, virtue, modest greatness, and excellence will all start to develop. It says to the children, "Give up messing around; there is Paradise to be won!" and teaches them self-control through instruction in the Qur'an. It says to the youth, "There is Hell-fire; give up your drunkenness!" and brings them to their senses. To the oppressor, it says, "There is severe torment; you will receive a blow!" and makes them bow to justice. To the elderly it says, "Awaiting you in the hereafter is everlasting happiness, far greater than all the happiness you have lost here, and immortal youth; try to win them!" It turns their tears into laughter. It shows its favorable effects in every group, particular and universal, and illuminates them. Sociologists and moralists, who are concerned with the social life of mankind, should take special note. If the rest of the thousands of benefits and advantages of belief in the hereafter are compared with the five or six we have alluded to, it will be understood that only belief is the means of happiness in this world and the next, and in the lives of both.

As these examples suggest, once people live by religious morality, it's easy to advise them, forbid them to commit evil, and turn them to the true path. Bediuzzaman often said that terror and anarchy could be destroyed only if people live by the morality of the Qur'an—commanding love, tolerance, peace, forgiveness, affection and compassion; standing against all forms of evil and wickedness. These words of his call on Muslims to embrace the truths of the Qur'an, again emphasizing that only prevailing religion can end anarchy in the world:

> *The only solution to the ruin and destruction caused by anarchy, which menaces and has wreaked terrible calamities on mankind, is the eternal and timeless truths of a sacred and divine religion.*

Bediuzzaman frequently stressed that the morality of the Qur'an, and its interpretation in the *Risale-i Nur* made a great contribution in eliminating terror and anarchy, and would continue to do so in future. Every effort to explain Qur'anic morality and invite people to the path of true Islam helps fulfill that duty and plays an important role in the struggle against terrorism. Bediuzzaman drew attention to the importance of that: "The *Risale-i Nur* definitely has no connection with politics. But since it has smashed absolute disbelief, it destroys and repulses anarchy, which underlies absolute disbelief, and absolute despotism, which overlies it."

In another statement, he sets out some essentials to get rid of anarchy: "Respect, compassion, refraining from sin, security, the giving up of lawlessness and being obedient to authority." Later in the same statement, he describes how the *Risale-i Nur* fulfills the duties they have taken on:

> When the Risale-i Nur looks to the life of society, it establishes and strengthens these five principles in a powerful and sacred fashion and preserves the cornerstone of public order... Over the last twenty years, the "Risale-i Nur" has made one hundred thousand people into harmless, beneficial members of this nation and country.

ART, WISDOM AND UNANIMITY OF PURPOSE

In his works, Bediuzzaman Said Nursi offers a detailed description of the form that struggle against terror, atheism, anarchy and the problems of the Islamic World should take: "Our enemies are ignorance, poverty and inner conflict. We shall fight these three foes with the weapons of wisdom, skill and unanimity of purpose." These vital words draw attention to three grave dangers: ignorance, poverty and conflict.

It's essential to warn the public against the first of these, ignorance. In today's Islamic world, the great majority has some a knowledge of religion and belief in God. Yet seldom does that same majority deeply examine religion and spiritual values. Because their knowledge is generally superficial and picked up secondhand, it's impossible for them to translate religion's proper morality to be, in its true sense, into life. It's essential, therefore, to do away with that lack of knowledge.

The poverty of the Muslim world is the second danger Bediuzzaman cites. The poverty prevents people from having a proper education and thus feeds ignorance. It also makes Muslims feel weak and thus feeds both frustration and radicalization. The third danger is the inner conflict over so many issues in the Muslim world. When parties can reach no agreement on basic values, their debate over ideas usually degenerates into hostilities, conflicts and even civil wars. Tolerance and mutual respect are not only inter-civilizational but also intra-civilizational necessities.

But the truth is, a constructive attitude can resolve these problems and conflicts. The paths of reason and conscience are one and the same. For that reason, truth needs to be stated openly, in the face of the chaos and strife that conflict brings with it. Against these three dangers, Bediuzzaman also stressed the measures to be taken.

The first of these, art, occupies an important place and means several things: First, that people should be taught to understand beauty and aesthetics. These blessings from God will turn human souls away from brute force. Knowing that art is a blessing from God, and giving thanks for it, increases peoples' spiritual depth. For that reason, it's most important to show the full beauty of the God's art all around us. Artists should act in that knowledge, and the devout need to turn to art with that same awareness. Every explanation of the morality of religion must bear artistic values in mind. It's highly important to demonstrate the devout's superior artistic understanding in all written works, with colored pictures, simple and clear language, and high-quality printing.

Wisdom embodied in the written word is equally a form of art. The words employed, the examples used, and the striking, effective means of expression all make a very important impressions on the reader. When it comes to explaining the beauties of religion, simple means of expression—as opposed to unclear, confusing and abstruse methods—make it much easier to grasp the truth and understand it.

The "wisdom" Bediuzzaman refers to means the possession of knowledge. Muslims need to be the masters of knowledge in the age in which they live. That, of cource includes science and social sciences. Because a Muslim is an earthly representative of the religion that God has chosen for Man, he needs to be well versed in the sciences, cultures, thought and technology of his time, as well as being able to employ that knowledge efficiently.

The final method Bediuzzaman recommends, unanimity of purpose, needs to be brought about by every Muslim who wants to achieve security and well being and to see the Islamic world flourish again. History shows that unification and harmony in the Islamic world have always brought success. The golden age of the Prophet (may god bless him and grant him peace) and the first caliphs, the Abbasid Empire, the empire of Saladin, or the Ottoman Empire; all these examples indicate that unification among the Muslims themselves created powerful and victorious, yet fair and tolerant states. In times of turmoil, both Muslims and non-Muslims suffered.

Thus, a revival of the Islamic world is due to the unification of Muslims all around the globe, transcending ethnic, sectarian or social disputes. Once this is achieved, the formation of a political unity — in terms of an Islamic Union — will also be at hand. Such a Union will resolve the disputes both among the Muslims themselves and among the Muslims and non-Muslims; heal the radical elements in the Islamic world by means of education and persuasion; and establish good relations between the Islamic civilization and other civilizations.

CONCLUSION

Unless necessary measures are taken, unless deep-rooted solutions are brought in, the 21st century will continue to be a time of terror and violence, just as the 20th was before it. The ideological fight against terrorism, therefore, must begin started with great and urgency, to include very great numbers of people. This fight will be fought on the level of ideas—between people who believe in the true religious morality, who are loving, forgiving, compassionate and in full possession of their conscience; and those who draw their strength from ignorance, arrogance and violence.

In one holy verse (Surah Hud: 116), our Lord asks, "Would there had been more people with a vestige of good among the generations of those who came before you, who forbade corruption in the earth…" Believers should possess the virtue that God describes in that verse. While terrorists hope to achieve their aims by violence, believers should know that true success can be achieved only by clinging tightly to the religion of God, and acting accordingly. If Jews, Christians, and Muslims join together in that struggle, in a spirit of respect for all beliefs and ideas and, by the will of God, they will enjoy definitive success.

A terrorist may learn by heart all the fundamental sources behind his beliefs. Yet such a person is still unaware of the one evident truth that will bring him happiness and inspiration, both in this world and the next. That's because all his life, he's been educated in radical ideologies, in the context of the idea that life is a battleground in which only the strong survive, where violence and oppression are the only means of survival. Anyone resorting to terrorism, no matter what his religion, race, or nation, must understand that he's acting under the influence of a misleading philosophy, that in the final analysis stems from materialist and Darwinist thinking, though it sometimes poses as a religious idea.

Those who resort to secular terrorism are unaware that God and the hereafter really do exist; that this world is merely a place of trial; and that only those who believe and carry out their religious obligations devoutly will be saved. Those who resort to allegedly "religious" terrorism, are far from understanding God's commandments against mischief and the value of human life, such as that "... If someone kills another person—unless it is in retaliation for someone else or for causing corruption in the earth—it is as if he had murdered all mankind. And if anyone gives life to another person, it is as if he had given life to all mankind." (Qur'an, 5: 32)

At this point, a great responsibility falls on all true believers, no matter what their religion. Jews must not ignore Old Testament statements calling mankind to peace and tolerance, and they must call on all other Jews to oppose terrorism — including the state terrorism employed by Israel in the occupied territories. So should Christians call on all other Christians, taking as their guide the morality most pleasing to God. They should also stress that "the war on terror" should not turn into violent revenge, and a peaceful "counter-terrorism" should be preferred, since the Christian faith proclaims that "blessed are the peacemakers". (Matthew, 5: 9) One should not forget that terrorism stems from wrong ideas and the basic struggle against terrorism should be on the level of ideas. Believers must explain that these ideas are wrong both in terms of their theory and practice. No idea can prevail by means of violence, oppression and cruelty; and despotism can never triumph.

Terrorist ideology is built on sand. Its foundations can easily be swept away by mobilizing a proper education campaign. Sincere believers in all parts of the world can help end the ignorance that breeds terrorism by searching for solutions, writing books and articles, promoting educational activities and disseminating their own cultural heritage.

7

The Evolution Misconception

Every detail in this universe points to a superior creation. By contrast, materialism, which seeks to deny the fact of creation in the universe, is nothing but an unscientific fallacy.

Once materialism is invalidated, all other theories based on this philosophy are rendered baseless. Foremost of them is Darwinism, that is, the theory of evolution. This theory, which argues that life originated from inanimate matter through coincidences, has been demolished with the recognition that Allah created the universe. American astrophysicist Hugh Ross explains this as follows:

Atheism, Darwinism, and virtually all the "isms" emanating from the eighteenth to the twentieth century philosophies are built upon the assumption, the incorrect assumption, that the universe is infinite. The singularity has brought us face to face with the cause – or causer – beyond/behind/before the universe and all that it contains, including life itself.

It is Allah Who created the universe and Who designed it down to its smallest detail. Therefore, it is impossible for the theory of evolution, which holds that living things are but products of chance, to be true.

Unsurprisingly, when we look at the theory of evolution, we see that this theory is denounced by scientific findings. The design in life is extremely complex and striking. In the inanimate world, for instance, we can explore how sensitive are the balances which atoms rest upon, and further, in the animate world, we can observe in what complex designs these atoms were brought together, and how extraordinary are the mechanisms and structures such as proteins, enzymes, and cells, which are manufactured with them.

This extraordinary design in life invalidated Darwinism at the end of the 20th century.

We have dealt with this subject in great detail in some of our other studies, and shall continue to do so. However, we think that, considering its importance, it will be helpful to make a short summary here as well.

THE SCIENTIFIC COLLAPSE OF DARWINISM

Although a doctrine going back as far as ancient Greece, the theory of evolution was advanced extensively in the 19th century. The most important development that made the theory the top topic of the world of science was the book by Charles Darwin titled The Origin of Species published in 1859. In this book, Darwin denied that Allah created different living species on the earth separately. According to Darwin, all living beings had a common ancestor and they diversified over time through small changes.

Darwin's theory was not based on any concrete scientific finding; as he also accepted, it was just an "assumption." Moreover, as Darwin confessed in the long chapter of his book titled "Difficulties of the Theory," the theory was failing in the face of many critical questions.

Darwin invested all his hopes in new scientific discoveries, which he expected to solve the "Difficulties of the Theory." However, contrary to his expectations, scientific findings expanded the dimensions of these difficulties.

The defeat of Darwinism against science can be reviewed under three basic topics:

1) The theory can by no means explain how life originated on the earth.

2) There is no scientific finding showing that the "evolutionary mechanisms" proposed by the theory have any power to evolve at all.
3) The fossil record proves completely the contrary of the suggestions of the theory of evolution.

In this section, we will examine these three basic points in general outlines:

THE FIRST INSURMOUNTABLE STEP: THE ORIGIN OF LIFE

The theory of evolution posits that all living species evolved from a single living cell that emerged on the primitive earth 3.8 billion years ago. How a single cell could generate millions of complex living species and, if such an evolution really occurred, why traces of it cannot be observed in the fossil record are some of the questions the theory cannot answer. However, first and foremost, of the first step of the alleged evolutionary process it has to be inquired: How did this "first cell" originate?

Since the theory of evolution denies creation and does not accept any kind of supernatural intervention, it maintains that the "first cell" originated coincidentally within the laws of nature, without any design, plan, or arrangement. According to the theory, inanimate matter must have produced a living cell as a result of coincidences. This, however, is a claim inconsistent with even the most unassailable rules of biology.

"LIFE COMES FROM LIFE"

In his book, Darwin never referred to the origin of life. The primitive understanding of science in his time rested on the assumption that living beings had a very simple structure. Since medieval times, spontaneous generation, the theory asserting that non-living materials came together to form living organisms, had been widely accepted. It was commonly believed that insects came into being from food leftovers, and mice from wheat. Interesting experiments were conducted to prove this theory. Some wheat was placed on a dirty piece of cloth, and it was believed that mice would originate from it after a while.

Similarly, worms developing in meat was assumed to be evidence of spontaneous generation. However, only some time later was it understood that worms did not appear on meat spontaneously, but were carried there by flies in the form of larvae, invisible to the naked eye.

Even in the period when Darwin wrote *The Origin of Species*, the belief that bacteria could come into existence from non-living matter was widely accepted in the world of science.

However, five years after the publication of Darwin's book, Louis Pasteur announced his results after long studies and experiments, which disproved spontaneous generation, a cornerstone of Darwin's theory. In his triumphal lecture at the Sorbonne in 1864, Pasteur said, "*Never will the doctrine of spontaneous generation recover from the mortal blow struck by this simple experiment.*"

Advocates of the theory of evolution resisted the findings of Pasteur for a long time. However, as the development of science unraveled the complex structure of the cell of a living being, the idea that life could come into being coincidentally faced an even greater impasse.

INCONCLUSIVE EFFORTS IN THE TWENTIETH CENTURY

The first evolutionist who took up the subject of the origin of life in the twentieth century was the renowned Russian biologist Alexander Oparin. With various theses he advanced in the 1930's, he tried to prove that the cell of a living being could originate by coincidence. These studies, however, were doomed to failure, and Oparin had to make the following confession: "Unfortunately, however, the problem of the origin of the cell is perhaps the most obscure point in the whole study of the evolution of organisms."

Evolutionist followers of Oparin tried to carry out experiments to solve the problem of the origin of life. The best known of these experiments was carried out by American chemist Stanley Miller in 1953. Combining the gases he alleged to have existed in the primordial earth's atmosphere in an experiment set-up, and adding energy to the mixture, Miller synthesized several organic molecules (amino acids) present in the structure of proteins.

Barely a few years had passed before it was revealed that this experiment, which was then presented as an important step in the name of evolution, was invalid, the atmosphere used in the experiment having been very different from real earth conditions.

After a long silence, Miller confessed that the atmosphere medium he used was unrealistic.

All the evolutionist efforts put forth throughout the twentieth century to explain the origin of life ended with failure. The geochemist Jeffrey Bada from San Diegó Scripps Institute accepts this fact in an article published in *Earth* Magazine in 1998:

> *Today as we leave the twentieth century, we still face the biggest unsolved problem that we had when we entered the twentieth century: How did life originate on Earth?*

THE COMPLEX STRUCTURE OF LIFE

The primary reason why the theory of evolution ended up in such a big impasse about the origin of life is that even the living organisms deemed the simplest have incredibly complex structures. The cell of a living being is more complex than all of the technological products produced by man. Today, even in the most developed laboratories of the world, a living cell cannot be produced by bringing organic chemicals together.

The conditions required for the formation of a cell are too great in quantity to be explained away by coincidences. The probability of proteins, the building blocks of cell, being synthesized coincidentally, is 1 in 10950 for an average protein made up of 500 amino acids. In mathematics, a probability smaller than 1 over 1050 is practically considered to be impossible.

The DNA molecule, which is located in the nucleus of the cell and which stores genetic information, is an incredible databank. It is calculated that if the information coded in DNA were written down, this would make a giant library consisting of 900 volumes of encyclopaedias of 500 pages each.

A very interesting dilemma emerges at this point: the DNA can only replicate with the help of some specialized proteins (enzymes). However, the synthesis of these enzymes can only be realized by the information coded in DNA. As they both depend on each other, they have to exist at the same time for replication. This brings the scenario that life originated by itself to a deadlock. Prof. Leslie Orgel, an evolutionist of repute from the University of San Diego, California, confesses this fact in the September 1994 issue of the *Scientific American* magazine:

> *It is extremely improbable that proteins and nucleic acids, both of which are structurally complex, arose spontaneously in the same place at the same time. Yet it also seems impossible to have one without the other. And so, at first glance, one might have to conclude that life could never, in fact, have originated by chemical means.*

No doubt, if it is impossible for life to have originated from natural causes, then it has to be accepted that life was "created" in a supernatural way. This fact explicitly invalidates the theory of evolution, whose main purpose is to deny creation.

IMAGINARY MECHANISMS OF EVOLUTION

The second important point that negates Darwin's theory is that both concepts put forward by the theory as "evolutionary mechanisms" were understood to have, in reality, no evolutionary power.

Darwin based his evolution allegation entirely on the mechanism of "natural selection". The importance he placed on this mechanism was evident in the name of his book: *The Origin of Species, By Means Of Natural Selection...*

Natural selection holds that those living things that are stronger and more suited to the natural conditions of their habitats will survive in the struggle for life. For example, in a deer herd under the threat of attack by wild animals, those that can run faster will survive. Therefore, the deer herd will be comprised of faster and stronger individuals. However, unquestionably, this mechanism will not cause deer to evolve and transform themselves into another living species, for instance, horses. Therefore, the mechanism of natural selection has no evolutionary power. Darwin was also aware of this fact and had to state this in his book *The Origin of Species*:

Natural selection can do nothing until favourable individual differences or variations occur.

LAMARCK'S IMPACT

So, how could these "favourable variations" occur? Darwin tried to answer this question from the standpoint of the primitive understanding of science in his age. According to the French biologist Lamarck, who lived before Darwin, living creatures passed on the traits they acquired during their lifetime to the next generation and these traits, accumulating from one generation to another, caused new species to be formed. For instance, according to Lamarck, giraffes evolved from antelopes; as they struggled to eat the leaves of high trees, their necks were extended from generation to generation.

Darwin also gave similar examples, and in his book *The Origin of Species*, for instance, said that some bears going into water to find food transformed themselves into whales over time.

However, the laws of inheritance discovered by Mendel and verified by the science of genetics that flourished in the 20th century, utterly demolished the legend that acquired traits were passed on to subsequent generations. Thus, natural selection fell out of favour as an evolutionary mechanism.

NEO-DARWINISM AND MUTATIONS

In order to find a solution, Darwinists advanced the "Modern Synthetic Theory", or as it is more commonly known, Neo-Darwinism, at the end of the 1930's. Neo-Darwinism added mutations, which are distortions formed in the genes of living beings because of external factors such as radiation or replication errors, as the "cause of favourable variations" in addition to natural mutation.

Today, the model that stands for evolution in the world is Neo-Darwinism. The theory maintains that millions of living beings present on the earth formed as a result of a process whereby numerous complex organs of these organisms such as the ears, eyes, lungs, and wings, underwent "mutations," that is, genetic disorders. Yet, there is an outright scientific fact that totally undermines this theory: Mutations do not cause living beings to develop; on the contrary, they always cause harm to them.

The reason for this is very simple: the DNA has a very complex structure and random effects can only cause harm to it. American geneticist B.G. Ranganathan explains this as follows:

First, genuine mutations are very rare in nature. Secondly, most mutations are harmful since they are random, rather than orderly changes in the structure of genes; any random change in a highly ordered system will be for the worse, not for the better. For example, if an earthquake were to shake a highly ordered structure such as a building, there would be a random change in the framework of the building which, in all probability, would not be an improvement.

Not surprisingly, no mutation example, which is useful, that is, which is observed to develop the genetic code, has been observed so far. All mutations have proved to be harmful. It was understood that mutation, which is presented as an "evolutionary mechanism," is actually a genetic occurrence that harms living beings, and leaves them disabled. (The most common effect of mutation on human beings is cancer). No doubt, a destructive mechanism cannot be an "evolutionary mechanism." Natural selection, on the other hand, "can do nothing by itself" as Darwin also accepted. This fact shows us that there is no "evolutionary mechanism" in nature. Since no evolutionary mechanism exists, neither could any imaginary process called evolution have taken place.

THE FOSSIL RECORD: NO SIGN OF INTERMEDIATE FORMS

The clearest evidence that the scenario suggested by the theory of evolution did not take place is the fossil record.

According to the theory of evolution, every living species has sprung from a predecessor. A previously existing species turned into something else in time and all species have come into being in this way. According to the theory, this transformation proceeds gradually over millions of years.

Had this been the case, then numerous intermediary species should have existed and lived within this long transformation period.

For instance, some half-fish/half-reptiles should have lived in the past which had acquired some reptilian traits in addition to the fish traits they already had.

Or there should have existed some reptile-birds, which acquired some bird traits in addition to the reptilian traits they already had. Since these would be in a transitional phase, they should be disabled, defective, crippled living beings. Evolutionists refer to these imaginary creatures, which they believe to have lived in the past, as "transitional forms."

If such animals had really existed, there should be millions and even billions of them in number and variety. More importantly, the remains of these strange creatures should be present in the fossil record. In *The Origin of Species*, Darwin explained:

> *If my theory be true, numberless intermediate varieties, linking most closely all of the species of the same group together must assuredly have existed... Consequently, evidence of their former existence could be found only amongst fossil remains.*

DARWIN'S HOPES SHATTERED

However, although evolutionists have been making strenuous efforts to find fossils since the middle of the 19th century all over the world, no transitional forms have yet been uncovered. All the fossils unearthed in excavations showed that, contrary to the expectations of evolutionists, life appeared on earth all of a sudden and fully-formed. A famous British paleontologist, Derek V. Ager, admits this fact, even though he is an evolutionist:

> *The point emerges that if we examine the fossil record in detail, whether at the level of orders or of species, we find - over and over again - not gradual evolution, but the sudden explosion of one group at the expense of another.*

This means that in the fossil record, all living species suddenly emerge as fully formed, without any intermediate forms in between. This is just the opposite of Darwin's assumptions. Also, it is very strong evidence that living beings are created. The only explanation of a living species emerging suddenly and complete in every detail without any evolutionary ancestor can be that this species was created. This fact is admitted also by the widely known evolutionist biologist Douglas Futuyma:

> *Creation and evolution, between them, exhaust the possible explanations for the origin of living things. Organisms either appeared on the earth fully developed or they did not. If they did not, they must have developed from pre-existing species by some process of modification. If they did appear in a fully developed state, they must indeed have been created by some omnipotent intelligence.*

Fossils show that living beings emerged fully developed and in a perfect state on the earth. That means that "the origin of species" is, contrary to Darwin's supposition, not evolution but creation.

THE TALE OF HUMAN EVOLUTION

The subject most often brought up by the advocates of the theory of evolution is the subject of the origin of man. The Darwinist claim holds that the modern men of today evolved from some kind of ape-like creatures. During this alleged evolutionary process, which is supposed to have started 4-5 million years ago, it is claimed that there existed some "transitional forms" between modern man and his ancestors. According to this completely imaginary scenario, four basic "categories" are listed:

1. Australopithecus
2. Homo habilis
3. Homo erectus
4. Homo sapiens

Evolutionists call the so-called first ape-like ancestors of men *"Australopithecus"* which means "South African ape." These living beings are actually nothing but an old ape species that has become extinct. Extensive research done on various Australopithecus specimens by two world famous anatomists from England and the USA, namely, Lord Solly Zuckerman and Prof. Charles Oxnard, has shown that these belonged to an ordinary ape species that became extinct and bore no resemblance to humans.

Evolutionists classify the next stage of human evolution as "homo," that is "man." According to the evolutionist claim, the living beings in the Homo series are more developed than Australopithecus. Evolutionists devise a fanciful evolution scheme by arranging different fossils of these creatures in a particular order. This scheme is imaginary because it has never been proved that there is an evolutionary relation between these different classes. Ernst Mayr, one of the most important proponents of the theory of evolution in the twentieth century, contends in his book *One Long Argument* that *"particularly historical [puzzles] such as the origin of life or of* Homo sapiens, *are extremely difficult and may even resist a final, satisfying explanation."*

By outlining the link chain as *"Australopithecus > Homo habilis > Homo erectus > Homo sapiens,"* evolutionists imply that each of these species is one another's ancestor. However, recent findings of paleoanthropologists have revealed that Australopithecus, Homo habilis and Homo erectus lived at different parts of the world at the same time.

Moreover, a certain segment of humans classified as Homo erectus have lived up until very modern times. *Homo sapiens neandarthalensis and Homo sapiens sapiens* (modern man) co-existed in the same region.

This situation apparently indicates the invalidity of the claim that they are ancestors of one another. A paleontologist from Harvard University, Stephen Jay Gould, explains this deadlock of the theory of evolution although he is an evolutionist himself:

> *What has become of our ladder if there are three coexisting lineages of hominids (A. africanus, the robust australopithecines, and H. habilis), none clearly derived from another? Moreover, none of the three display any evolutionary trends during their tenure on earth.*

Put briefly, the scenario of human evolution, which is sought to be upheld with the help of various drawings of some "half ape, half human" creatures appearing in the media and course books, that is, frankly, by means of propaganda, is nothing but a tale with no scientific ground.

Lord Solly Zuckerman, one of the most famous and respected scientists in the U.K., who carried out research on this subject for years, and particularly studied Australopithecus fossils for 15 years, finally concluded, despite being an evolutionist himself, that there is, in fact, no such family tree branching out from ape-like creatures to man.

Zuckerman also made an interesting "spectrum of science." He formed a spectrum of sciences ranging from those he considered scientific to those he considered unscientific. According to Zuckerman's spectrum, the most "scientific" – that is, depending on concrete data – fields of science are chemistry and physics. After them come the biological sciences and then the social sciences. At the far end of the spectrum, which is the part considered to be most "unscientific," are "extra-sensory perception" – concepts such as telepathy and sixth sense–and finally "human evolution." Zuckerman explains his reasoning:

> We then move right off the register of objective truth into those fields of presumed biological science, like extrasensory perception or the interpretation of man's fossil history, where to the faithful [evolutionist] anything is possible - and where the ardent believer [in evolution] is sometimes able to believe several contradictory things at the same time.

The tale of human evolution boils down to nothing but the prejudiced interpretations of some fossils unearthed by certain people, who blindly adhere to their theory.

TECHNOLOGY IN THE EYE AND THE EAR

Another subject that remains unanswered by evolutionary theory is the excellent quality of perception in the eye and the ear.

Before passing on to the subject of the eye, let us briefly answer the question of "how we see". Light rays coming from an object fall oppositely on the retina of the eye. Here, these light rays are transmitted into electric signals by cells and they reach a tiny spot at the back of the brain called the centre of vision. These electric signals are perceived in this centre of the brain as an image after a series of processes. With this technical background, let us do some thinking.

The brain is insulated from light. That means that the inside of the brain is solid dark, and light does not reach the location where the brain is situated. The place called the centre of vision is a solid dark place where no light ever reaches; it may even be the darkest place you have ever known. However, you observe a luminous, bright world in this pitch darkness.

The image formed in the eye is so sharp and distinct that even the technology of the 20th century has not been able to attain it. For instance, look at the book you read, your hands with which you hold it, then lift your head and look around you. Have you ever seen such a sharp and distinct image as this one at any other place? Even the most developed television screen produced by the greatest television producer in the world cannot provide such a sharp image for you. This is a three-dimensional, colored, and extremely sharp image. For more than 100 years, thousands of engineers have been trying to achieve this sharpness. Factories, huge premises were established, much research has been done, plans and designs have been made for this purpose. Again, look at a TV screen and the book you hold in your hands. You will see that there is a big difference in sharpness and distinction. Moreover, the TV screen shows you a two-dimensional image, whereas with your eyes, you watch a three-dimensional perspective having depth.

For many years, tens of thousands of engineers have tried to make a three-dimensional TV, and reach the vision quality of the eye. Yes, they have made a three-dimensional television system but it is not possible to watch it without putting on glasses; moreover, it is only an artificial three-dimension. The background is more blurred, the foreground appears like a paper setting. Never has it been possible to produce a sharp and distinct vision like that of the eye. In both the camera and the television, there is a loss of image quality.

Evolutionists claim that the mechanism producing this sharp and distinct image has been formed by chance. Now, if somebody told you that the television in your room was formed as a result of chance, that all its atoms just happened to come together and make up this device that produces an image, what would you think? How can atoms do what thousands of people cannot?

If a device producing a more primitive image than the eye could not have been formed by chance, then it is very evident that the eye and the image seen by the eye could not have been formed by chance. The same situation applies to the ear. The outer ear picks up the available sounds by the auricle and directs them to the middle ear; the middle ear transmits the sound vibrations by intensifying them; the inner ear sends these vibrations to the brain by translating them into electric signals. Just as with the eye, the act of hearing finalises in the centre of hearing in the brain.

The situation in the eye is also true for the ear. That is, the brain is insulated from sound just like it is from light: it does not let any sound in. Therefore, no matter how noisy is the outside, the inside of the brain is completely silent. Nevertheless, the sharpest sounds are perceived in the brain. In your brain, which is insulated from sound, you listen to the symphonies of an orchestra, and hear all the noises in a crowded place. However, if the sound level in your brain was measured by a precise device at that moment, it would be seen that a complete silence is prevailing there.

As is the case with imagery, decades of effort have been spent in trying to generate and reproduce sound that is faithful to the original. The results of these efforts are sound recorders, high-fidelity systems, and systems for sensing sound.

Despite all this technology and the thousands of engineers and experts who have been working on this endeavour, no sound has yet been obtained that has the same sharpness and clarity as the sound perceived by the ear. Think of the highest-quality HI-FI systems produced by the biggest company in the music industry. Even in these devices, when sound is recorded some of it is lost; or when you turn on a HI-FI you always hear a hissing sound before the music starts. However, the sounds that are the products of the technology of the human body are extremely sharp and clear. A human ear never perceives a sound accompanied by a hissing sound or with atmospherics as does HI-FI; it perceives sound exactly as it is, sharp and clear. This is the way it has been since the creation of man.

So far, no visual or recording apparatus produced by man has been as sensitive and successful in perceiving sensory data as are the eye and the ear.

However, as far as seeing and hearing are concerned, a far greater fact lies beyond all this.

TO WHOM DOES THE CONSCIOUSNESS THAT SEES AND HEARS WITHIN THE BRAIN BELONG?

Who is it that watches an alluring world in its brain, listens to symphonies and the twittering of birds, and smells the rose?

The stimulations coming from the eyes, ears, and nose of a human being travel to the brain as electro-chemical nervous impulses. In biology, physiology, and biochemistry books, you can find many details about how this image forms in the brain. However, you will never come across the most important fact about this subject: Who is it that perceives these electro-chemical nervous impulses as images, sounds, odours and sensory events in the brain? There is a consciousness in the brain that perceives all this without feeling any need for eye, ear, and nose. To whom does this consciousness belong? There is no doubt that this consciousness does not belong to the nerves, the fat layer and neurons comprising the brain. This is why Darwinist-materialists, who believe that everything is comprised of matter, cannot give any answer to these questions.

For this consciousness is the spirit God created. The spirit needs neither the eye to watch the images, nor the ear to hear the sounds. Furthermore, nor does it need the brain to think.

Everyone who reads this explicit and scientific fact should ponder on Almighty God, should fear Him and seek refuge in Him, He Who squeezes the entire universe in a pitch-dark place of a few cubic centimetres in a three-dimensional, colored, shadowy, and luminous form.

A MATERIALIST FAITH

The information we have presented so far shows us that the theory of evolution is a claim evidently at variance with scientific findings. The theory's claim on the origin of life is inconsistent with science, the evolutionary mechanisms it proposes have no evolutionary power, and fossils demonstrate that the intermediate forms required by the theory never existed. So, it certainly follows that the theory of evolution should be pushed aside as an unscientific idea. This is how many ideas such as the earth-centered universe model have been taken out of the agenda of science throughout history.

However, the theory of evolution is pressingly kept on the agenda of science. Some people even try to represent criticisms directed against the theory as an "attack on science." Why?

The reason is that the theory of evolution is an indispensable dogmatic belief for some circles. These circles are blindly devoted to materialist philosophy and adopt Darwinism because it is the only materialist explanation that can be put forward for the workings of nature.

Interestingly enough, they also confess this fact from time to time. A well known geneticist and an outspoken evolutionist, Richard C. Lewontin from Harvard University, confesses that he is "first and foremost a materialist and then a scientist":

> *It is not that the methods and institutions of science somehow compel us accept a material explanation of the phenomenal world, but, on the contrary, that we are forced by our a priori adherence to material causes to create an apparatus of investigation and a set of concepts that produce material explanations, no matter how counter-intuitive, no matter how mystifying to the uninitiated. Moreover, that materialism is absolute, so we cannot allow a Divine Foot in the door.*

These are explicit statements that Darwinism is a dogma kept alive just for the sake of adherence to the materialist philosophy. This dogma maintains that there is no being save matter. Therefore, it argues that inanimate, unconscious matter created life. It insists that millions of different living species; for instance, birds, fish, giraffes, tigers, insects, trees, flowers, whales and human beings originated as a result of the interactions between matter such as the pouring rain, the lightning flash, etc., out of inanimate matter. This is a precept contrary both to reason and science. Yet Darwinists continue to defend it just so as "not to allow a Divine Foot in the door."

Anyone who does not look at the origin of living beings with a materialist prejudice will see this evident truth: All living beings are works of a Creator, Who is All-Powerful, All-Wise and All-Knowing. This Creator is God, Who created the whole universe from non-existence, designed it in the most perfect form, and fashioned all living beings.

THE THEORY OF EVOLUTION IS THE MOST POTENT SPELL IN THE WORLD

It needs to be made clear that anyone free of prejudice and the influence of any particular ideology, who uses only his reason and logic, will clearly understand that belief in the theory of evolution, which brings to mind the superstitions of societies with no knowledge of science or civilization, is quite impossible.

As has been explained above, those who believe in the theory of evolution think that a few atoms and molecules thrown into a huge vat could produce thinking, reasoning professors, university students, scientists such as Einstein and Galileo, artists such as Humphrey Bogart, Frank Sinatra and Pavarotti, as well as antelopes, lemon trees and carnations.

Moreover, the scientists and professors who believe in this nonsense are educated people. That is why it is quite justifiable to speak of the theory of evolution as "the most potent spell in history." Never before has any other belief or idea so taken away peoples' powers of reason, refused to allow them to think intelligently and logically and hidden the truth from them as if they had been blindfolded. This is an even worse and unbelievable blindness than the Egyptians worshipping the Sun God Ra, totem worship in some parts of Africa, the people of Saba worshipping the Sun, the tribe of the Prophet Abraham worshipping idols they had made with their own hands or the people of the Prophet Moses worshipping the Golden Calf.

In fact, this situation is a lack of reason Allah pointed to in the Qur'an. He reveals in many verses that some peoples' minds will be closed and that they will be powerless to see the truth. Some of these verses are as follows:

> *As for those who disbelieve, it makes no difference to them whether you warn them or do not warn them, they will not believe. God has sealed up their hearts and hearing and over their eyes is a blindfold. They will have a terrible punishment. (Qur'an, 2: 6-7)*

> *... They have hearts they do not understand with. They have eyes they do not see with. They have ears they do not hear with. Such people are like cattle. No, they are even further astray! They are the unaware. (Qur'an, 7: 179)*

> *Even if We opened up to them a door into heaven, and they spent the day ascending through it, they would only say, "Our eyesight is befuddled! Or rather we have been put under a spell!" (Qur'an, 15: 14-15)*

Words cannot express just how astonishing it is that this spell should hold such a wide community in thrall, keep people from the truth, and not be broken for 150 years. It is understandable that one or a few people might believe in impossible scenarios and claims full of stupidity and illogicality. However, "magic" is the only possible explanation for people from all over the world believing that unconscious and lifeless atoms suddenly decided to come together and form a universe that functions with a flawless system of organization, discipline, reason and consciousness, the planet Earth with all its features so perfectly suited to life, and living things full of countless complex systems.

In fact, Allah reveals in the Qur'an in the incident of the Prophet Moses and Pharaoh that some people who support atheistic philosophies actually influence others by magic. When Pharaoh was told about the true religion, he told the Prophet Moses to meet with his own magicians. When the Prophet Moses did so, he told them to demonstrate their abilities first. The verses continue:

> *He said, "You throw." And when they threw, they cast a spell on the people's eyes and caused them to feel great fear of them. They produced an extremely powerful magic. (Qur'an, 7: 116)*

As we have seen, Pharaoh's magicians were able to deceive everyone, apart from the Prophet Moses and those who believed in him. However, the evidence put forward by the Prophet Moses broke that spell, or "swallowed up what they had forged" as the verse puts it.

We revealed to Moses, "Throw down your staff." And it immediately swallowed up what they had forged. So the Truth took place and what they did was shown to be false. (Qur'an, 7: 117-119)

As we can see from that verse, when it was realized that what these people who had first cast a spell over others had done was just an illusion, they lost all credibility. In the present day too, unless those who under the influence of a similar spell believe in these ridiculous claims under their scientific disguise and spend their lives defending them abandon them, they too will be humiliated when the full truth emerges and the spell is broken. In fact, Malcolm Muggeridge, an atheist philosopher and supporter of evolution admitted he was worried by just that prospect:

> *I myself am convinced that the theory of evolution, especially the extent to which it's been applied, will be one of the great jokes in the history books in the future. Posterity will marvel that so very flimsy and dubious an hypothesis could be accepted with the incredible credulity that it has.84*

That future is not far off: On the contrary, people will soon see that "chance" is not a god, and will look back on the theory of evolution as the worst deceit and the most terrible spell in the world. That spell is already rapidly beginning to be lifted from the shoulders of people all over the world. Many people who see the true face of the theory of evolution are wondering with amazement how it was that they were ever taken in by it.

Terrorism: The Rite Of The Antichrist

We have so far looked at the kind of movement the Antichrist, the greatest purveyor of discord in the days leading up to doomsday, represents, and what kind of people are ensnared by it. In this chapter, we shall consider terrorism, one of the gravest contributors to this strife.

Although it is one of the most commonly heard terms in the world today, there is still no definition of it that all can agree on. One of the main reasons for this is that people who are regarded as terrorists by some, are regarded by others as those engaged in a just struggle. Whatever the aim may be, it is never possible to regard any group that resorts to violence and targets innocent people as just. Individuals or societies may desire different things, and these aspirations may be entirely valid. Yet, violence is not the way to bring them about. Force should only be used in self-defense. For that reason, any act of violence aimed at innocent people may be regarded as an act of terrorism.

The fundamental strategy of terrorism is the spreading of fear, and by it to gain influence. Instead of working for their aspirations through more peaceable and reasonable means, terrorist groups turn to violence, which they regard is far more effective. According to them, the more ruthless and destructive an act of terrorism is, the more terrifying it is, in other words the nearer it will have come to achieving its aim.

One of the most dreadful aspects of terrorism is the fact that it is devoid of all moral values and recognizes no rules. People who turn to terrorism lack all love, affection, compassion and tolerance, and are solely governed by feelings of hatred, anger and revenge. Unconsciously, such people's intention is to relieve their anger and take revenge, without considering the result of their actions. The idea of the damage that their actions might result in causes not the slightest stirrings of their conscience. Because, conscience of the kind of person who regards terrorism as any kind of solution is obstructed, as, therefore, are his reason, foresight and understanding.

According to the morality of the Qur'an, however, there is no room for anger. God has revealed that so long as people act in the light of individual emotions, such as anger, there will be corruption and chaos in the world. He has therefore commanded us for all time to behave with a tolerant, peaceful and brotherly spirit. When people abide by that morality, however, the system of the Antichrist, based as it is in violence, will completely collapse, terror and anarchy will disappear, and the climate of chaos that currently prevails in the world will come to an end. This is how God recommends that morality in one verse;

Make allowances for people, command what is right, and turn away from the ignorant. (Qur'an, 7: 199)

Those who Engage in Terrorism in the Name of Religion

The morality of religion forbids all kinds of terrorist acts, and yet, a number of terrorist groups still claim that they are acting in its name. Yet, when one has a close look at the world-views of those who carry out massacres or employ violence as a method, it is quite clear that such people are deviant. They have no idea of truth of religion, and are unable to live by or comprehend its morality. Anyone who genuinely believes in the existence of God, who truly fears Him and abides by the book revealed by Him would never be able to take any kind of action that might harm innocent and defenseless people. Those who carry out acts of terrorism and violence in the name of Islam, therefore, cannot possibly be called religious groups.

The true message of a religion or other system of ideas may sometimes be twisted by its so-called supporters, or interpreted incorrectly. That applies to Judaism as well as Christianity. The Crusaders, for instance, were European Christians who set out from Europe at the end of the 11th century with the aim of liberating the Holy Land. They may have set out with an alleged religious agenda, but they spread fear and barbarity wherever they went.

The savagery of these barbarians who misinterpreted Christianity, which is a religion of love and certainly has no room for violence, clearly had nothing to do with genuine religion at all.

Most of those who resort to terror in the name of religion are fanatical groups linked to pagan beliefs or newly developed mystical teachings, not the divine religions at all. These groups, and especially those in America and Japan, carry out terrible acts of violence against their own members as well as other people. These include the groups that burned themselves to death on a farm, or committed mass suicide in their beds, or the people who harmed others by releasing poison gas in the Japanese underground system. Other groups that have come to notice, due to their acts of terrorism, include fanatical racists such as the Ku Klux Klan and neo-Nazi groups. Over the last 20 years in particular, there has been a visible increase in racist and fascist ideas among young people, and that has led to an increase in the number of acts of violence. The attacks perpetrated against Turks in Germany a few years ago, the abuse and assaults aimed at people of Asian and African origin in other European countries, and the acts of violence against Blacks and Arabs that still take place in the United States even today, can all be included among the range of methods employed by such groups.

It must not be forgotten that, at the basis of all deviant movements, both those considered in this book and others that we have not dealt with, lies the fact that people have turned their backs on the morality of religion, and have been raised without true knowledge of the religion The common religious morality of Islam, Christianity and Judaism is diametrically opposed to the system of the Antichrist, built as it is on violence and savagery. At the root of religion lies love, affection and compassion. God has commanded us to treat one another with justice, tolerance, understanding, compassion and respect. Furthermore, people are charged with effecting that kind of behavior no matter what the religion, language, race or gender of the person they are dealing with. For that reason, it is impossible for there to be violence in a society where the morality of religion prevails. The morality of religion is the only system that can lead people to peace and security. God reveals in one verse:

You who believe! Enter absolutely into peace (Islam). Do not follow in the footsteps of the Devil. He is an outright enemy to you. (Qur'an, 2: 208) The following pages contain some information about groups and organizations that regard violence as normal and essential. The aim behind the preparation of this section is not to provide information about these terrorist organizations. It is to reveal the ideological system of the Antichrist, which deceives these groups that regard violence as a solution, no matter what their respective ideologies may be. The information here is of the utmost importance from the point of view of demonstrating the complexity of the system of the Antichrist, one which is currently so prevalent in the world.

RACIST TERROR

World War II was madness sparked off by a racist and fascist ideology. Violence and conflict, the so-called sacred values of these ideologies, briskly infected the entire world, leading to 55 million people falling victim to fascist savagery. Though the fact that victory fell upon the Allies meant that fascism was defeated, it did not disappear. It merely went underground. As a whole, there has been a discernable rise in the number of racist and fascist organizations and acts of violence in the world over the last 10 years. While Europe battles with acts of violence perpetrated by neo-Nazis, the United States has had to deal with a resurgence of the Ku Klux Klan and similar "white supremacy" organizations. Today, both the neo-Nazis and the members of the Ku Klux Klan are carrying out attacks and encouraging their members to commits acts of terror and violence.

Many people may imagine that the Ku Klux Klan had carried out most of its attacks on and oppression of Blacks merely in the 1920s and 1930s, but that in modern times it had been consigned to the waste bin of history. The Klan is still alive, however. Today, in the United States as a whole, there are a great many Ku Klux Klan churches, even if they happen to go by other names, and many racist organizations linked to that church's teachings. That church and the organizations linked to it are not just against Blacks, but oppose all non-European races, especially the Muslims living in America, believing that a concerted struggle needs to be waged against them. That "struggle" includes the formation of armed units.

It is no secret that the basis of the Klan's teachings is that European whites are superior to all other races, and that the white race should never be polluted by those others. In order to prevent such contamination, other races must not be permitted to live in areas inhabited by the white race. The idea is that the other races have no right to the kinds of opportunities enjoyed by the whites. These races are regarded as parasites trying to contaminate the purity and superiority of the whites, and it is believed that all kinds of measures need to be taken to oppose them. These views of the Klan are the basis for the attacks carried out against other races in America. At the root of these ideas, lies hatred and aggression instead of love, tolerance and dialogue.

The so-called scientific justification for the concept of the superiority of the white race is Darwin's theory of evolution. Darwin had suggested that certain races, the European race for instance, had progressed further than other races during the evolutionary process. Those outside these advanced races were in his view primitive creatures little better than apes. To put it another way, while some races had made enormous evolutionary progress, others were still at a level not far removed from man's primitive ancestor, the ape. Darwin indulged in racist speculation about the future, and wrote:

> At some future period, not very distant as measured by centuries, the civilised races of man will almost certainly exterminate, and replace, the savage races throughout the world. At the same time the anthropomorphous (manlike) apes, ...will no doubt be exterminated. The break between man and his nearest allies will then be wider.

These racist views of Darwin's became an important justification used in the service of the colonialist powers of the time to disguise their own brutality. The claim that Darwin put forward to demonstrate his theory is extremely interesting in the point of view of revealing his ignorance and prejudice. In a letter to a scientist named W. Graham in 1881, Darwin cited the Turkish nation as a proof of his theory. According to this nonsense of Darwin's, the Turkish nation was one of those backward peoples that would soon disappear:

I could show fight on natural selection having done and doing more for the progress of civilization than you seem inclined to admit. Remember what risk the nations of Europe ran, not so many centuries ago of being overwhelmed by the Turks, and how ridiculous such an idea now is! The more civilised so-called Caucasian races have beaten the Turkish hollow in the struggle for existence. Looking to the world at no very distant date, what an endless number of the lower races will have been eliminated by the higher civilized races throughout the world.16

Even today we still hear of churches belonging to Blacks in various states in America being burned, of attacks on mosques and synagogues, and assaults of members of other races. Following the terrorist attack on the World Trade Center on September 11, 2001, in particular, certain circles influenced by this and similar organizations stepped up their attacks. Businesses, mosques and associations belonging to Muslims in a number of states were attacked. Muslim students were not allowed into school, and Muslim children were assaulted in the streets. Everyone not totally devoid of reason and logic knows that the Islamic world, and innocent Muslim civilian and children in particular, cannot be held responsible for those ruthless attacks. (In fact, following September 11, there emerged a significant reaction, on the part of those with intelligence and common sense, which instead began to look into Islam. There was also an increase in the number of people turning to Islam). On the other hand, the situation was merely one indication of what a menace the encouragement of hatred based on race or belief could pose.

Members of the Klan do not agree, however. They are busily preparing for a great war between the races, which they believe will take place in the 21st century.

The Dimensions of Racism in America

The Ku Klux Klan was established in the 1870s, and became very powerful in America in the wake of the First World War. By the 1920s, it had some 3-4 million members.17

Like those of all other racist ideologies, the ideological roots of the teachings of the Klan, which start from the premise that "We will slaughter our enemies when the war to protect the white race begins," is the view that the white race is at the top of the evolutionary scale, while other races are to be located further down, for which reason they merit all kinds of inhuman treatment. A great number of people in America still hold to this view. It is fair to say that these groups, organized under different names, such as the National Alliance, the World Church of the Creator and Arian Nation, actually operate under the umbrella of the Ku Klux Klan.

The most important common factor between the views of these organizations, some of which we shall be looking at below, is that they have no qualms about using violence to achieve their aims, but rather often regard violence and aggression as necessary.

World Church of the Creator (WCOTC)

The WCOTC is one of those active racist organizations in America that is growing stronger by the day. This deviant organization denies the existence of God, the day of judgment, heaven and hell, and also has a large number of followers outside the United States. The idea of the superiority of the white race constitutes the basis of the organization's ideology. On its web site, Ben Klassen, the founder of this racist group, has this to say about their ideology:

> *[The] objective [of our religion] would be: The Survival, Expansion and Advancement of the White Race. It [our religion] is based on love—love for the White Race.... We, therefore, reject ...angels and devils and gods.... Our Golden Rule briefly can be summarized as follows: That which is good for the White Race is the highest virtue; that which is bad for the White Race is the ultimate sin... Nature tells us to take care of our own kind and only our own kind. We*

> *do not regard any of the mud races to be our own kind... The niggers, undoubtedly, are at the very bottom of the ladder, not far above monkeys and chimpanzees... We have no intention of helping the mud races prosper, multiply, and crowd us off the limited space of this planet.*

This perverse idea, as we have seen, is treated as a religion by its followers, its members subscribing to it wholly. However, it is totally unfounded, of course, to call this perversity a religion. We would be more correct in calling it a brand of Social Darwinism, the fundamental teaching of which is the future struggle against other races. That notion is actually referred to by the slogan "Rahowa," (Racial Holy War), and is regarded by the group as one of its core values. In another address, Ben Klassen informed his followers what Rahowa actually means, and felt no scruples about calling them to take up arms:

RAHOWA! In this one word we sum up the total goal and program of not only the Church of the Creator, but of the total White Race, and it is this: We take up the challenge. We gird for total war against the Jews and the rest of the goddamned mud races of the world—politically, militantly, financially, morally and religiously. In fact we regard it as the heart of our religious creed, and as the most sacred credo of all. We regard it as a holy war to the finish—a racial holy war.

The expected war between the races is one of the major aims of Klan organizations. The subject is stressed at just about every meeting. During speeches, Klan members are filled with enthusiasm for the war, and many references to it are made in their writings. Incitement towards this war, which has now assumed mythical status among them, is frequently to be seen in Klan publications. For instance, the journal *Knight-Ridder*, which covered a national rally held in Columbia, included the following lines:

King is the leader of the Christian Knights, who dreams of a resurgent Ku Klux Klan... He points down the street where both he and a neighbor decorate their front yards with robed Klansmen yard statues. He says: "A race war is coming. The Klan is the only hope for the white race."20

As is the case with many racist organizations, Rahowa is founded fundamentally on the belief in evolution. Such a degree of hostility towards other races, and the lack of any compunction over the using of violence as a means, are all the result of the belief in the theory of evolution. Nothing can prevent anyone who regards somebody else as an animal from abusing, attacking and, if necessary, killing that individual.

The following words of Matt Hale, who became leader of the organization after Ben Klassen, are just one example of the close connection between the idea which they treat as a religion and belief in evolution:

But we *are* animals. That's the thing. We don't accept this idea that just because we can think and speak and walk on two legs that we are not bound by nature's laws. We are.

These words are an indication of the organization's peculiar, unique view of religion. Naturally, that religion has absolutely nothing to do with Christianity, which promotes humility, love and tolerance. And, the leaders of the organization do not hesitate to admit the fact. The following extract from an interview with Matt Hale nicely sums up their view of religion:

Rather than a religion such as Christianity, which tells them to love their enemies, love the meek and the inferior. We need a religion, which exalts our own people and our own people alone... So we need to recognize this and do away with the idea that all men are created equal and idiotic notions of that kind... what we believe in doing is ending all aid to all non-white races. We believe that without this aid the non-white races would very quickly shrink their own numbers. They could not feed themselves... We believe that a perfect world is much more possible by having only white people, white racial comrades around the world. And we believe that once the non-white races are gone, and the white race is united with a pro living, a pro-life creed such as Creativity, there will be peace and prosperity for our white people.

Yet those who maintain the superiority of one race, and believe that their characteristics make them superior to others, are ignoring one very important truth. None of these values are permanent. Every human being, be he a believer or an unbeliever, will sooner or later die, leaving behind everything that he possessed in this world, and render account for himself to our Lord. On that day, nobody will be able to help anyone else, nobody's race, color or ancestry will be of the slightest importance, nothing he possessed in this world will be of the slightest advantage to him, and nobody will be able to put forward any excuses to justify his actions. God describes this in a verse:

Then when the Trumpet is blown, no ties of kinship will exist between them on that day, nor may they question one another. (Qur'an, 23: 101)

Klan Teachings

The following articles were taken from a speech by Matt Hale at a Klan rally on January 14, 2001:

Saying the races are equal is an insult to our race.

We despise and abhor integration, interracial marriage and the flooding of this country with non-White hoards.

Interracial marriage is a sin against our people.

The Civil Rights movement was wrong for us. It was wrong for our interests.

The white race is intellectually superior to all other races.

When we have our day, when we are in power in this world as we wish to be, as we will be, certainly we will subsidize the best of our race, the most intelligent of our race to have the most children.

The future is going to be one in which we have a land that is White and we will repatriate the other races.

They would be pushed on the boats by force—within the law! That's going to be the law.

Non-Whites are absolutely irrelevant. If they were lying in a pool of blood, it would be absolutely irrelevant. It simply means nothing to me. What I care about is my own racial family.

The brain makes the races different. The races have different shapes and sizes of brains.

On why most serial killers have been White … White people plan what they do. White people actually think. Most of the crimes that Blacks commit are impulsive. White people think about the crime they are going to commit. White people are involved in this type of crime because it takes a lot of planning.

These words strikingly reveal the thinking of a Klan member. This mentality is of such a kind that even the acts of a serial murder can become the cause for boasting, and savagery justified in the name of racial superiority.

The National Alliance

One of the fascist organizations enjoying increasing support from young people in America is the National Alliance. The organization was first founded in 1970 by Dr. William Pierce, a young professor of physics at Oregon State University, as the National Youth Alliance. Its outstanding characteristic was the way it targeted colleges and universities. Age of membership was restricted to 30 and under. Later, however, that age barrier was lifted and a new organization was created called the National Alliance. One of the principle objectives of this organization attaches great importance to the rearing up of young people with racist ideas. That, it is believed, will enable future generations to emerge in the awareness of racial superiority. Like all other racist groups, the National Alliance aims to defend the superiority of the white race under all circumstances. Dr. Pierce summed up this objective during an interview he gave in 1997:

Ultimately, we must separate ourselves from the Blacks and other non-Whites and keep ourselves separate, no matter what it takes to accomplish this... Eventually we must hunt them down and get rid of them.

That, of course, is not the only similarity between the National Alliance and other fascist organizations. As with others who believe in the theory of evolution, it is also prominent in the National Alliance. No matter how much organization members may claim to be religious, their statements reveal their beliefs to be totally opposed to religion. In general, they will state the following:

We see ourselves as integral with a unitary world around us, which evolves according to natural law. In the simplest words: There is only one reality, which we call Nature: ...We are part of Nature and subject to Nature's laws. Within the scope of these laws we are able to determine our own destiny... In other words, we ourselves are responsible for everything over which we have the power of choice: in particular, for the state of our environment and for the destiny of our race. This view may be contrasted with the Semitic view.

As we have seen, the use of religious principles in speeches by fascist and racist groups, and their efforts to portray themselves as people who live by the morality of religion, are nothing more than a sham tactic. Studies and researches by sociologists and academics have emphasized this fact. One of these academics is Jack Levin, director for the study of Violence and Social Conflict at Boston's Northeastern University. Levin states that the reason the groups use biblical references is to "lend an air of religious credibility" to their message of hate.

NEO-NAZISM: AN IDEOLOGY BASED ON VIOLENCE AND TERROR

While racist groups that represent racism and xenophobia come together under the umbrella of the Ku Klux Klan in America, the neo-Nazis perform the same role in Europe. European racism began with the skinheads in Great Britain, and turned into a neo-Nazi movement in the 1990s. The main characteristics of these groups which define themselves as neo-Nazis are the way that, just like the Ku Klux Klan, they maintain the superiority of the white race and attack foreigners and those living in poorer areas.

Neo-Nazi movements have grown increasingly powerful over the last 10 years, and their sphere of influence has widened considerably. Their members now number around 70,000. The neo-Nazis have set themselves various targets in different countries. According to one study, Turks in Germany, Gypsies in Hungary, Slovakia and the Czech Republic, Asians in Great Britain, North Africans in France and Northeasterners in Brazil, are among their slated victims. The neo-Nazis' distinguishing characteristics are violence, hatred, intimidation, the use of threat and destruction.

According to official German figures, in 1997 alone there were 10,037 incidents linked to racism and xenophobia. The figure for 2000 was more than 10,000. In Britain, there were 10,982 racism-linked incidents between April and September alone. More than half of these crimes consisted of threats, menaces and intimidation. The rest were made up of murders, assaults, vandalism of homes and businesses, etc.

Louis Beam and William Pierce, extreme right-wing American ideologues, share a very important place in the neo-Nazi movement that developed during the 1990s. The concepts of "leaderless resistance" and "white revolution" put forward by these men have now come to dominate the thought of the neo-Nazi movement. At the root of various acts of terror, such as bombings, looting, and the destruction of workplaces in numerous countries of the world, can continually be found their concept of "leaderless resistance." According to their idea, neo-Nazi actions aught to be carried out on either an individual basis or else by very small gangs.

The books *Hunter* and *The Turner Diaries* by William Pierce are regarded as the principle inspiration behind neo-Nazi terror. The pamphlet *A Practical Guide to Aryan Revolution* by the French Nationalist

Socialist Movement, which took those books as its theoretical basis, contains all the information a neo-Nazi would require. The pamphlet is a detailed, practical terrorist handbook, divided into such chapter headings as *Methods of Covert Direct Action, Escape and Evasion, Assasination, Terror Bombing, Sabotage, Racial War, How To Create A Revolutionary Situation, and Rules of Engagement – Regulations Concerning the Conduct of Soldiers of the Aryan Liberation Army.*

Even if they do not play an active role within these groups, many people nevertheless support fascism and are influenced by these books. *The Turner Diaries,* for instance, describe how one underground group organized against the state and what kind of activities it engaged in. In his defense, a man by the name of John William King, who killed a Black man named James Byrd Jr. in 1998 by tying him and dragging him behind his pick-up truck, was reported to having said, "We're going to start The Turner Diaries early."

Following the 1993 Oklahoma bombing by Timothy McVeigh, attention turned to William Pierce's book *Hunter,* in which Pierce described the actions of a bomber who acted alone. The hero of the book was not supported by any group or organization, but consciously carried out a terrorist attack single-handedly, just as Timothy McVeigh did.

The Oklahoma Bomber Was a Neo-Nazi

Up until September 11, 2001, the worst terrorist attack the American people had witnessed was that of on federal building in Oklahoma by Timothy McVeigh, as a result of which 168 people lost their lives, including a number of children. What is interesting about that bombing is that Timothy McVeigh was both the member of a deviant cult as well as a neo-Nazi.

McVeigh claimed to have carried out that bombing in revenge for David Koresh and his followers who burned to death on a farm in 1993. According to McVeigh, Koresh and the cult members did not kill themselves, but were actually murdered by the American state. He therefore decided to take revenge on that state, and planned to bomb the people working in its name in the Federal Building. Exactly two years after the deaths of Koresh and his cult followers, on the second anniversary in fact, McVeigh cold-bloodedly parked a lorry full of explosives in front of the Federal Building and the rest is history. After the attack, McVeigh was helped by another neo-Nazi, Terry Nichols. The most important fact to recognize about those who supported Nichols and McVeigh before the attack, who helped locate the explosives and knew what McVeigh was up to, is that they were all neo-Nazis.

Shortly before his execution, McVeigh sent a letter to *The Buffalo News* in which he said he was not sorry about the bombing, which he saw as a "legit tactic," in his solitary war against the federal government. That attack, the product of a disturbed mind, is once again an appalling indication of what terrible destruction the movements we are presently discussing can wreak on people and society.

As we should now be able to recognize from these numerous examples, those who are caught up in the system of the Antichrist believe it is entirely justified to discriminate between people on the grounds of race, language and gender, and to exercise brutality against them. What is more, that discrimination between communities can turn into the type of hysteria that leads to war and destruction. People are attacked solely because of their language, religion or race, and needlessly suffer all sorts of abuse. One of the reasons for this, as is made clear in the Qur'an, is that the Devil portrays "fanatical rage" as right and honorable. Most of the groups who at the present are encouraging terrorism, or who carry such acts, are caught up by this temptation, and base their attacks on racist statements. It is clear from the following verse exactly to what extent such racist provocation violates the principles of Islam:

Those who disbelieve filled their hearts with fanatical rage—the fanatical rage of the Time of Ignorance—and God sent down serenity to His Messenger and to the believers, and obliged them to respect the formula of heedfulness which they had most right to and were most entitled to. God has knowledge of all things. (Qur'an, 48:26)

The different peoples of the world have been created in order for human beings to come to know each other, to have good relations with each other, not to be enemies of one another. In the Qur'an, God has revealed that the ideology of the "master race," which foments the climate of terror desired by the Antichrist, is utterly false. Only better morality proffers societies, cultures or individuals with superiority. It is of absolutely no importance what race people belong to, what language they speak, or what color their skins are. Trying to ascribe superiority on the basis of such values, and harboring feelings of hatred towards other societies, are products of the ideology of the Antichrist. This is how God has revealed that the differences between races are a means by which friendship and cultural exchange can be brought about, and that superiority depends solely on piety, in other words, on faith and morality:

Mankind! We created you from a male and female, and made you into peoples and tribes so that you might come to know each other.The noblest among you in God's sight is the one who best performs his duty. God is All-Knowing, All-Aware. (Qur'an, 49: 13)

SATANISM; THE TERROR OF THE DEVIL

Satanism is a perverted ideology that makes violence and savagery a ritual in its creed. Satanists, who describe themselves as such, make deeds of inhumanity and brutality into acts of worship.

When the word Satanism is mentioned most people think merely of its widespread psychological influence on young people, and regard it as a kind of insignificant mystical movement. Also, due to the influence of the media, they may think of Satanists as performing strange rituals, much unlike what ordinary and well-balanced people would otherwise do. It is true that Satanists are part of a culture of violence and perform strange and horrible rites, yet, what most people fail to see is that Satanism is a materialist and atheist ideology that supports violence and which dates back to the

1800s. Furthermore, the ideology has a large number of followers throughout the world.

The fundamental principle of Satanism is that it rejects all religious values, takes the Devil as its deity, and claims that hell is a kind of salvation. According to the belief of Satanism, people have no responsibilities, apart from that of following their own desires. If his desires lead a person to anger, hatred, revenge, deceit, theft, the harming others or even murder, then that is acceptable. The basic logic that Satanism relies on, in support of that belief, is the claim that the avoidance of evil is a kind of insincerity. In other words, this perverted belief maintains that if his desires impel someone to kill another, and if he acts according to that impulse, then he has behaved sincerely.

Virtues such as love, tolerance, patience and forgiveness, which are highly esteemed by most people, and are elements of the true morality, are loathed by Satanists. This deviant ideology maintains that there should be no restrictions on evil and such feelings as hatred, anger and vengeance. Article 5 of *The Satanic Bible*, widely regarded as the fundamental textbook of Satanism, states, instead of the biblical principle that says "To him who strikes you on the cheek, offer the other also." that "Satan represents vengeance, instead of turning the other cheek." Elsewhere in that same book appears the commandment:

Hate your enemies with a whole heart, and if a man smite you on one cheek, SMASH him on the other!

It is obvious that according to such thinking it will be impossible to prevent any kind wickedness. Such an atmosphere will inevitably lead to chaos and strife. It is impossible to speak of order, peace, stability, security, forgiveness or tolerance in any society in which people do not listen to the voice of their consciences, and are thus unable to distinguish between good and bad, and to use their will and judgment to act for good. In an environment of that sort, anyone who feels anger towards somebody else will be unable to restrain that anger and behave with moderation, and will inevitably seek his revenge. Alternatively, instead of being patient in times of need and poverty, and attempting to address those needs in a sensible manner, these people will resort to theft and other sorts of crime. Satanism is their justification for doing so.

The kind of society proposed by the ideology of Satanism recognizes no rules and no bounds. Its aim is the free expression of selfish desires and evil. In his book *The Satanic Bible*, Anton LaVey, regarded as the founder of modern Satanism, recommends to his followers that they live by and promote wickedness as they so please. In an interview, LaVey even said: "I feel laws are, obviously, made to be broken ... I see nothing wrong with robbing somebody on the street.

Satanism's refusal to recognize any bounds does not stop there, of course. People would not only harm themselves and those around them, but would direct their hostility and anger at all. That refusal to recognize any limits, moreover, leads to the regard of violence as an intrinsic part of life. According to Satanism, violence is a fact of nature, and thus inescapable. Therefore, this distorted view maintains that it is perfectly permissible for people to resort to violence. Since any attempt to prevent or minimize violence is a violation of what is natural, any attempt to do so is futile, and it is therefore illogical to do so.

As we have seen, Satanism holds utterly perverse beliefs, which encourage people to be aggressive, to commit murder, and even mass slaughter. In America in particular, academics have established that Satanism lies at the root of national terror, and that serious steps need to be taken in order to deal with it. One of these academics is Carl Roschke, a professor at Denver University, who has stressed the importance of the subject in the words, "We're really dealing with the way satanic ideology has become a basis for domestic terrorism." Roschke says that the most important step in the war to be waged against Satanism is to make it clear that its followers are not just "harmless wackoes," but that when their crimes are examined, one can understand just how harmful someone claiming to be a Satanist can be. There is no doubt that the most important fight against a movement of this sort must be ideological. That being the case, we must establish which ideologies Satanism is founded on.

Darwinism is the Ideological Basis of Satanism

One of the most common ways Satanists use to describe themselves, in their books, magazines and publications, as well as their websites, is to regard man as a "kind of developed animal," and to maintain that "only the fittest can survive." This is the most important piece of evidence to corroborate that Darwinism lies at the very root of the Satanists' beliefs. In fact, many Satanists do not hesitate to admit the fact. In *A Description of Satanism*, a Satanist writer describes the ideology in these terms:

...First of all, Humans are social animals... all people and animals share a common source in mere biology. Satanism is the belief that Humans are nothing more than higher animals—we have no special place in creation other than being lucky to have evolved and survived...

Another Satanist publication, *The Church of Satan,* describes how they believe that human beings are a kind of developed animal:

Since Satanism stands for acceptance of Man as an animal, there have often been creators in many past cultures who embraced this insight and explored it in the context of their society, thus we seek out these artistic philosophical expressions and see them to be the roots of our current awareness.

It is clear from the preceding that Satanism regards Darwin's theory, that human beings evolved from animals, as the source of its own ideological "awareness." The introduction to an interview with Anton LaVey, carried in the music journal *MF Magazine*, describes the relationship between Satanism and Darwinism:

In the late 1960s, Anton LaVey brought forth an easily understandable doctrine of social Darwinism, and strong positive thinking (magic) to the growing mass of individuals sick of both hippieism and the stagnant morals of Christianity.

Magister Peter H. Gilmore, a priest of the Church of Satan, describes this perverted religion in the following terms:

... Let us instead look at contemporary Satanism for what it really is: a brutal religion of elitism and social Darwinism that seeks to re-establish the reign of the able over the idiotic, of swift justice over injustice, and for a wholesale rejection of egalitarianism as a myth that has crippled the advancement of the human species for the last two thousand years.

Of course, the idea of justice, as set out above, has absolutely no resemblance to the notion of justice as we know it should be, that is, established on the principle of equality. The above version is a Satanist idea of justice, and as will be seen from what follows, it is a version that endows anyone who regards himself as superior to others to usurp all such powers and rights.

The way Satanism shares so many parallels with Social Darwinism, which regards Western society as superior to others, has led to cooperation between it and a number of other racist and chauvinistic movements, especially fascism. One can find many individuals who believed in Satanism among the ranks of Hitler's National Socialists and Mussolini's Blackshirts. Anton LaVey makes this reference to that collaboration:

It's an unholy alliance. Many different types of such people have made contact with us in the past. The anti-Christian strength of National Socialist Germany is part of the appeal to Satanists—the drama, the lighting, the choreography with which they moved millions of people.39

Darwinism is the primary ground shared between these tendencies and Satanism. Social Darwinism, which lies at the heart of all these deviant ideologies, is defended by Satanists as follows:

The principle of the survival of the strong is advocated on all levels of society, from allowing an individual to stand or fall, to even letting those nations that cannot handle themselves take the consequences of this inability... There would be a concomitant reduction in the world's population as the weak are allowed to experience the consequences of social Darwinism. Thus has nature always acted to cleanse and strengthen her children... We embrace reality and do not try to transform it into some utopia that is contrary to the very fabric of existence.

Another expression of the Satanists' attachment to Social Darwinism is their fierce support for the theory of eugenics, itself the product of fascism. The theory of eugenics maintained that the sick and the crippled ought to be eliminated from society, and the number of healthy individuals increased through breeding. The theory was most prominently implemented in Nazi Germany. According to the theory of eugenics, in the same way that healthy animal stock is bred by mating healthy species, by this way a race of humans also be improved. Those elements obstructing such improvement (the sick, crippled, mentally handicapped etc.) need to be eradicated. When this line of thinking was adopted in Nazi Germany, tens of thousands of people with genetic and mental diseases were slaughtered ruthlessly.

Satanism is also in favor of the same terrible mercilessness. Their own publications reveal their view on eugenics:

Satanists also seek to enhance the laws of nature by concentrating on fostering the practice of eugenics... It is the practice of encouraging people of talent and ability to reproduce, to enrich the gene pool from which our species can grow. This was commonly practiced throughout the world... Until the genetic code is cracked and we can choose the character of our offspring at will, Satanists seek to mate the best with the best.

The Perverse Rites of Satanism

Black masses, and the terrible things that are conducted during them, is what most often comes to peoples' minds whenever Satanism is mentioned. Yet, many people believe that it is make-believe only portrayed in films, and that nothing of the sort actually takes place in real life. However, the terrible scenes we are used to watching in films are really parts and aspects of Satanist masses and rituals.

The real purpose behind these rituals is to make contact with the Devil and learn his so-called teachings. In order to see just how important these devilish rites are in Satanism, a brief look at their own books and websites is more than sufficient. The common feature of these publications is the way they devote considerable space to gloomy subjects and insist on the importance of the black mass. In a well-known Satanist website, which carries various Satanist messages for the under-18s, these so-called masses are emphasized as being one of the fundamental elements of Satanism, and that young people who cannot attend group ceremonies should nevertheless hold such services on their own. The details of the services these young people are instructed to hold are then given:

Don't be disturbed or frightened or think you're crazy when you feel contacted by the Dark Ones… Approach the Dark Masters with the proper degree of respect and decorum—that's what rituals are for, to establish a relationship… You don't need everything mentioned in Dr. LaVey's books to do an effective ritual. Maybe you don't have the money to obtain, or the private space to store, items such as swords, chalices, black robes, gongs and elaborate altars. Here is a powerful ritual you can perform… Light the candle and set it before you… As you gaze at the flame, say in your mind or out loud, "I am ready, oh, Dark Lord. I feel your strength within me and wish to honor you in my life. I am one of the Devil's Own. Hail Satan!"… This is a simple way of conjuring Satan into your life.

One can recognize such perversion, immorality and savagery in any society that takes Satan as its guide. For Satanists, these things are inspired by the Devil himself, and must be adhered to. Satanists, who do adhere to them, fall into forms of sexual perversions, torture humans as well as animals, and even perform such disgusting things as the drinking of the blood of the creatures or people they kill. In many countries of the world, young people who describe themselves as Satanists hold drug-parties at which all kinds of immorality and perversion take place, and which frequently end in the killing of one of their number in the Devil's name.

The way Satanists attach such importance to the shedding of blood at their rituals is a small-scale example of the plan Satan has for mankind. Satan hates mankind, and wants to inflict as much suffering on it as possible. It is therefore his aim to fill the world with bloodshed. The ideologies of the Antichrist we discussed earlier, such as fascism, racism and communism, all serve his purpose. All the wars, massacres, killings, and acts of terrorism, linked to these and similar atheistic ideologies, are all "Satanic masses" aimed at satisfying the Devil's lust for blood.

Those who openly describe themselves as Satanists carry out the shedding of blood as an act of worship. Those who incite terror and anarchy in the world are actually performing the same rite, in a more secret but with far wider ramifications. In short, the Devil, and the system of the Antichrist established by him for the world are using those they have managed to take in and are trying to turn the world into a brutal battleground.

Satanism is an Ideology That Has Already Been Defeated

We need to bear in mind the Satanists' own views when considering the threat posed by it. When Satanists are asked how many of them there are, they claim to have large numbers of followers, because there are many people who actually live by the tenets of Satanism without being aware of the fact. In a way, that is actually the case. Many people, consciously or unconsciously, share the views of the Satanists. That is because, refusing to listen to the voice of one's conscience, or to live by proper morality, therefore following one's own desires, is the same as obeying the commands of the Devil. When one considers all the destruction caused by Satanists up to the present day, it is quite clear in what a terrible state a society consisting of such people is going to end up to be.

The claim that man is a species of animal, on which Satanism is founded, is utter nonsense. Mankind did not come into being as the result of blind chance. The Creator of mankind, and of the order and splendor of the entire universe, is the infinitely powerful, superior and All-Wise God, who has no weaknesses of any kind. He created man with the ability to think and reason, to distinguish between right and wrong, and also with a responsibility towards his Creator. Just as each individual's ego direct him towards evil, so his conscience protects him from it, and commands him to turn away from it. It is man's duty to listen to the voice of his conscience, not to his ego and adopt the kind of morality that is pleasing to God. That morality will not only allow the individual concerned, and the society in which he lives, to enjoy a peaceful and secure existence, but will also, by the will of God, lead to the sublimest reward in the hereafter.

One important fact that must not be lost sight of is that the life Satan offers, which he dresses up to appear so very attractive, is mere deception. Satan may make all kinds of promises about the possibilities of the life of this world, and may try to turn people away form the true path, yet, it must not be forgotten that the road he beckons man to follow will only lead to ultimate destruction for those who take it. That is because Satan and his followers have already been defeated. As God explains in a verse:

... What they call on is an arrogant Satan whom God has cursed. He said, "I will take a certain fixed proportion of Your servants. I will lead them astray and fill them with false hopes. I will command them and they will cut off cattle's ears. I will command them and they will change God's creation." Anyone who takes the Devil as his protector in place of God has clearly lost everything.. (Qur'an, 4: 117-119)

DEVIANT SECTS OFFER OTHER FORMS OF VIOLENCE

We have already discussed in earlier chapters the existence in a number of countries of the world, and especially the United States, of superstitious cults that adhere to deviant belief-systems, and how such groups engage in acts of terror. These mystical groups destroy the order of society, encourage nations towards violence, and lead to killings and even suicides. Some of the best-known of these are: David Koresh and his followers who committed mass suicide, the Heaven's Gate cult who did the same, and the Aum Shinrikyo cult who harmed hundreds of people by releasing poison gas into the Japanese underground transit system.

In addition to these, however, every day in America are attacks perpetrated by unknown groups as well as mass suicide. The worst mass suicide so far was that of "The People's Temple" cult.

Established at the end of the 1970s, under the leadership of Jim Jones, this cult lived isolated from the rest of the world in a forest area in Southern America. Following a number of complaints, in 1978, US Congressman Leo Ryan visited the Jonestown area on a fact-finding mission. As Ryan was leaving Jonestown, 18 temple members who wanted to leave the cult tried to accompany him, at which point violence erupted. Cult members opened fire on those who attempted to leave it. Congressman Ryan, three journalists, and one of the departing members were killed. Eleven people were injured. A few hours after that incident, the leader of the cult ordered their members to commit mass suicide by drinking potassium cyanide. Children died first; babies were killed by poison squirted into their mouths with a syringe. Then more than 900 people, children included, poisoned themselves.

By the 1990s, however, the group that attracted the most attention through mass death was the cult of David Koresh. When security units wished to inspect a farm in Texas on February 28, 1993, cult members opened fire on them. A siege that would last 51 days then ensued. When one member of the security forces tried to get into the farm on the 51st day, smoke suddenly began rising. The security forces announced that David Koresh had set fire to the farm, and that booby traps installed in various parts of it had turned the place into an inferno, in which some 90 people burned to death. Deviant cults again hit the headlines in 1997, when some 40 people wearing black T-shirts and sports-shoes committed mass suicide in the north of San Diego. Aged between 26 and 72, they had killed themselves out of a belief that the Hale-Bopp comet, which was then passing by the earth, would carry them to a higher level of evolution. This is how their ideas were expressed on their website:

> The joy is that our Older Member in the Evolutionary Level above human has made it clear to us that Hale-Bopp's approach is the "marker" we've been waiting for. … Our 22 years of classroom here on planet Earth is finally coming to conclusion "graduation" from the Human Evolutionary Level. We are happily prepared to leave "this world" and go with Ti's crew. (Ti refers to Bonnie Lu Trusdale a cofounder of the cult who died of cancer in 1985)

These accounts may seem to have very little to do with the lives of most people who are reading this book. Yet, nobody should be deceived by that fact as we have only considered three examples in detail. A large number of deviant cults and organizations are influencing young people in many countries of the world. The fact that some people regard these movements as being far removed from themselves does not mean that they are not causing terrible harm to individuals and to society as a whole. On the contrary, they reveal the different forms the strife of the Antichrist can take and how widespread it actually is.

The Japanese Cult's Underground Attack

The harm that such cults cause for the lives and property of their members is by no means the only threat they pose. The deviant ideas and lifestyles promoted by these cults also damage the very fabric of society. From time to time, some of them organize attacks directly aimed at the civilian population. One recent example of this was the Japanese cult Aum Shinrikyo, and its release of poison gas into a Tokyo metro station. The cult was also held responsible for a similar gas attack in Matsumoto near Tokyo, in which seven people died and 144 were injured. According to the teachings of the leader of the cult, Shoko Asahara, a person can only cleanse his soul by killing. World domination is only possible by implementing the violence that he teaches his followers. Acts that normal people would regard as cold-blooded, are for the members of the cult true examples of morality.

The first target of the attacks, which began in 1994, were the judges who had filed charges against the cult and lived in accommodations provided by the Ministry of Justice . The first attack resulted in seven deaths. At the same time, the cult had begun the construction of a 70-ton capacity sarin gas production facility, on the orders of Asahara, who also instructed that 1,000 automatic rifles and a million bullets be manufactured. With the help of Russian experts hired by the cult, there were also efforts being made to construct a kind of nuclear weapon. Also within Asahara's sphere of activities were kidnappings and murder, especially of lawyers and public prosecutors opposed to the cult's activities.

The attack on the underground system resulted in a much more severe reaction against the cult. Thousands of commuters on their way to work were affected. Twelve people died and more than 5,000 received treatment in hospital, and the attack became a terrifying example of the threat such groups now pose to the public.

As we have seen from the above examples, any kind of immorality is to be expected from groups that develop their own beliefs far removed from the morality of religion. The members of such organizations are wholly capable of any kind of deviance, from drug abuse to theft, and from kidnapping to torture, though they often only end up in bringing an end to their own lives.

One must never forget that it should come as no surprise that people who do not believe in God, have no fear of Him, and refuse to recognize true morality, engage in such acts of violence. That is because, they do not believe they will have to account for their deeds, nor that they will receive their just due in the Hereafter. In addition, they would probably adopt entirely inappropriate or false beliefs on the subject of life after death, all in accordance with their desires. The only true path however, is that revealed by God to His servants. Anyone who knows of the religion of God, and lives by it, is moderate and well-balanced. Furthermore, in the Qur'an, God has commanded man to think and use his reason. It is thus impossible for true believers to get caught-up in any belief system without listening to their consciences and employing their powers of reasoning. The faithful act in accordance with the dictates of their conscience at every moment in their lives, and behave reasonably. That, in turn, protects them from all forms of immorality and perversion. True believers are those who stay firmly rooted on the path revealed by God. It is clear, however, that such cults and organizations have long since turned away from that path.

There is no question that the acts of violence and terror we have been considering are not the only manifestations of terror in the world today. Very many terrorist organizations in a great many countries have for many years been spreading fear, terror, as well as leading to the deaths of many innocent people. These include the IRA, which for many years has been a major thorn in the side of the government of Great Britain; ETA in the Basque region of Spain, ASALA, the Armenian terrorist organization which for many years attacked Turkish diplomats serving abroad, and the Kurdistan Workers' Party (PKK). Although they all have different ideological motives, all terrorist groups and people who support the use of violence, whether listed here or not, and whether they are aware of the fact or not, agree on one thing. That is, the rejection of religion. Whatever their ideology and world-view may be, the true reason why anyone turns to anarchy and violence is that they lack any beliefs and conscience to prevent them from doing so.

CONCLUSION

As we have stressed right through this book, it is peoples' refusal to listen to the voice of their consciences that turns them in the direction of violence and savagery. They totally ignore the fact that they are responsible to God and that they will have to account for all their actions in the hereafter. The most effective means of turning such people away from violence and terrorism, therefore, is in addressing the ignorance that directs them down that road in the first place. While most nations turn to law-enforcement agencies, and political and economic strategies when dealing with terrorism, none of these are sufficient to resolve the problem on their own. What really needs to be done is to destroy the ideological foundation of terrorism. That requires a war on the level of ideas against all ideologies that promote hatred and anger, and their replacement with the moral virtues taught by religion.

As we have seen throughout the course of this book, Darwinism is the principle foundation of such ideologies. The only reason why that theory, which has today lost all scientific credibility, and has been shown to be devoid of all reason and logic, is still being artificially kept alive, is an ideological attachment to it. When that foundation is eventually done away with, therefore, the ideologies built on it will necessarily collapse. For that reason, the war of ideas against Darwinism is essential for bringing peace and security to mankind.

One important strategy of that war consists of revealing the true source of the ideologies in question, together with all their errors and deceptions. Another important stage is explaining the morality of religion, which will bring with it true peace and security. Since most people today have little idea of what the true religion is, they fall under the influence of atheism. That is why explaining the true religion, and the presentation of the morality commanded by God to the entire world, is the duty of every person who knows and lives by it.

Today, in the world as a whole, the system of the Antichrist prevails, in other words, anarchy, strife and chaos are rife. Throughout history, God has destroyed a great many evil and corrupt communities. All societies and movements founded on cruelty and ruthlessness, which resort to violence and terrorism and oppress others, face the same inevitable end. All anarchists and terrorist are doomed to destruction. All nations that support anarchy and terror will be eliminated. Cruelty can never endure. This is how the end of a wrongdoing society is described in the Qur'an,

So the last remnant of the people who did wrong was cut off. Praise belongs to God, the Lord of all the worlds! (Qur'an, 6: 45)

The Antichrist will also come to the same end. Of that there is no doubt. Those who resort to violence and terrorism must therefore turn away from them for fear of suffering the same fate. God reveals that He will forgive those who repent for their sins and turn towards that which is good. God will not hold them responsible for actions they committed out of ignorance or because they did not know the morality of religion. God is merciful and compassionate. So those who promote anarchy and harm other people must not think that it is "too late to turn back." It is never too late to turn away from anarchy and terror. All they need do is to repent to God, with a sincere heart, and stop what they are doing. The following verse reveals how God promises to forgive those who commit evil out of ignorance and then seek forgiveness:

When those who believe in Our Signs come to you, say, "Peace be upon you!' God has made mercy incumbent on Himself. If anyone among you does evil out of ignorance and then afterwards repents and puts things right, He is Ever-Forgiving, Most Merciful. (Qur'an, 6: 54)

8

THE EVOLUTION DECEPTION

Every detail in this universe points to a superior creation. By contrast, materialism, which seeks to deny the fact of creation in the universe, is nothing but an unscientific fallacy.

Once materialism is invalidated, all other theories based on this philosophy are rendered baseless. Foremost of them is Darwinism, that is, the theory of evolution. This theory, which argues that life originated from inanimate matter through coincidences, has been demolished with the recognition that the universe was created by God. American astrophysicist Hugh Ross explains this as follows:

Atheism, Darwinism, and virtually all the "isms" emanating from the eighteenth to the twentieth century philosophies are built upon the assumption, the incorrect assumption, that the universe is infinite. The singularity has brought us face to face with the cause – or causer – beyond/behind/before the universe and all that it contains, including life itself.

It is God Who created the universe and Who designed it down to its smallest detail. Therefore, it is impossible for the theory of evolution, which holds that living beings are not created by God, but are products of coincidences, to be true.

Unsurprisingly, when we look at the theory of evolution, we see that this theory is denounced by scientific findings. The design in life is extremely complex and striking. In the inanimate world, for instance, we can explore how sensitive are the balances which atoms rest upon, and further, in the animate world, we can observe in what complex designs these atoms were brought together, and how extraordinary are the mechanisms and structures such as proteins, enzymes, and cells, which are manufactured with them.

This extraordinary design in life invalidated Darwinism at the end of the 20th century.

We have dealt with this subject in great detail in some of our other studies, and shall continue to do so. However, we think that, considering its importance, it will be helpful to make a short summary here as well.

The Scientific Collapse of Darwinism

Although a doctrine going back as far as ancient Greece, the theory of evolution was advanced extensively in the 19th century. The most important development that made the theory the top topic of the world of science was the book by Charles Darwin titled *The Origin of Species* published in 1859. In this book, Darwin denied that different living species on the earth were created separately by God. According to Darwin, all living beings had a common ancestor and they diversified over time through small changes.

Darwin's theory was not based on any concrete scientific finding; as he also accepted, it was just an "assumption." Moreover, as Darwin confessed in the long chapter of his book titled "Difficulties of the Theory," the theory was failing in the face of many critical questions.

Darwin invested all his hopes in new scientific discoveries, which he expected to solve the "Difficulties of the Theory." However, contrary to his expectations, scientific findings expanded the dimensions of these difficulties.

The defeat of Darwinism against science can be reviewed under three basic topics:

1) The theory can by no means explain how life originated on the earth.

2) There is no scientific finding showing that the "evolutionary mechanisms" proposed by the theory have any power to evolve at all.
3) The fossil record proves completely the contrary of the suggestions of the theory of evolution.

In this section, we will examine these three basic points in general outlines:

The First Insurmountable Step: The Origin of Life

The theory of evolution posits that all living species evolved from a single living cell that emerged on the primitive earth 3.8 billion years ago. How a single cell could generate millions of complex living species and, if such an evolution really occurred, why traces of it cannot be observed in the fossil record are some of the questions the theory cannot answer. However, first and foremost, of the first step of the alleged evolutionary process it has to be inquired: How did this "first cell" originate?

Since the theory of evolution denies creation and does not accept any kind of supernatural intervention, it maintains that the "first cell" originated coincidentally within the laws of nature, without any design, plan, or arrangement. According to the theory, inanimate matter must have produced a living cell as a result of coincidences. This, however, is a claim inconsistent with even the most unassailable rules of biology.

"Life Comes from Life"

In his book, Darwin never referred to the origin of life. The primitive understanding of science in his time rested on the assumption that living beings had a very simple structure. Since medieval times, spontaneous generation, the theory asserting that non-living materials came together to form living organisms, had been widely accepted. It was commonly believed that insects came into being from food leftovers, and mice from wheat. Interesting experiments were conducted to prove this theory. Some wheat was placed on a dirty piece of cloth, and it was believed that mice would originate from it after a while.

Similarly, worms developing in meat was assumed to be evidence of spontaneous generation. However, only some time later was it understood that worms did not appear on meat spontaneously, but were carried there by flies in the form of larvae, invisible to the naked eye.

Even in the period when Darwin wrote *The Origin of Species*, the belief that bacteria could come into existence from non-living matter was widely accepted in the world of science.

However, five years after the publication of Darwin's book, Louis Pasteur announced his results after long studies and experiments, which disproved spontaneous generation, a cornerstone of Darwin's theory. In his triumphal lecture at the Sorbonne in 1864, Pasteur said, *"Never will the doctrine of spontaneous generation recover from the mortal blow struck by this simple experiment."*

Advocates of the theory of evolution resisted the findings of Pasteur for a long time. However, as the development of science unraveled the complex structure of the cell of a living being, the idea that life could come into being coincidentally faced an even greater impasse.

Inconclusive Efforts in the 20th Century

The first evolutionist who took up the subject of the origin of life in the 20th century was the renowned Russian biologist Alexander Oparin. With various theses he advanced in the 1930's, he tried to prove that the cell of a living being could originate by coincidence. These studies, however, were doomed to failure, and Oparin had to make the following confession: *"Unfortunately, however, the problem of the origin of the cell is perhaps the most obscure point in the whole study of the evolution of organisms."*

Evolutionist followers of Oparin tried to carry out experiments to solve the problem of the origin of life. The best known of these experiments was carried out by American chemist Stanley Miller in 1953. Combining the gases he alleged to have existed in the primordial earth's atmosphere in an experiment set-up, and adding energy to the mixture, Miller synthesized several organic molecules (amino acids) present in the structure of proteins.

Barely a few years had passed before it was revealed that this experiment, which was then presented as an important step in the name of evolution, was invalid, the atmosphere used in the experiment having been very different from real earth conditions.

After a long silence, Miller confessed that the atmosphere medium he used was unrealistic.

All the evolutionist efforts put forth throughout the 20th century to explain the origin of life ended with failure. The geochemist Jeffrey Bada from San Diego Scripps Institute accepts this fact in an article published in *Earth* Magazine in 1998:

> *Today as we leave the twentieth century, we still face the biggest unsolved problem that we had when we entered the twentieth century: How did life originate on Earth?*

The Complex Structure of Life

The primary reason why the theory of evolution ended up in such a big impasse about the origin of life is that even the living organisms deemed the simplest have incredibly complex structures. The cell of a living being is more complex than all of the technological products produced by man. Today, even in the most developed laboratories of the world, a living cell cannot be produced by bringing inorganic materials together.

The conditions required for the formation of a cell are too great in quantity to be explained away by coincidences. The probability of proteins, the building blocks of cell, being synthesized coincidentally, is 1 in 10950 for an average protein made up of 500 amino acids. In mathematics, a probability smaller than 1 over 1050 is practically considered to be impossible.

The DNA molecule, which is located in the nucleus of the cell and which stores genetic information, is an incredible databank. It is calculated that if the information coded in DNA were written down, this would make a giant library consisting of 900 volumes of encyclopaedias of 500 pages each.

A very interesting dilemma emerges at this point: the DNA can only replicate with the help of some specialized proteins (enzymes). However, the synthesis of these enzymes can only be realized by the information coded in DNA. As they both depend on each other, they have to exist at the same time for replication. This brings the scenario that life originated by itself to a deadlock. Prof. Leslie Orgel, an evolutionist of repute from the University of San Diego, California, confesses this fact in the September 1994 issue of the *Scientific American* magazine:

> *It is extremely improbable that proteins and nucleic acids, both of which are structurally complex, arose spontaneously in the same place at the same time. Yet it also seems impossible to have one without the other. And so, at first glance, one might have to conclude that life could never, in fact, have originated by chemical means.*

No doubt, if it is impossible for life to have originated from natural causes, then it has to be accepted that life was "created" in a supernatural way. This fact explicitly invalidates the theory of evolution, whose main purpose is to deny creation.

Imaginary Mechanisms of Evolution

The second important point that negates Darwin's theory is that both concepts put forward by the theory as "evolutionary mechanisms" were understood to have, in reality, no evolutionary power.

Darwin based his evolution allegation entirely on the mechanism of "natural selection". The importance he placed on this mechanism was evident in the name of his book: *The Origin of Species, By Means Of Natural Selection*...

Natural selection holds that those living things that are stronger and more suited to the natural conditions of their habitats will survive in the struggle for life. For example, in a deer herd under the threat of attack by wild animals, those that can run faster will survive. Therefore, the deer herd will be comprised of faster and stronger individuals. However, unquestionably, this mechanism will not cause deer to evolve and transform themselves into another living species, for instance, horses.

Therefore, the mechanism of natural selection has no evolutionary power. Darwin was also aware of this fact and had to state this in his book *The Origin of Species:*

> *Natural selection can do nothing until favourable individual differences or variations occur.*

Lamarck's Impact

So, how could these "favourable variations" occur? Darwin tried to answer this question from the standpoint of the primitive understanding of science in his age. According to the French biologist Lamarck, who lived before Darwin, living creatures passed on the traits they acquired during their lifetime to the next generation and these traits, accumulating from one generation to another, caused new species to be formed.

For instance, according to Lamarck, giraffes evolved from antelopes; as they struggled to eat the leaves of high trees, their necks were extended from generation to generation.

Darwin also gave similar examples, and in his book *The Origin of Species*, for instance, said that some bears going into water to find food transformed themselves into whales over time.

However, the laws of inheritance discovered by Mendel and verified by the science of genetics that flourished in the 20th century, utterly demolished the legend that acquired traits were passed on to subsequent generations. Thus, natural selection fell out of favour as an evolutionary mechanism.

Neo-Darwinism and Mutations

In order to find a solution, Darwinists advanced the "Modern Synthetic Theory", or as it is more commonly known, Neo-Darwinism, at the end of the 1930's. Neo-Darwinism added mutations, which are distortions formed in the genes of living beings because of external factors such as radiation or replication errors, as the "cause of favourable variations" in addition to natural mutation.

Today, the model that stands for evolution in the world is Neo-Darwinism. The theory maintains that millions of living beings present on the earth formed as a result of a process whereby numerous complex organs of these organisms such as the ears, eyes, lungs, and wings, underwent "mutations," that is, genetic disorders. Yet, there is an outright scientific fact that totally undermines this theory: Mutations do not cause living beings to develop; on the contrary, they always cause harm to them.

The reason for this is very simple: the DNA has a very complex structure and random effects can only cause harm to it. American geneticist B.G. Ranganathan explains this as follows:

First, genuine mutations are very rare in nature. Secondly, most mutations are harmful since they are random, rather than orderly changes in the structure of genes; any random change in a highly ordered system will be for the worse, not for the better. For example, if an earthquake were to shake a highly ordered structure such as a building, there would be a random change in the framework of the building which, in all probability, would not be an improvement.

Not surprisingly, no mutation example, which is useful, that is, which is observed to develop the genetic code, has been observed so far. All mutations have proved to be harmful. It was understood that mutation, which is presented as an "evolutionary mechanism," is actually a genetic occurrence that harms living beings, and leaves them disabled. (The most common effect of mutation on human beings is cancer). No doubt, a destructive mechanism cannot be an "evolutionary mechanism." Natural selection, on the other hand, "can do nothing by itself" as Darwin also accepted. This fact shows us that there is no "evolutionary mechanism" in nature. Since no evolutionary mechanism exists, neither could any imaginary process called evolution have taken place.

The Fossil Record: No Sign of Intermediate Forms

The clearest evidence that the scenario suggested by the theory of evolution did not take place is the fossil record.

According to the theory of evolution, every living species has sprung from a predecessor. A previously existing species turned into something else in time and all species have come into being in this way. According to the theory, this transformation proceeds gradually over millions of years.

Had this been the case, then numerous intermediary species should have existed and lived within this long transformation period.

For instance, some half-fish/half-reptiles should have lived in the past which had acquired some reptilian traits in addition to the fish traits they already had.

Or there should have existed some reptile-birds, which acquired some bird traits in addition to the reptilian traits they already had. Since these would be in a transitional phase, they should be disabled, defective, crippled living beings. Evolutionists refer to these imaginary creatures, which they believe to have lived in the past, as "transitional forms."

If such animals had really existed, there should be millions and even billions of them in number and variety. More importantly, the remains of these strange creatures should be present in the fossil record. In *The Origin of Species*, Darwin explained:

> *If my theory be true, numberless intermediate varieties, linking most closely all of the species of the same group together must assuredly have existed... Consequently, evidence of their former existence could be found only amongst fossil remains.*

Darwin's Hopes Shattered

However, although evolutionists have been making strenuous efforts to find fossils since the middle of the 19th century all over the world, no transitional forms have yet been uncovered. All the fossils unearthed in excavations showed that, contrary to the expectations of evolutionists, life appeared on earth all of a sudden and fully-formed.

A famous British paleontologist, Derek V. Ager, admits this fact, even though he is an evolutionist:

> *The point emerges that if we examine the fossil rec,ord in detail, whether at the level of orders or of species, we find - over and over again - not gradual evolution, but the sudden explosion of one group at the expense of another.*

This means that in the fossil record, all living species suddenly emerge as fully formed, without any intermediate forms in between. This is just the opposite of Darwin's assumptions. Also, it is very strong evidence that living beings are created. The only explanation of a living species emerging suddenly and complete in every detail without any evolutionary ancestor can be that this species was created. This fact is admitted also by the widely known evolutionist biologist Douglas Futuyma: Creation and evolution, between them, exhaust the possible explanations for the origin of living things. Organisms either appeared on the earth fully developed or they did not. If they did not, they must have developed from pre-existing species by some process of modification. If they did appear in a fully developed state, they must indeed have been created by some omnipotent intelligence.

Fossils show that living beings emerged fully developed and in a perfect state on the earth. That means that "the origin of species" is, contrary to Darwin's supposition, not evolution but creation.

The Tale of Human Evolution

The subject most often brought up by the advocates of the theory of evolution is the subject of the origin of man. The Darwinist claim holds that the modern men of today evolved from some kind of ape-like creatures. During this alleged evolutionary process, which is supposed to have started 4-5 million years ago, it is claimed that there existed some "transitional forms" between modern man and his ancestors. According to this completely imaginary scenario, four basic "categories" are listed:

1. Australopithecus
2. Homo habilis
3. Homo erectus
4. Homo sapiens

Evolutionists call the so-called first ape-like ancestors of men "*Australopithecus*" which means "South African ape." These living beings are actually nothing but an old ape species that has become extinct. Extensive research done on various *Australopithecus* specimens by two world famous anatomists from England and the USA, namely, Lord Solly Zuckerman and Prof. Charles Oxnard, has shown that these belonged to an ordinary ape species that became extinct and bore no resemblance to humans.

Evolutionists classify the next stage of human evolution as "homo," that is "man." According to the evolutionist claim, the living beings in the *Homo* series are more developed than Australopithecus. Evolutionists devise a fanciful evolution scheme by arranging different fossils of these creatures in a particular order. This scheme is imaginary because it has never been proved that there is an evolutionary relation between these different classes. Ernst Mayr, one of the most important proponents of the theory of evolution in the 20th century, contends in his book *One Long Argument* that *"particularly historical [puzzles] such as the origin of life or of Homo sapiens, are extremely difficult and may even resist a final, satisfying explanation."*

By outlining the link chain as "*Australopithecus* > *Homo habilis* > *Homo erectus* > *Homo sapiens*," evolutionists imply that each of these species is one another's ancestor. However, recent findings of paleoanthropologists have revealed that *Australopithecus*, *Homo habilis* and *Homo erectus* lived at different parts of the world at the same time.

Moreover, a certain segment of humans classified as *Homo erectus* have lived up until very modern times. *Homo sapiens neandarthalensis* and *Homo sapiens sapiens* (modern man) co-existed in the same region.

This situation apparently indicates the invalidity of the claim that they are ancestors of one another. A paleontologist from Harvard University, Stephen Jay Gould, explains this deadlock of the theory of evolution although he is an evolutionist himself:

> *What has become of our ladder if there are three coexisting lineages of hominids (A. africanus, the robust australopithecines, and H. habilis), none clearly derived from another? Moreover, none of the three display any evolutionary trends during their tenure on earth.*

Put briefly, the scenario of human evolution, which is sought to be upheld with the help of various drawings of some "half ape, half human" creatures appearing in the media and course books, that is, frankly, by means of propaganda, is nothing but a tale with no scientific ground.

Lord Solly Zuckerman, one of the most famous and respected scientists in the U.K., who carried out research on this subject for years, and particularly studied *Australopithecus* fossils for 15 years, finally concluded, despite being an evolutionist himself, that there is, in fact, no such family tree branching out from ape-like creatures to man.

Zuckerman also made an interesting "spectrum of science." He formed a spectrum of sciences ranging from those he considered scientific to those he considered unscientific. According to Zuckerman's spectrum, the most "scientific"—that is, depending on concrete data—fields of science are chemistry and physics. After them come the biological sciences and then the social sciences. At the far end of the spectrum, which is the part considered to be most "unscientific," are "extra-sensory perception"—concepts such as telepathy and sixth sense–and finally "human evolution." Zuckerman explains his reasoning:

> *We then move right off the register of objective truth into those fields of presumed biological science, like extrasensory perception or the interpretation of man's fossil history, where to the faithful [evolutionist] anything is possible - and where the ardent believer [in evolution] is sometimes able to believe several contradictory things at the same time.*

The tale of human evolution boils down to nothing but the prejudiced interpretations of some fossils unearthed by certain people, who blindly adhere to their theory.

Technology in the Eye and the Ear

Another subject that remains unanswered by evolutionary theory is the excellent quality of perception in the eye and the ear.

Before passing on to the subject of the eye, let us briefly answer the question of "how we see". Light rays coming from an object fall oppositely on the retina of the eye. Here, these light rays are transmitted into electric signals by cells and they reach a tiny spot at the back of the brain called the centre of vision. These electric signals are perceived in this centre of the brain as an image after a series of processes. With this technical background, let us do some thinking.

The brain is insulated from light. That means that the inside of the brain is solid dark, and light does not reach the location where the brain is situated. The place called the centre of vision is a solid dark place where no light ever reaches; it may even be the darkest place you have ever known. However, you observe a luminous, bright world in this pitch darkness.

The image formed in the eye is so sharp and distinct that even the technology of the 20th century has not been able to attain it. For instance, look at the book you read, your hands with which you hold it, then lift your head and look around you. Have you ever seen such a sharp and distinct image as this one at any other place? Even the most developed television screen produced by the greatest television producer in the world cannot provide such a sharp image for you. This is a three-dimensional, coloured, and extremely sharp image. For more than 100 years, thousands of engineers have been trying to achieve this sharpness. Factories, huge premises were established, much research has been done, plans and designs have been made for this purpose. Again, look at a TV screen and the book you hold in your hands. You will see that there is a big difference in sharpness and distinction. Moreover, the TV screen shows you a two-dimensional image, whereas with your eyes, you watch a three-dimensional perspective having depth.

For many years, ten of thousands of engineers have tried to make a three-dimensional TV, and reach the vision quality of the eye. Yes, they have made a three-dimensional television system but it is not possible to watch it without putting on glasses; moreover, it is only an artificial three-dimension. The background is more blurred, the foreground appears like a paper setting. Never has it been possible to produce a sharp and distinct vision like that of the eye. In both the camera and the television, there is a loss of image quality.

Evolutionists claim that the mechanism producing this sharp and distinct image has been formed by chance. Now, if somebody told you that the television in your room was formed as a result of chance, that all its atoms just happened to come together and make up this device that produces an image, what would you think? How can atoms do what thousands of people cannot?

If a device producing a more primitive image than the eye could not have been formed by chance, then it is very evident that the eye and the image seen by the eye could not have been formed by chance. The same situation applies to the ear. The outer ear picks up the available sounds by the auricle and directs them to the middle ear; the middle ear transmits the sound vibrations by intensifying them; the inner ear sends these vibrations to the brain by translating them into electric signals. Just as with the eye, the act of hearing finalises in the centre of hearing in the brain. The situation in the eye is also true for the ear. That is, the brain is insulated from sound just like it is from light: it does not let any sound in. Therefore, no matter how noisy is the outside, the inside of the brain is completely silent. Nevertheless, the sharpest sounds are perceived in the brain. In your brain, which is insulated from sound, you listen to the symphonies of an orchestra, and hear all the noises in a crowded place. However, if the sound level in your brain was measured by a precise device at that moment, it would be seen that a complete silence is prevailing there.

As is the case with imagery, decades of effort have been spent in trying to generate and reproduce sound that is faithful to the original. The results of these efforts are sound recorders, high-fidelity systems, and systems for sensing sound. Despite all this technology and the thousands of engineers and experts who have been working on this endeavour, no sound has yet been obtained that has the same sharpness and clarity as the sound perceived by the ear. Think of the highest-quality HI-FI systems produced by the biggest company in the music industry. Even in these devices, when sound is recorded some of it is lost; or when you turn on a HI-FI you always hear a hissing sound before the music starts. However, the sounds that are the products of the technology of the human body are extremely sharp and clear. A human ear never perceives a sound accompanied by a hissing sound or with atmospherics as does HI-FI; it perceives sound exactly as it is, sharp and clear. This is the way it has been since the creation of man.

So far, no visual or recording apparatus produced by man has been as sensitive and successful in perceiving sensory data as are the eye and the ear.

However, as far as seeing and hearing are concerned, a far greater fact lies beyond all this.

To Whom Does the Consciousness that

Sees and Hears Within the Brain Belong?

Who is it that watches an alluring world in its brain, listens to symphonies and the twittering of birds, and smells the rose?

The stimulations coming from the eyes, ears, and nose of a human being travel to the brain as electro-chemical nervous impulses. In biology, physiology, and biochemistry books, you can find many details about how this image forms in the brain. However, you will never come across the most important fact about this subject: Who is it that perceives these electro-chemical nervous impulses as images, sounds, odours and sensory events in the brain? There is a consciousness in the brain that perceives all this without feeling any need for eye, ear, and nose. To whom does this consciousness belong? There is no doubt that this consciousness does not belong to the nerves, the fat layer and neurons comprising the brain. This is why Darwinist-materialists, who believe that everything is comprised of matter, cannot give any answer to these questions.

For this consciousness is the spirit created by God. The spirit needs neither the eye to watch the images, nor the ear to hear the sounds. Furthermore, nor does it need the brain to think.

Everyone who reads this explicit and scientific fact should ponder on Almighty God, should fear Him and seek refuge in Him, He Who squeezes the entire universe in a pitch-dark place of a few cubic centimetres in a three-dimensional, coloured, shadowy, and luminous form.

A Materialist Faith

The information we have presented so far shows us that the theory of evolution is a claim evidently at variance with scientific findings. The theory's claim on the origin of life is inconsistent with science, the evolutionary mechanisms it proposes have no evolutionary power, and fossils demonstrate that the intermediate forms required by the theory never existed. So, it certainly follows that the theory of evolution should be pushed aside as an unscientific idea. This is how many ideas such as the earth-centered universe model have been taken out of the agenda of science throughout history.

However, the theory of evolution is pressingly kept on the agenda of science. Some people even try to represent criticisms directed against the theory as an "attack on science." Why?

The reason is that the theory of evolution is an indispensable dogmatic belief for some circles. These circles are blindly devoted to materialist philosophy and adopt Darwinism because it is the only materialist explanation that can be put forward for the workings of nature.

Interestingly enough, they also confess this fact from time to time. A well known geneticist and an outspoken evolutionist, Richard C. Lewontin from Harvard University, confesses that he is "first and foremost a materialist and then a scientist":

> *It is not that the methods and institutions of science somehow compel us accept a material explanation of the phenomenal world, but, on the contrary, that we are forced by our a priori adherence to material causes to create an apparatus of investigation and a set of concepts that produce material explanations, no matter how counter-intuitive, no matter how mystifying to the uninitiated. Moreover, that materialism is absolute, so we cannot allow a Divine Foot in the door.*

These are explicit statements that Darwinism is a dogma kept alive just for the sake of adherence to the materialist philosophy. This dogma maintains that there is no being save matter. Therefore, it argues that inanimate, unconscious matter created life. It insists that millions of different living species; for instance, birds, fish, giraffes, tigers, insects, trees, flowers, whales and human beings originated as a result of the interactions between matter such as the pouring rain, the lightning flash, etc., out of inanimate matter. This is a precept contrary both to reason and science. Yet Darwinists continue to defend it just so as "not to allow a Divine Foot in the door."

Anyone who does not look at the origin of living beings with a materialist prejudice will see this evident truth: All living beings are works of a Creator, Who is All-Powerful, All-Wise and All-

Knowing. This Creator is God, Who created the whole universe from non-existence, designed it in the most perfect form, and fashioned all living beings.

The Theory of Evolution is the Most Potent Spell in the World

It needs to be made clear that anyone free of prejudice and the influence of any particular ideology, who uses only his reason and logic, will clearly understand that belief in the theory of evolution, which brings to mind the superstitions of societies with no knowledge of science or civilization, is quite impossible.

As has been explained above, those who believe in the theory of evolution think that a few atoms and molecules thrown into a huge vat could produce thinking, reasoning professors, university students, scientists such as Einstein and Galileo, artists such as Humphrey Bogart, Frank Sinatra and Pavarotti, as well as antelopes, lemon trees and carnations. Moreover, the scientists and professors who believe in this nonsense are educated people. That is why it is quite justifiable to speak of the theory of evolution as "the most potent spell in history." Never before has any other belief or idea so taken away peoples' powers of reason, refused to allow them to think intelligently and logically and hidden the truth from them as if they had been blindfolded. This is an even worse and unbelievable blindness than the Egyptians worshipping the Sun God Ra, totem worship in some parts of Africa, the people of Saba worshipping the Sun, the tribe of the Prophet Ibrahim worshipping idols they had made with their own hands or the people of the Prophet Musa worshipping the Golden Calf.

In fact, this situation is a lack of reason pointed to by God in the Qur'an. He reveals in many verses that some peoples' minds will be closed and that they will be powerless to see the truth. Some of these verses are as follows:

As for those who disbelieve, it makes no difference to them whether you warn them or do not warn them, they will not believe. God has

> *sealed up their hearts and hearing and over their eyes is a blindfold. They will have a terrible punishment. (Surat al-Baqara: 6-7)*

> *...They have hearts they do not understand with. They have eyes they do not see with. They have ears they do not hear with. Such people are like cattle. No, they are even further astray! They are the unaware. (Surat al-A'raf: 179)*

> *Even if We opened up to them a door into heaven, and they spent the day ascending through it, they would only say, "Our eyesight is befuddled! Or rather we have been put under a spell!" (Surat al-Hijr: 14-15)*

Words cannot express just how astonishing it is that this spell should hold such a wide community in thrall, keep people from the truth, and not be broken for 150 years. It is understandable that one or a few people might believe in impossible scenarios and claims full of stupidity and illogicality. However, "magic" is the only possible explanation for people from all over the world believing that unconscious and lifeless atoms suddenly decided to come together and form a universe that functions with a flawless system of organization, discipline, reason and consciousness, the planet Earth with all its features so perfectly suited to life, and living things full of countless complex systems.

In fact, God reveals in the Qur'an in the incident of the Prophet Musa and Pharaoh that some people who support atheistic philosophies actually influence others by magic. When Pharaoh was told about the true religion, he told the Prophet Musa to meet with his own magicians. When the Prophet Musa did so, he told them to demonstrate their abilities first. The verses continue:

> *He said, "You throw." And when they threw, they cast a spell on the people's eyes and caused them to feel great fear of them. They produced an extremely powerful magic. (Surat al-A'raf: 116)*

As we have seen, Pharaoh's magicians were able to deceive everyone, apart from the Prophet Musa and those who believed in him. However, the evidence put forward by the Prophet Musa broke that spell, or "swallowed up what they had forged" as the verse puts it.

We revealed to Musa, "Throw down your staff." And it immediately swallowed up what they had forged. So the Truth took place and what they did was shown to be false. (Surat al-A'raf: 117-119)

As we can see from that verse, when it was realized that what these people who had first cast a spell over others had done was just an illusion, they lost all credibility. In the present day too, unless those who under the influence of a similar spell believe in these ridiculous claims under their scientific disguise and spend their lives defending them abandon them, they too will be humiliated when the full truth emerges and the spell is broken. In fact, Malcolm Muggeridge, an atheist philosopher and supporter of evolution admitted he was worried by just that prospect:

> *I myself am convinced that the theory of evolution, especially the extent to which it's been applied, will be one of the great jokes in the history books in the future. Posterity will marvel that so very flimsy and dubious an hypothesis could be accepted with the incredible credulity that it has.*

That future is not far off: On the contrary, people will soon see that "chance" is not a god, and will look back on the theory of evolution as the worst deceit and the most terrible spell in the world. That spell is already rapidly beginning to be lifted from the shoulders of people all over the world. Many people who see the true face of the theory of evolution are wondering with amazement how it was that they were ever taken in by it.

BY HARUN YAHYA

When a person examines his own body or any other living thing in nature, the world or the whole universe, in it he sees a great design, art, plan and intelligence. All this is evidence proving God's being, unit, and eternal power.

For Men of Understanding was written to make the reader see and realise some of the evidence of creation in nature. *For Men of Understanding* is also available in Indonesian, German, French, Urdu and Russian.

Many people think that Darwin's Theory of Evolution is a proven fact. Contrary to this conventional wisdom, recent developments in science completely disprove the theory. The only reason Darwinism is still foisted on people by means of a worldwide propaganda campaign lies in the ideological aspects of the theory. All secular ideologies and philosophies try to provide a basis for themselves by relying on the theory of evolution.

This book clarifies the scientific collapse of the theory of evolution in a way that is detailed but easy to understand. It reveals the frauds and distortions committed by evolutionists to "prove" evolution. Finally it analyzes the powers and motives that strive to keep this theory alive and make people believe in it.

Anyone who wants to learn about the origin of living things, including mankind, needs to read this book. *The Evolution Deceit* is also available in Italian, Albanian, Spanish, Indonesian, Malay, Russian, Arabic, Bulgarian, French, German and (Bosnian).

How was matter and time created from nothingness? What does the Big Bang theory signify about the creation of the universe? What is the parallelism between Einstein's Theory of Relativity and the Qur'anic verses?

All of these questions are answered in this book. If you want to learn the truths about space, matter, time and fate, read this book.

People who are oppressed, who are tortured to death, innocent babies, those who cannot afford even a loaf of bread, who must sleep in tents or even in streets in cold weather, those who are massacred just because they belong to a certain tribe, women, children, and old people who are expelled from their homes because of their religion... Eventually, there is only one solution to the injustice, chaos, terror, massacres, hunger, poverty, and oppression: the values of the Qur'an. Today, science has proven that the universe was created from nothing with a Big Bang. Moreover, all physical balances of the universe are designed to support human life. Everything from the nuclear reactions in stars to the chemical properties of a carbon atom or a water molecule, is created in a glorious harmony. This is the exalted and flawless creation of God, the Lord of All the Worlds. *The Creation of the Universe* is also available in French, Russian and Indonesian.

This book deals with how the theory of evolution is invalidated by scientific findings and experiments in a concise and simple language.

Many societies that rebelled against the will of God or regarded His messengers as enemies were wiped off the face of the earth completely... Perished Nations examines these penalties as revealed in the verses of the Quran and in light of archaeological discoveries. This book is also available in German, French, Spanish, Russian, Indonesian and Portuguese.

Fascism and communism, which made humanity suffer dark times, are fed from the same source, on the grounds of which they can attract masses to their side. This source is the materialist philosophy and its adaptation to nature, which is Darwinism. The acknowledgement of the scientific invalidity of this theory will bring about the end of all these detrimental ideologies. This book is also available in French.

This book gets into detail on the issue of origins and makes a comprehensive and technical refutation of Darwinist theory. As it is mentioned in the book, anyone who still defends the theory of evolution has to come into terms with this book and face its challenge. Otherwise, he will de facto accept that his allegiance to the theory of evolution is a non-scientific approach but a materialistic dogma.

The purpose of this book is to warn people against the day on which they will say "If only we did not rebel against God. If only we listened to the messengers..." and therefore feel deep regret. This is a summons to live for the cause of God when there is still time. *Before You Regret* is also available in French and German.

In a body that is made up of atoms, you breathe in air, eat food, and drink liquids that are all composed of atoms. Everything you see is nothing but the result of the collision of electrons of atoms with photons.

In this book, the implausibility of the spontaneous formation of an atom, the building-block of everything, living or non-living, is related and the flawless nature of God's creation is demonstrated. *The Miracle in the Atom* is also available in Indonesian.

A study that examines and seeks to remind us of the basic moral principles of the Qur'an, particularly those that are most likely to be forgotten or neglected at times. This book is also available in Bengoli.

In the Qur'an, there is an explicit reference to the "second coming of the Jesus to the world" which is heralded in a hadith. The realisation of some information revealed in the Qur'an about Jesus can only be possible by Jesus' second coming… This book is also available in German.

Darwin said: "If it could be demonstrated that any complex organ existed, which could not possibly have been formed by numerous, successive, slight modifications, my theory would absolutely break down." When you read this book, you will see that Darwin's theory has absolutely broken down, just as he feared it would. A thorough examination of the feathers of a bird, the sonar system of a bat or the wing structure of a fly reveal amazingly complex designs. And these designs indicate that they are created flawlessly by God. The book is also available in Russian.

Colours, patterns, spots even lines of each living being existing in nature have a meaning. An attentive eye would immediately recognise that not only the living beings, but also everything in nature are just as they should be. Furthermore, he would realise that everything is given to the service of man: the comforting blue colour of the sky, the colourful view of flowers, the bright green trees and meadows, the moon and stars illuminating the world in pitch darkness together with innumerable beauties surrounding man. This book is also available in Arabic and Indonesian.

The plan, design, and delicate balance existing in our bodies and reaching into even the remotest corners of the incredibly vast universe must surely have a superior Creator. Man is unable to see his Creator yet he can nevertheless grasp His existence, strength, and wisdom by means of his intellect. This book is a summons to think. A summons to ponder over the universe and living beings and see how they have been created flawlessly. The book is also available in Urdu, French and Indonesian.

In the Qur'an, conscience has a meaning and importance beyond its common and everyday use. This book introduces the real concept of conscience that is related in the Qur'an and draws our attention to the kind of understanding, thought, and wisdom that a truly conscientious person has. This book is also available in German and French.

There are questions about religion that people seek answers to and hope to be enlightened in the best way. However in most cases, people base their opinions on hearsay rather than acquiring them from the real source of religion: the Qur'an. In these booklets, you will find the most accurate answers to all the questions you seek answers for and learn your responsibilities towards your Creator. This book is also available in German.

When the events of "sickness" and "recovering" take place, our bodies become a battleground in which a bitter struggle is taking place. Microbes invisible to our eyes intrude into our body and begin to increase rapidly. The body however has a mechanism that combats them. Known as the "immune system", this mechanism is the most disciplined, most complex and successful army of the world. This system proves that the human body is the outcome of a unique design that has been planned with a great wisdom and skill. In other words, the human body is the evidence of a flawless creation, which is the peerless creation of God. This book is also available in Indonesian.

Man is a being to which God has granted the faculty of thinking. Yet a majority of people fail to employ this faculty as they should… The purpose of this book is to summon people to think in the way they should and to guide them in their efforts to think. This book is also available in Indonesian.

The unprecedented style and the superior wisdom inherent in the Qur'an is conclusive evidence confirming that it is the Word of God. Apart from this, there are a number of miracles verifying the fact that the Qur'an is the revelation of God, one of them being that, 1,400 years ago, it declared a number of scientific facts that have only been established thanks to the technological breakthroughs of the 20th century. In this book, in addition to the scientific miracles of the Qur'an, you will also find messages regarding the future. *Mracles of the Qur'an* is also available in Serbo-Croat (Bosnian), Chinese and Russian.

The world is a temporary place specially created by God to test man. That is why, it is inherently flawed and far from satisfying man's endless needs and desires. Each and every attraction existing in the world eventually wears out, becomes corrupt, decays and finally disappears. This is the never-changing reality of life. This book explains this most important essence of life and leads man to ponder the real place to which he belongs, namely the Hereafter.

The content of this book is an extremely important truth that astounded large numbers of people, and caused their outlook on life to change drastically. We can sum up this reality like this: "All events, people, buildings, cities, cars, places, which are a part of our life in this world, in short, everything we see, hold, touch, smell, taste and hear, are actually illusions and sensations that form in our brain."

The purpose of this book is to display the miraculous features of plants and hence to make people see "the creation miracle" in things -they often encounter in the flow of their daily lives and sidestep.

This book opens new horizons on these issues for people who, throughout their lives, -think only about their own needs and hence fail to see the evidence of God's existence. Reading and understanding this book will be an important step in coming to an understanding of one's Creator.

The information hidden inside DNA controls the thousands of different events that take place in the cells of the human body and in the functioning of its systems, as well as all the physical features, from the colour of a person's hair and eyes to his height. In the same way that every book has a writer and owner, so does the information in DNA:and that Creator is our Lord God, the All-Wise.

Just as a tiny key opens a huge door, this book will open new horizons for its readers. And the reality behind that door is the most important reality that one can come across in one's lifetime. Relating the amazing and admirable features of spiders known by few people and asking the questions of "how" and "why" in the process, this book reveals the excellence and perfection inherent in God's creation.

In societies distant from religion, right is often presented as wrong, and vice versa. Unbecoming behaviour which will not please God may be favoured and encouraged. Romanticism is one of those wrong sentiments which is assumed to be "right". This book reveals what a serious threat romanticism – which is imagined to be a simple character trait – poses to societies and individuals, and shows how easy it is to eliminate this danger.

These millimeter-sized animals that we frequently come across but don't care much about have an excellent ability for organization and specialization that is not to be matched by any other being on earth. These aspects of ants create in one a great admiration for God's superior power and unmatched creation. The book is also available inUrdu and Indonesian.

This book maintains that the source of the scourge of terrorism does not come from a divine religion, and that there is no room for terrorism in Islam. It is revealed, in the light of the verses of the Koran and with examples from history, that Islam forbids terrorism and aims to bring peace and security to the world. *Islam Denounces Terrorism* is also available in German.

This book is about the enthusiasm of believers that keeps growing until the end of their lives. The main aim of the book is to increase the enthusiasm of believers showing them what a great blessing enthusiasm is, and how it enhances the power of believers.

That people do not adopt the moral values of the Qur'an and submit to God underlie the personal and social depression, pain, fears and lack of confidence that is widely experienced today. This book explains the detriments that disbelief gives to people and discloses the only way to salvation, which is submission to God.

The plan, design, and delicate balance existing in our bodies and reaching into even the remotest corners of the incredibly vast universe must surely have a superior Creator. Man is unable to see his Creator yet he can nevertheless grasp His existence, strength, and wisdom by means of his intellect. This book is a summons to think. A summons to ponder over the universe and living beings and see how they have been created flawlessly.

Scientific progress makes it clear that living beings have an extremely complex structure and an order that is too perfect to have come into being by accident. Recently, for example, the perfect structure in the human gene became a top issue as a result of the completion of the Human Genome Project. In this book, the unique creation of God is once again disclosed for all to see.

Moses is the prophet whose life is most narrated in the Qur'an. The Qur'an provides a very detailed account of his struggle with Pharaoh, the unfavourable conduct of his people and the way the Prophet Moses summoned them to the way of God. This book provides a thorough examination into the life of the Prophet Moses in the light of the Qur'anic verses. Fascism is an ideology that has brought great disasters to humanity. Not only has it caused millions of people to be killed and tortured simply because of their race, but it has also attempted to abolish all human values. The main purpose of the book is to present various fascist tendencies which appear under different methods and guises, and expose their real origins and objectives. The book also attempts to tear down the mask of fascism, and reveal that fascism is definitely an anti-religionist system.

The Qur'an has been revealed to us so that we may read and ponder. The Basic Concepts of the Qur'an is a useful resource prepared as a guide to thinking. Some basic Islamic concepts like the soul, conscience, wisdom, loyalty, submission to God, brotherhood, modesty, prayer, patience, are discussed in the light of Qur'anic verses. This book is also available in Portuguese.

The way to examine the universe and all the beings therein and to discover God's art of creation and announce it to humanity is "science". Therefore, religion adopts science as a way to reach the details of God's creation and therefore encourages science. Just as religion encourages scientific research, so does scientific research that is guided by the facts communicated by religion yield very repid and definite results. This is because religion is the unique source that provides the most correct and definite answer to the question of how the universe and life came into being. This book is also available in Russian.

One of the principal deceptions that impels people into delinquency and makes them pursue their own desires is their heedlessness of death. Both human beings and the universe they live in are mortal. What awaits the disbelievers in the next world is more dreadful: the eternal wrath of hell. This book, based on the verses of the Qur'an, makes a detailed depiction of the moment of death, the day of judgement, and the penalties in hell, and it sounds a warning about the great danger facing us. *Death Resurrection Hell* is also available in Polish.

The most serious mistake a man makes is not pondering. It is not possible to find the truth unless one thinks about basic questions such as "How and why am I here?", "Who created me?", or "Where am I going?." Failing to do so, one becomes trapped in the vicious circle of daily life and turns into a selfish creature caring only for himself. *Ever Thought About the Truth?* summons people to think on such basic questions and to discover the real meaning of life. This bookis also available in French.

In this book you will find explanations about eternity, timelessness and spacelessness that you will never have encountered anywhere else and you will be confronted by the reality that eternity has already begun. The real answers to many questions people always ponder such as the true nature of death, resurrection after death, the existence of an eternal life, and the time when all these things will happen are to be found here...

Never plead ignorance of God's evident existence, that everything was created by God, that everything you own was given to you by God for your subsistence, that you will not stay so long in this world, of the reality of death, that the Qur'an is the Book of truth, that you will give account for your deeds, of the voice of your conscience that always invites you to righteousness, of the existence of the hereafter and the day of account, that hell is the eternal home of severe punishment, and of the reality of fate.

One of the principal deceptions that impel people into delinquency is the fact that they constantly forget the basic facts of life. This book summons man to remember facts that his soul prompts him to forget.

While watching television or reading the paper, you see many items which you would not like to see or hear: destitute people, murders, quarrels, ill-treatment, and much more... Certainly, you, too, would like to live in a peaceful and secure society where people live in harmony and friendship. However just waiting for such a world to come about by itself one day is of no use. This book is a summons to those who want goodness to prevail: it calls on them to do goodness and to form an alliance with other good people like themselves.

The Qur'an has been sent down as a book easily understandable to everyone. Everyone who believes in God and follows his conscience can take counsel from the verses of the Qur'an and obey the commands in the verses. However, those who follow their lower self fail to measure God with His true scale, entertain doubts about the hereafter, interpret the verses of the Qur'an wrongly in their own crooked reasoning. In this book, the reasons why those who do not use their intellect misinterpret the Qur'an are examined and some examples of the unwise interpretations and objections they make concerning the verses are reviewed and answered.

In the Qur'an, God tells people many secrets. People who are unaware of these secrets experience the trouble and distress caused by this throughout their lives. For those who learn these secrets of the Qur'an, however, the life of this world is very easy, and full of joy and excitement. This book deals with the subjects God related to people as a secret.

"Everything that constitutes our life is a totality of perceptions received by our soul. The things, people, places and events that make our world and our lives meaningful are like a dream; we perceive them only as images in our brain, and have nothing to do with their truth or reality..."

In the book, which consists of a conversation between four people, the prejudices that prevent people from understanding this great truth are removed, and the misconceptions they have are explained. Driven by pride and arrogance, man forgets that he is solely a servant of God. The first representative of arrogance is Satan, who rebelled against God. Throughout history, people who out of their pride worshipped themselves, have been mimicking the arrogance of Satan.

Everyone has some knowledge and convictions about Islam. However, the majority of these convictions have their origins in inadequate or incorrect sources. Actually, what one has to do to know Islam is to study the Qur'an, which comprises the origin and basis of Islam. Based on the information conveyed in the Qur'an, this book gives an account of God's attributes, our purpose in this world, what we have to do to fulfill this purpose.

God, in the Qur'an, calls the culture of people who are not subject to the religion of God "ignorance." Only a comparison of this culture with the honourable thoughts and moral structure of the Qur'an can reveal its primitive and corrupted nature. The purpose of this book is to take this comparison further, displaying the extent of the "crude understanding" of ignorant societies.

God createsevery word one utters, and every event one experiences, from the moment one is born into tis world. For a believer who understands this fact, uninterrupted joy of faith becomes an unchanging quality of life. The fate decreed by God is flawless. In this entity made up of millions of events, there is only goodness, benevolence, and wisdom for everyone who looks at them with an eye for goodness.

In order for justice to reign on the Earth, a morality that will make people leave their own interests aside in favour of justice is needed. This morality is the Qur'anic morality that God teaches and commands us. In Surat an-Nisa, God commands believers to act justly, albeit against themselves. The purpose of this book is to describe the true justice in the Qur'an.

In this book, all ideologies based on disbelief are referred to as "the religions of irreligion." That is simply because these ideologies have in time evolved to become religions with a complete system of beliefs, practices, and rules for conducting one's daily life.

A Muslim's life is described as follows in the Qur'an: "Truly, my prayer and my worship, my life and my death, are (all) for God" (The Qur'an, 6:162) A believer who decides to live for the cause of God must abandon all the idols of the society of ignorance *Devoted to God* is a summons to overthrow these idols for good.

CONCLUSION: RECOMMENDATIONS TO THE WESTERN WORLD AND MUSLIMS

Today, the Western world is concerned about the organisations that use terror under the guise of Islam and this concern is not misplaced. It is obvious that those carrying out terror and their supporters should be tried according to international judicial criteria. However, a more important point to consider is the long-term strategies that have to be pursued to discover viable solutions to these problems.

The assessments above reveal that terror has no place in Islam and that it is a crime committed against humanity. They further show the inherently contradictory nature of the concept of "Islamic terror". This provides us with an important vantage point:

1) The time ahead requires all countries to act with caution, sensitivity and wisdom. The bleak scenario that unfolds with the "Clash of civilisations", is one to the detriment of the whole world, and from which no one benefits. The world community at large must take the opportunity to learn to live side by side in peaceful interchange, learning from each other, studying each other's history, accomplishments in religion, art, literature, philosophy, science, technology, and culture, all of which mutually enrich one another's lives.

2) The activities serving the presentation of true Islam must be widespread. The solution to combat radical factions in Islamic countries should not be "compulsory secularisation". On the contrary, such a policy will incite more reaction from the masses. The solution is the dissemination of true Islam and the appearance of a Muslim model which embraces the Qur'anic values such as human rights, democracy, freedom, high morality, science, spirituality, aesthetics, and which offers happiness and bliss to humanity. Muslims must explain and live by the moral values commanded by the Qur'an and as exemplified by Muhammad, the Messenger of God. Muslims have the responsibility to take Islam out from the hands of

those who misapply it, (which leads to further misunderstanding of Islam) and place it back into the hands of those who live by the teachings of Islamic virtue and by the example of Muhammad, the Messenger of God.

3) The source of terrorism is in ignorance and bigotry and the solution to terrorism is education. To the circles who feel sympathy with terror, it should be made clear that terror is utterly against Islam and that it only serves to harm Islam, Muslims and humanity at large.

4) Long-term cultural solutions must be devised to combat terrorism which has its roots in communist, fascist and racist ideologies. Today in countries all over the world, Darwinist precepts form the basis of the education system. However, as we have stressed earlier, Darwinism is an erroneous ideology that sees man as an animal who developed only by fighting for survival - something which constitutes the likely basis of all forms of terrorism. An ideology that predicts only those holding power will survive and considers war as a virtue is like a huge morass that will never cease to visit disaster on the world. This being the case, beside the judicial and other measures that will be introduced to combat terrorism, there is also a need for a vigorous education campaign to be launched all over the world. Disclosure of the real face of the deception of Darwinism and materialism and instruction in the good values God has revealed for people must be the fundamentals of this education. Peace and stability are attainable only through living by the good values of true religion. Without draining the morass, it is not possible to rid the world of disaster.

Our hope is that these measures will help to the world get rid of terrorism and all other bigoted, brutal, barbarous structures. With the Christian culture it represents, the United States that defines itself as "a nation under God" is in fact a real friend of the Muslims. In the Qur'an, God draws attention to this fact and informs us that

Christians are those who are "most affectionate to those who believe". (Qur'an, 5:82) In history, some ignorant people (for instance, the Crusaders) failed to understand this fact and caused conflicts between these two religions. To prevent the repetition of this scenario, which is propagated with mottos like "Clash of Civilizations" or "Holy War against the West", true Christians and Muslims need to come together and co-operate. Indeed, the developments which took place in the aftermath of these grievous events indicate that the seeds of this co-operation have already been sowed. This grave act of terrorism, which has drawn the Christian and Muslim communities closer, led many Christians come to know more about the religion of Islam and encouraged Muslims to make greater efforts to communicate true Islamic morality described in the Qur'an. All these developments are the glad tidings that people will understand Islamic values better and be able to rid themselves of any prejudices they had held. By the Will of God, the 21st century will be the time when people will truly acknowledge that the dissemination of the values of Islam is the unique way of achieving much longed-for peace on the planet.

THE MISCONCEPTION OF EVOLUTION

Darwinism, which seeks to deny the fact of creation in the universe, is nothing but an unscientific fallacy. This theory, which argues that life originated from inanimate matter through coincidences, has been demolished with the recognition that the universe was created by God. It is God Who created the universe and Who designed it down to its smallest detail. Therefore, it is impossible for the theory of evolution, which holds that living beings are not created by God, but are products of coincidences, to be true.

Unsurprisingly, when we look at the theory of evolution, we see that this theory is denounced by scientific findings. The design in life is extremely complex and striking. In the inanimate world, for instance, we can explore how sensitive are the balances which atoms rest upon, and further, in the animate world, we can observe in what complex designs these atoms were brought together, and how extraordinary are the mechanisms and structures such as proteins, enzymes, and cells, which are manufactured with them. This extraordinary design in life invalidated Darwinism at the end of the 20th century. We have dealt with this subject in great detail in some of our other studies, and shall continue to do so. However, we think that, considering its importance, it will be helpful to make a short summary here as well.

The Scientific Collapse of Darwinism

Although a doctrine going back as far as ancient Greece, the theory of evolution was advanced extensively in the 19th century. The most important development that made the theory the top topic of the world of science was the book by Charles Darwin titled “” published in 1859. In this book, Darwin denied that different living species on the earth were created separately by God.

According to Darwin, all living beings had a common ancestor and they diversified over time through small changes. Darwin's theory was not based on any concrete scientific finding; as he also accepted, it was just an “assumption.” Moreover, as Darwin confessed in the long chapter of his book titled “Difficulties of the Theory,” the theory was failing in the face of many critical questions. Darwin invested all his hopes in new scientific discoveries, which he expected to solve the “Difficulties of the Theory.” However, contrary to his expectations, scientific findings expanded the dimensions of these difficulties. The defeat of Darwinism against science can be reviewed under three basic topics:

1) The theory can by no means explain how life originated on the earth.
2) There is no scientific finding showing that the “evolutionary mechanisms” proposed by the theory have any power to evolve at all.
3) The fossil record proves completely the contrary of the suggestions of the theory of evolution.

In this section, we will examine these three basic points in general outlines:

The First Insurmountable Step: The Origin of Life

The theory of evolution posits that all living species evolved from a single living cell that emerged on the primitive earth 3.8 billion years ago. How a single cell could generate millions of complex living species and, if such an evolution really occurred, why traces of it cannot be observed in the fossil record are some of the questions the theory cannot answer. However, first and foremost, of the first step of the alleged evolutionary process it has to be inquired: How did this "first cell" originate?

Since the theory of evolution denies creation and does not accept any kind of supernatural intervention, it maintains that the "first cell" originated coincidentally within the laws of nature, without any design, plan, or arrangement. According to the theory, inanimate matter must have produced a living cell as a result of coincidences. This, however, is a claim inconsistent with even the most unassailable rules of biology.

"Life Comes from Life"

In his book, Darwin never referred to the origin of life. The primitive understanding of science in his time rested on the assumption that living beings had a very simple structure. Since medieval times, spontaneous generation, the theory asserting that non-living materials came together to form living organisms, had been widely accepted. It was commonly believed that insects came into being from food leftovers, and mice from wheat. Interesting experiments were conducted to prove this theory. Some wheat was placed on a dirty piece of cloth, and it was believed that mice would originate from it after a while. Similarly, worms developing in meat were assumed to be evidence of spontaneous generation. However, only some time later was it understood that worms did not appear on meat spontaneously, but were carried there by flies in the form of larvae, invisible to the naked eye.

Even in the period when Darwin wrote, the belief that bacteria could come into existence from non-living matter was widely accepted in the world of science.

However, five years after Darwin's book was published, the discovery of Louis Pasteur disproved this belief, which constituted the groundwork of evolution. Pasteur summarized the conclusion he reached after time-consuming studies and experiments: "The claim that inanimate matter can originate life is buried in history for good."

Advocates of the theory of evolution resisted the findings of Pasteur for a long time. However, as the development of science unraveled the complex structure of the cell of a living being, the idea that life could come into being coincidentally faced an even greater impasse.

Inconclusive Efforts in the 20th Century

The first evolutionist who took up the subject of the origin of life in the 20th century was the renowned Russian biologist Alexander Oparin. With various theses he advanced in the 1930's, he tried to prove that the cell of a living being could originate by coincidence. These studies, however, were doomed to failure, and Oparin had to make the following confession: "Unfortunately, the origin of the cell remains a question which is actually the darkest point of the entire evolution theory."

Evolutionist followers of Oparin tried to carry out experiments to solve the problem of the origin of life. The best known of these experiments was carried out by American chemist Stanley Miller in 1953. Combining the gases he alleged to have existed in the primordial earth's atmosphere in an experiment set-up, and adding energy to the mixture, Miller synthesized several organic molecules (amino acids) present in the structure of proteins.

Barely a few years had passed before it was revealed that this experiment, which was then presented as an important step in the name of evolution, was invalid, the atmosphere used in the experiment having been very different from real earth conditions.

After a long silence, Miller confessed that the atmosphere medium he used was unrealistic. All the evolutionist efforts put forth throughout the 20th century to explain the origin of life ended with failure. The geochemist Jeffrey Bada from San Diego Scripps Institute accepts this fact in an article published in *Earth* Magazine in 1998:

> *Today as we leave the twentieth century, we still face the biggest unsolved problem that we had when we entered the twentieth century: How did life originate on Earth?*

The Complex Structure of Life

The primary reason why the theory of evolution ended up in such a big impasse about the origin of life is that even the living organisms deemed the simplest have incredibly complex structures. The cell of a living being is more complex than all of the technological products produced by man. Today, even in the most developed laboratories of the world, a living cell cannot be produced by bringing inorganic materials together.

The conditions required for the formation of a cell are too great in quantity to be explained away by coincidences. The probability of proteins, the building blocks of cell, being synthesized coincidentally, is 1 in 10 for an average protein made up of 500 amino acids. In mathematics, a probability smaller than 1 over 10 is practically considered to be impossible.

The DNA molecule, which is located in the nucleus of the cell and which stores genetic information, is an incredible databank. It is calculated that if the information coded in DNA were written down, this would make a giant library consisting of 900 volumes of encyclopaedias of 500 pages each.

A very interesting dilemma emerges at this point: the DNA can only replicate with the help of some specialized proteins (enzymes). However, the synthesis of these enzymes can only be realized by the information coded in DNA. As they both depend on each other, they have to exist at the same time for replication. This brings the scenario that life originated by itself to a deadlock. Prof. Leslie Orgel, an evolutionist of repute from the University of San Diego, California, confesses this fact in the September 1994 issue of the *Scientific American* magazine:

It is extremely improbable that proteins and nucleic acids, both of which are structurally complex, arose spontaneously in the same place at the same time. Yet it also seems impossible to have one without the other. And so, at first glance, one might have to conclude that life could never, in fact, have originated by chemical means.

No doubt, if it is impossible for life to have originated from natural causes, then it has to be accepted that life was "created" in a supernatural way. This fact explicitly invalidates the theory of evolution, whose main purpose is to deny creation.

Imaginary Mechanisms of Evolution

The second important point that negates Darwin's theory is that both concepts put forward by the theory as "evolutionary mechanisms" were understood to have, in reality, no evolutionary power. Darwin based his evolution allegation entirely on the mechanism of "natural selection". The importance he placed on this mechanism was evident in the name of his book: , *By Means Of Natural Selection...*

Natural selection holds that those living things that are stronger and more suited to the natural conditions of their habitats will survive in the struggle for life. For example, in a deer herd under the threat of attack by wild animals, those that can run faster will survive. Therefore, the deer herd will be comprised of faster and stronger individuals. However, unquestionably, this mechanism will not cause deer to evolve and transform themselves into another living species, for instance, horses.

Therefore, the mechanism of natural selection has no evolutionary power. Darwin was also aware of this fact and had to state this in his book :

Natural selection can do nothing until favourable variations chance to occur.

Lamarck's Impact

So, how could these "favourable variations" occur? Darwin tried to answer this question from the standpoint of the primitive understanding of science in his age. According to the French biologist Lamarck, who lived before Darwin, living creatures passed on the traits they acquired during their lifetime to the next generation and these traits, accumulating from one generation to another, caused new species to be formed. For instance, according to Lamarck, giraffes evolved from antelopes; as they struggled to eat the leaves of high trees, their necks were extended from generation to generation.

Darwin also gave similar examples, and in his book, for instance, said that some bears going into water to find food transformed themselves into whales over time.

However, the laws of inheritance discovered by Mendel and verified by the science of genetics that flourished in the 20th century, utterly demolished the legend that acquired traits were passed on to subsequent generations. Thus, natural selection fell out of favour as an evolutionary mechanism.

Neo-Darwinism and Mutations

In order to find a solution, Darwinists advanced the "Modern Synthetic Theory", or as it is more commonly known, Neo-Darwinism, at the end of the 1930's. Neo-Darwinism added mutations, which are distortions formed in the genes of living beings because of external factors such as radiation or replication errors, as the "cause of favourable variations" in addition to natural mutation.

Today, the model that stands for evolution in the world is Neo-Darwinism. The theory maintains that millions of living beings present on the earth formed as a result of a process whereby numerous complex organs of these organisms such as the ears, eyes, lungs, and wings, underwent "mutations," that is, genetic disorders. Yet, there is an outright scientific fact that totally undermines this theory: Mutations do not cause living beings to develop; on the contrary, they always cause harm to them.

The reason for this is very simple: the DNA has a very complex structure and random effects can only cause harm to it. American geneticist B.G. Ranganathan explains this as follows:

> *Mutations are small, random, and harmful. They rarely occur and the best possibility is that they will be ineffectual. These four characteristics of mutations imply that mutations cannot lead to an evolutionary development. A random change in a highly specialised organism is either ineffectual or harmful. A random change in a watch cannot improve the watch. It will most probably harm it or at best be ineffectual. An earthquake does not improve the city, it brings destruction.*

Not surprisingly, no mutation example, which is useful, that is, which is observed to develop the genetic code, has been observed so far. All mutations have proved to be harmful. It was understood that mutation, which is presented as an "evolutionary mechanism," is actually a genetic occurrence that harms living beings, and leaves them disabled. (The most common effect of mutation on human beings is cancer). No doubt, a destructive mechanism cannot be an "evolutionary mechanism." Natural selection, on the other hand, "can do nothing by itself" as Darwin also accepted. This fact shows us that there is no "evolutionary mechanism" in nature. Since no evolutionary mechanism exists, neither could any imaginary process called evolution have taken place.

The Fossil Record: No Sign of Intermediate Forms

The clearest evidence that the scenario suggested by the theory of evolution did not take place is the fossil record.

According to the theory of evolution, every living species has sprung from a predecessor. A previously existing species turned into something else in time and all species have come into being in this way. According to the theory, this transformation proceeds gradually over millions of years. Had this been the case, then numerous intermediary species should have existed and lived within this long transformation period. For instance, some half-fish/half-reptiles should have lived in the past which had acquired some reptilian traits in addition to the fish traits they already had. Or there should have existed some reptile-birds, which acquired some bird traits in addition to the reptilian traits they already had. Since these would be in a transitional phase, they should be disabled, defective, crippled living beings. Evolutionists refer to these imaginary creatures, which they believe to have lived in the past, as "intermediate forms."

If such animals had really existed, there should be millions and even billions of them in number and variety. More importantly, the remains of these strange creatures should be present in the fossil record. In , Darwin explained:

If my theory be true, numberless intermediate varieties, linking most closely all of the species of the same group together must assuredly have existed... Consequently, evidence of their former existence could be found only amongst fossil remains.

Darwin's Hopes Shattered

However, although evolutionists have been making strenuous efforts to find fossils since the middle of the 19th century all over the world, no transitional forms have yet been uncovered. All the fossils unearthed in excavations showed that, contrary to the expectations of evolutionists, life appeared on earth all of a sudden and fully-formed. A famous British paleontologist, Derek V. Ager, admits this fact, even though he is an evolutionist:

The point emerges that if we examine the fossil record in detail, whether at the level of orders or of species, we find – over and over again – not gradual evolution, but the sudden explosion of one group at the expense of another.

This means that in the fossil record, all living species suddenly emerge as fully formed, without any intermediate forms in between. This is just the opposite of Darwin's assumptions. Also, it is very strong evidence that living beings are created. The only explanation of a living species emerging suddenly and complete in every detail without any evolutionary ancestor can be that this species was created. This fact is admitted also by the widely known evolutionist biologist Douglas Futuyma: Creation and evolution, between them, exhaust the possible explanations for the origin of living things. Organisms either appeared on the earth fully developed or they did not. If they did not, they must have developed from pre-existing species by some process of modification. If they did appear in a fully developed state, they must indeed have been created by some omnipotent intelligence. Fossils show that living beings emerged fully developed and in a perfect state on the earth. That means that is, contrary to Darwin's supposition, not evolution but creation.

The Tale of Human Evolution

The subject most often brought up by the advocates of the theory of evolution is the subject of the origin of man. The Darwinist claim holds that the modern men of today evolved from some kind of ape-like creatures. During this alleged evolutionary process, which is supposed to have started 4-5 million years ago, it is claimed that there existed some "transitional forms" between modern man and his ancestors. According to this completely imaginary scenario, four basic "categories" are listed:

1. *Australopithecus*
2. *Homo habilis*
3. *Homo erectus*
4. *Homo sapiens*

Evolutionists call the so-called first ape-like ancestors of men "Australopithecus" which means "South African ape." These living beings are actually nothing but an old ape species that has become extinct. Extensive research done on various *Australopithecus* specimens by two world famous anatomists from England and the USA, namely, Lord Solly Zuckerman and Prof. Charles Oxnard, has shown that these belonged to an ordinary ape species that became extinct and bore no resemblance to humans.

Evolutionists classify the next stage of human evolution as "homo," that is "man." According to the evolutionist claim, the living beings in the Homo series are more developed than Australopithecus. Evolutionists devise a fanciful evolution scheme by arranging different fossils of these creatures in a particular order. This scheme is imaginary because it has never been proved that there is an evolutionary relation between these different classes. Ernst Mayr, one of the foremost defenders of the theory of evolution in the 20th century, admits this fact by saying that "the chain reaching as far as *Homo sapiens* is actually lost."

By outlining the link chain as "*Australopithecus* > *Homo habilis* > *Homo erectus* > *Homo sapiens*," evolutionists imply that each of these species is one another's ancestor. However, recent findings of paleoanthropologists have revealed that Australopithecus, *Homo habilis* and *Homo erectus* lived at different parts of the world at the same time. Moreover, a certain segment of humans classified as *Homo erectus* have lived up until very modern times. *Homo sapiens* neandarthalensis and *Homo sapiens* sapiens (modern man) co-existed in the same region.

This situation apparently indicates the invalidity of the claim that they are ancestors of one another. A paleontologist from Harvard University, Stephen Jay Gould, explains this deadlock of the theory of evolution although he is an evolutionist himself:

> *What has become of our ladder if there are three coexisting lineages of hominids (*A. africanus, *the robust australopithecines, and* H. habilis*), none clearly derived from another? Moreover, none of the three display any evolutionary trends during their tenure on earth.*

Put briefly, the scenario of human evolution, which is sought to be upheld with the help of various drawings of some "half ape, half human" creatures appearing in the media and course books, that is, frankly, by means of propaganda, is nothing but a tale with no scientific ground. Lord Solly Zuckerman, one of the most famous and respected scientists in the U.K., who carried out research on this subject for years, and particularly studied *Australopithecus* fossils for 15 years, finally concluded, despite being an evolutionist himself, that there is, in fact, no such family tree branching out from ape-like creatures to man.

Zuckerman also made an interesting "spectrum of science." He formed a spectrum of sciences ranging from those he considered scientific to those he considered unscientific. According to Zuckerman's spectrum, the most "scientific"–that is, depending on concrete data–fields of science are chemistry and physics. After them come the biological sciences and then the social sciences. At the far end of the spectrum, which is the part considered to be most "unscientific," are "extra-sensory perception"–concepts such as telepathy and sixth sense–and finally "human evolution." Zuckerman explains his reasoning:

We then move right off the register of objective truth into those fields of presumed biological science, like extrasensory perception or the interpretation of man's fossil history, where to the faithful (evolutionist) anything is possible - and where the ardent believer (in evolution) is sometimes able to believe several contradictory things at the same time.

The tale of human evolution boils down to nothing but the prejudiced interpretations of some fossils unearthed by certain people, who blindly adhere to their theory.

Technology In The Eye and The Ear

Another subject that remains unanswered by evolutionary theory is the excellent quality of perception in the eye and the ear.

Before passing on to the subject of the eye, let us briefly answer the question of "how we see". Light rays coming from an object fall oppositely on the retina of the eye. Here, these light rays are transmitted into electric signals by cells and they reach a tiny spot at the back of the brain called the centre of vision. These electric signals are perceived in this centre of the brain as an image after a series of processes. With this technical background, let us do some thinking.

The brain is insulated from light. That means that the inside of the brain is solid dark, and light does not reach the location where the brain is situated. The place called the centre of vision is a solid dark place where no light ever reaches; it may even be the darkest place you have ever known. However, you observe a luminous, bright world in this pitch darkness.

The image formed in the eye is so sharp and distinct that even the technology of the 20th century has not been able to attain it. For instance, look at the book you read, your hands with which you hold it, then lift your head and look around you. Have you ever seen such a sharp and distinct image as this one at any other place? Even the most developed television screen produced by the greatest television producer in the world cannot provide such a sharp image for you. This is a three-dimensional, coloured, and extremely sharp image. For more than 100 years, thousands of engineers have been trying to achieve this sharpness. Factories, huge premises were established, much research has been done, plans and designs have been made for this purpose. Again, look at a TV screen and the book you hold in your hands. You will see that there is a big difference in sharpness and distinction. Moreover, the TV screen shows you a two-dimensional image, whereas with your eyes, you watch a three-dimensional perspective having depth.

For many years, ten of thousands of engineers have tried to make a three-dimensional TV, and reach the vision quality of the eye. Yes, they have made a three-dimensional television system but it is not possible to watch it without putting on glasses; moreover, it is only an artificial three-dimension. The background is more blurred, the foreground appears like a paper setting. Never has it been possible to produce a sharp and distinct vision like that of the eye. In both the camera and the television, there is a loss of image quality. Evolutionists claim that the mechanism producing this sharp and distinct image has been formed by chance. Now, if somebody told you that the television in your room was formed as a result of chance, that all its atoms just happened to come together and make up this device that produces an image, what would you think? How can atoms do what thousands of people cannot?

If a device producing a more primitive image than the eye could not have been formed by chance, then it is very evident that the eye and the image seen by the eye could not have been formed by chance. The same situation applies to the ear. The outer ear picks up the available sounds by the auricle and directs them to the middle ear; the middle ear transmits the sound vibrations by intensifying them; the inner ear sends these vibrations to the brain by translating them into electric signals. Just as with the eye, the act of hearing finalises in the centre of hearing in the brain. The situation in the eye is also true for the ear. That is, the brain is insulated from sound just like it is from light: it does not let any sound in. Therefore, no matter how noisy is the outside; the inside of the brain is completely silent. Nevertheless, the sharpest sounds are perceived in the brain. In your brain, which is insulated from sound, you listen to the symphonies of an orchestra, and hear all the noises in a crowded place. However, if the sound level in your brain was measured by a precise device at that moment, it would be seen that a complete silence is prevailing there.

As is the case with imagery, decades of effort have been spent in trying to generate and reproduce sound that is faithful to the original. The results of these efforts are sound recorders, high-fidelity systems, and systems for sensing sound. Despite all this technology and the thousands of engineers and experts who have been working on this endeavour, no sound has yet been obtained that has the same sharpness and clarity as the sound perceived by the ear.

Think of the highest-quality HI-FI systems produced by the biggest company in the music industry. Even in these devices, when sound is recorded some of it is lost; or when you turn on a HI-FI you always hear a hissing sound before the music starts. However, the sounds that are the products of the technology of the human body are extremely sharp and clear. A human ear never perceives a sound accompanied by a hissing sound or with atmospherics as does HI-FI; it perceives sound exactly as it is, sharp and clear. This is the way it has been since the creation of man.

So far, no visual or recording apparatus produced by man has been as sensitive and successful in perceiving sensory data as are the eye and the ear.

However, as far as seeing and hearing are concerned, a far greater fact lies beyond all this.

To Whom Does the Consciousness that Sees and Hears Within the Brain Belong?

Who is it that watches an alluring world in its brain, listens to symphonies and the twittering of birds, and smells the rose?

The stimulations coming from the eyes, ears, and nose of a human being travel to the brain as electro-chemical nervous impulses. In biology, physiology, and biochemistry books, you can find many details about how this image forms in the brain. However, you will never come across the most important fact about this subject: Who is it that perceives these electro-chemical nervous impulses as images, sounds, odours and sensory events in the brain? There is a consciousness in the brain that perceives all this without feeling any need for eye, ear, and nose. To whom does this consciousness belong? There is no doubt that this consciousness does not belong to the nerves, the fat layer and neurons comprising the brain. This is why Darwinist-materialists, who believe that everything is comprised of matter, cannot give any answer to these questions.

For this consciousness is the spirit created by God. The spirit needs neither the eye to watch the images, nor the ear to hear the sounds. Furthermore, nor does it need the brain to think.

Everyone who reads this explicit and scientific fact should ponder on Almighty God, should fear Him and seek refuge in Him, He Who squeezes the entire universe in a pitch-dark place of a few cubic centimeters in a three-dimensional, coloured, shadowy, and luminous form.

A Materialist Faith

The information we have presented so far shows us that the theory of evolution is a claim evidently at variance with scientific findings. The theory's claim on the origin of life is inconsistent with science, the evolutionary mechanisms it proposes have no evolutionary power, and fossils demonstrate that the intermediate forms required by the theory never existed. So, it certainly follows that the theory of evolution should be pushed aside as an unscientific idea. This is how many ideas such as the earth-centered universe model have been taken out of the agenda of science throughout history.

However, the theory of evolution is pressingly kept on the agenda of science. Some people even try to represent criticisms directed against the theory as an "attack on science." Why? The reason is that the theory of evolution is an indispensable dogmatic belief for some circles. These circles are blindly devoted to materialist philosophy and adopt Darwinism because it is the only materialist explanation that can be put forward for the workings of nature.

Interestingly enough, they also confess this fact from time to time. A well known geneticist and an outspoken evolutionist, Richard C. Lewontin from Harvard University, confesses that he is "first and foremost a materialist and then a scientist":

> *It is not that the methods and institutions of science somehow compel us accept a material explanation of the phenomenal world, but, on the contrary, that we are forced by our a priori adherence to material causes to create an apparatus of investigation and a set of concepts that produce material explanations, no matter how counter-intuitive, no matter how mystifying to the uninitiated. Moreover, that materialism is absolute, so we cannot allow a Divine Foot in the door.*

These are explicit statements that Darwinism is a dogma kept alive just for the sake of adherence to the materialist philosophy. This dogma maintains that there is no being save matter. Therefore, it argues that inanimate, unconscious matter created life. It insists that millions of different living species; for instance, birds, fish, giraffes, tigers, insects, trees, flowers, whales and human beings originated as a result of the interactions between matter such as the pouring rain, the lightning flash, etc., out of inanimate matter. This is a precept contrary both to reason and science. Yet Darwinists continue to defend it just so as "not to allow a Divine Foot in the door." Anyone who does not look at the origin of living beings with a materialist prejudice will see this evident truth: All living beings are works of a Creator, Who is All-Powerful, All-Wise and All-Knowing. This Creator is God, Who created the whole universe from non-existence, designed it in the most perfect form, and fashioned all living beings.

Bibliography

Amery, Reeves : *The Anatomy of Peace,* Oxford, New York, 2001.

Aurobindo, Sri : *The Foundations of Islamic Culture,* New York, 1973.

Fatima, T. : *Islamic Law and Judiciary,* Deep & Deep Publications, New Delhi, 2001.

Francis Darwin: *The Life and Letters of Charles Darwin,* D. Appleton and Company, New York, 1888.

John L. Esposito: *Islam: The Straight Path,* Oxford University Press, 1998.

Narayan : *Pan Islamism,* MacMillan, New York, 1953.

Oudha, Abdul Qadir : *Criminal Law of Islam,* Kitab Bhavan, New Delhi, 1999.

Poole, Lane, S. : *The Mohammedan Dynasties,* MacMillan & Co., London, 1895.

Qureshi, A. Iqbal : *Islam and the Theory of Interest,* Kitab Bhavan, New Delhi, 1994.

Rizvi, Hasan Askari : *Islami Reassertion : a Socio Political Study,* Progressive Publishers, Lahore, 1981.

Robert M. Young: *Darwinian Evolution and Human History,* Historical Studies on Science and Belief, 1980.

Saban Dogen, *Mehdi ve Deccal (Mahdi and Dajjal),* Gençlik Yayincilik, Istanbul, 1998.

Sidney Fox: *Klaus Dose, Molecular Evolution and The Origin of Life,* New York: Marcel Dekker, 1977.

Thomas Arnold: *The Spread of Islam in the World, A History of Peaceful Preaching,* Goodword Books, 2001.

Valliuddin, Mir : *The Quranic Sufism,* Motilal Banarsi Das Publishers, New Delhi, 1989.

INDEX